The Spiritual Situation
in Our Technical Society

The Spiritual Situation
in Our Technical Society

Paul Tillich

Edited and Introduced by
J. Mark Thomas

MERCER

ISBN 0-86554-292-9

*The Spiritual Situation
in Our Technical Society*
Copyright © 1988
Mercer University Press
Macon, Georgia 31207
All rights reserved
Printed in the United States of America

Library of Congress Cataloging-in-Publication Data
Tillich, Paul, 1886-1965.
The spiritual situation in our technical society.

Includes index.
1. Technology—religious aspects—Christianity.
2. Technology—Moral and ethical aspects. 3. Religion—
and science—1946–. 4. Civilization, Modern—
20th century. I. Thomas, J. Mark, 1937–.
II. Title.
BR115.T42T55   1988   261.5   87-34984
ISBN 0-86554-292-9 (alk. paper)

Contents

Part IV
Dehumanization in Technical Society   109

Acknowledgments

"The Lost Dimension in Religion," *Saturday Evening Post* 230 (14 June 1958): 28-29, 76, 78-79. Reprinted from the *Saturday Evening Post,* copyright 1958, the Curtis Publishing Co.

"Participation and Knowledge: Problems of an Ontology of Cognition." In *Sociologica,* 201-209. Edited by Theodor W. Adorno and Walter Dirks. Frankfurt am Main: Europasche Verlagsanstalt, 1955. Reprinted with permission of the publisher.

"How Has Science in the Last Century Changed Man's View of Himself?" In *The Current* 6:1-2 (1965): 85-89. Published with permission of the Harvard-Radcliff Catholic Student Center.

"The Decline and the Validity of the Idea of Progress." In *The Future of Religions.* Edited by Jerald C. Brauer. New York: Harper & Row, 1966. Published with permission of the publisher.

"Environment and the Individual," *Journal of the American Institute of Architects* 28 (June 1957): 90-92. Published with permission of the publisher.

"Conformity," *Social Research* 24 (Autumn 1957): 354-60. Published with permission of the publisher.

"The Relationship Today between Science and Religion." In *The Student Seeks an Answer,* 296-306. Edited by John A. Clark. Waterville ME: Colby College Press, 1960. Reprinted with permission of the publisher.

"Science and the Contemporary World in the View of a Theologian." In *Public and Private Association in the International Educational and Cultural Relations,* 67-70. Washington: U.S. Department of State, 15 February 1961. Published with permission of the publisher.

"Has Man's Conquest of Space Increased or Diminished His Stature?" In *The Great Ideas Today.* Chicago: Encyclopaedia Britannica, 1963. Reprinted with permission of Encyclopaedia Britannica, Inc., copyright 1963.

"Seven Theses concerning the Nuclear Dilemma." This short essay was published as a contribution to "The Nuclear Dilemma—A Discussion." *Christianity and Crisis* 21 (1961): 203-204. Reprinted with permission. Copyright 1961, *Christianity and Crisis,* 537 West 121st Street, New York, New York 10027.

Introduction

Three powerful spiritual forces determine the contemporary religious situation: "mathematical natural science, technique and capitalist economy." This is how Paul Tillich interpreted the "spiritual situation" of modernity in 1926 and throughout his intellectual life. In his books and essays that address these forces directly, and as an element of his systematic understanding in his other works, they appear again and again as constituting the "unconscious, self-evident faith" grounding the dynamics of Western society.[1] For him, to comprehend the structure and meaning of science, technology, and capitalism is to grasp the *situation* within which theology and ethics must be done. The essays in this volume, spanning the period from 1927 to 1964, offer a significant addition to this understanding. In addition, they run counter to the claim that once Tillich came to America, he abandoned his social-political interpretation in favor of an individual-existentialist one.[2]

For Tillich, the "situation" is one pole of all theological work representing the "creative interpretation of existence" in a period, including the "scientific and artistic, the economic, political, and ethical forms" in which

---

[1]Paul Tillich, *The Religious Situation*, trans. H. Richard Niebuhr (New York: Meridian Books, 1956) 40, 42.

[2]E.g., "What Tillich did . . . was essentially to abandon his earlier preoccupations with the broad social-political dimensions of history in order to offer a formulation ('New Being') more open to individualistic applications." David Hopper, *Tillich: A Theological Portrait* (Philadelphia: J. B. Lippincott, 1968) 100. Tillich *did* respond to psychological self-interpretations, of course, as is demonstrated by Perry LeFerre, *The Meaning of Health: Essays in Existentialism, Psychoanalysis, and Religion* (Chicago: Exploration Press, 1984) and *The Courage to Be* (New Haven: Yale University Press, 1952). But, as this latter volume shows, even the personal affirmation of one's being takes place against the situation of technical society: "The safety which is guaranteed by well-functioning mechanisms for the technical control of nature, by the refined psychological control of the person, by the rapidly increasing organizational control of society—this safety is bought at a high price: man, for whom all this was invented as a means, becomes a means himself in the service of means." (138)

this interpretation is expressed.[3] As Reinhold Niebuhr approached his ethical judgments with the Bible in one hand and a newspaper in the other, Paul Tillich's mediating theology demands a thoroughgoing knowledge of both religious symbols and the contemporary world to which they must speak. Doing theology today without an understanding of the dynamics of our technological era would have been, for him, impossible.

The situation, as one pole of the theological task, however, is never without religious meaning. If one understands culture as the form of religion, and religion as the substance of culture—as Tillich does—then the situation itself manifests religious and ethical dimensions. The interpretation of the situation represents an attempt to decipher "the style of an autonomous culture in all of its characteristic expressions, to discover their hidden religious significance."[4] And any theology that addresses the ethical question must begin with a "theology of culture applying not only to ethics but to all the functions of culture."[5]

Tillich's evaluation of the contemporary situation succumbs to neither the mere celebration of nor the "romantic enmity against technical civilizations."[6] Technical society is, rather, ambiguous in its realization; it is both creative and destructive. In this judgment, Tillich demonstrates his location as a theologian on the boundary.[7]

In the first part of this volume, Tillich describes the contemporary situation in terms of the development of bourgeois civilization and the eventual loss of religious depth in it. "The World Situation" has been determined by the loss of reason as the principle of truth and justice, the contemporary hegemony of technical reasoning, and the revolt against these developments in efforts at planning reason. Modernity is characterized by the struggle to regain control over the "Leviathan" of a scientifically and

---

[3]Paul Tillich, *Systematic Theology*, 3 vols. (Chicago: University of Chicago Press, 1951-1963) 1:3-4.

[4]Paul Tillich, *The Protestant Era*, trans. James Luther Adams (Chicago: University of Chicago Press, 1948) 58.

[5]Paul Tillich, *What Is Religion?*, trans. and intro. James Luther Adams (New York: Harper & Row, 1969) 160.

[6]*The Interpretation of History*, trans. N. A. Rasetzki and Elisa L. Talmey (New York: Charles Scribner's Sons, 1936) 6.

[7]For a fuller explication of Tillich's understanding of technology, see J. Mark Thomas, *Ethics and Technoculture* (Lanham MD: University Press of America, 1987).

technologically based world market system that shapes persons to its purposes. Thus, the lost dimension in technical society is also "The Lost Dimension in Religion": the dimension of depth. In running ahead horizontally, in making everything in nature (including human beings) into a tool, the question of the ultimate meaning of life is no longer answered or even asked with seriousness.

In the second part, Tillich describes the structure and meaning of science in its relation to society, the university, and to other realms of knowledge. The "Logos and Mythos of Technology" explores the rational structures and types of technology, their relation to other forms of interpretation (logos), and the meaning of technology within the totality of life (mythos). He specifies the conditions for the existence of science in "The Freedom of Science," especially that it must be free from ideological determination, and he analyzes the ontological structure of cognition in "Participation and Knowledge."

The role of science and technology in transforming the interpretation of human being and destiny is the focus of the third part. Each of the essays in this section is especially concerned with the way in which science and religion have been conceived—and misconceived—as modes of cognition. Science does not conflict with religion, Tillich claims, because religion operates at the level of meaning and symbol, not of factual object and conclusions. "How Has Science in the Last Century Changed Man's View of Himself?" reviews the change in the definition of the fundamental telos of human being from the classical-humanist to the transcendental-religious to the scientific-technical one, and the contemporary reaction to this change. The essay "The Decline and the Validity of the Idea of Progress" traces this central symbol of technical society in its historical development and in its applicability to the various dimensions of culture. In all of these essays, a normative judgment concerning the technological objectification of nature and persons is anticipated. The relationship between the "Expressions of Man's Self-Understanding in Philosophy and the Sciences" is the question of the final article in this section. The scientific and technical objectification of persons and things gives rise to protests from the existentialist and related movements.

In the essays for part 4, the moral meaning of technological society is more sharply drawn. The ambiguities of the relation between "Thing and Self" are manifest in a society that deprives both of subjectivity. And "The Person in a Technical Society" confronts a fate that threatens the personal itself, raising one of the great religious questions of our age: the meaning of the person in an impersonal world. The meaning of the human world that transcends mere surroundings is the central point of "Environment and the Individual." Technology and meaning unite, fundamentally, in the kind of space that humans structure for themselves. Finally, the person who struggles to maintain a self in a world of objectification must also struggle against the forces generated toward "Conformity."

The fifth part pursues the question of the relationship between science, philosophy, religion, and technology. The essay concerning "The Relationship Today between Science and Religion" distinguishes between religious and scientific knowledge and shows how religious symbols become absurd when made into literal statements. This "confusion of dimensions" causes the conflicts between religion and science that today should be obsolete. "Religion, Science, and Philosophy" carries on the theme of the difference between scientific and theological statements and indicates the philosophical and religious elements in every scientific view.

The ambiguities of science and technology, and their meaning as both instruments and symbols, is the subject of the sixth and final part. The essay "Science and the Contemporary World in the View of a Theologian" links the earlier discussion of the outdated conflict between science and religion to a focus on the destructiveness of technical science. Should the ambiguity of science bring about a restriction on its pursuit of truth? Consistent with his earliest reflections on the necessity of freedom in science, Tillich says no. "The Technical City as Symbol" reflects upon the way technical objects—including the technical city itself—are both things and symbols, bearers of functions and of meanings. And, in this essay, Tillich asks again about the meaning of our "well furnished house of the earth." What is its ultimate end? The ambiguity of science and technology is manifest poignantly in space travel. Tillich asks "Has Man's Conquest of Space Increased or Diminished His Stature?" He characterizes the lack of a final purpose in moving into transterresterial space with the concept of "forwardism," and he speaks of the ethical shadow that follows space exploration in its military purposes. This final negativity—the capacity of science and technology to end the existence of the earth—is discussed in the last two essays: "Seven Theses concerning the Nuclear Dilemma" and "The Hydrogen Cobalt Bomb." The radical ambiguity of our technical society is that it is capable of both ameliorating life on this planet and bringing it to an abrupt end.

The Spiritual Situation in Our Technical Society draws together a thread of interpretation running through all of Tillich's work over a period of some forty years. As he indicates in lecture notes for the essay from which this book title is taken, his method is "to describe determining structures and decisive trends." And what is the trend of modernity? It is not, he says, that society is determined by industry as such, but by "the methods and organization of industry."[8] From *The System of the Sciences* and *The Religious Situation* to *Systematic Theology,* he pursues the questions and problems arising from the ambiguity attending the central forces of the contemporary era: science, technology, and capitalism. The struggle with our real situation was itself a sign to Tillich that we were not completely lost in our age. Where there is questioning, there is the possibility of transcendence. And so, the best thing for us to do may be to ask with all those who have experienced the ambiguity of our time, what is the meaning of the technological world we are bringing into being, and how ought we to respond to it?

---

[8]"The Spiritual Situation in Our Technical Society" is one of several lectures Tillich delivered on science, technology, and religion, for which only handwritten lecture notes now exist. The Paul Tillich Archives, Andover-Harvard Theological Library, Harvard University, Cambridge MA.

Notes on Methodology

Documentary Sources

The essays in this volume come from diverse sources and times. They represent several types of documents, written in German and English, some previously unpublished and some published elsewhere. Most of these essays were originally delivered as lectures in Germany and America, but some were written as journal articles or as contributions to larger works.

Editing and Reediting Essays

The differences in time and place associated with the essays of this collection give rise to necessary shifts in literary style. Two things moderate these shifts, however. The first is that Tillich's thought remains relatively consistent from the earliest essays in ths volume to the latest. The second is that Tillich's lectures are themselves somewhat formal and theoretical so that there is less contrast between his lectures and formal writing than is sometimes the case.

While the systematic character of Tillich's thought gives a certain theoretical coherence to these essays, it was necessary to edit them to give a formal coherence as well.[1] Spellings have been modernized throughout, and usages have been made standard. While the editor values the contemporary use of inclusive language, Tillich's published essays have been left in their original state.

Headings have been used in the volume to aid the reader in following the text and to indicate important ideas. Tillich's outlines have been used to section some essays. Where other editors have supplied headings, these have been kept or altered in accordance with how well they fit the essays, the overall theme, and the thread of interpretation of this volume as a whole. Essays published without section headings have often been given headings to integrate them into the overall style of the volume.

---

[1] The standard reference used throughout this volume is *The Chicago Manual of Style*, 13th ed., rev. (Chicago: University of Chicago Press, 1982).

Some previously published essays have been reedited. This has been done as conservatively as possible. Grammar and usage have been brought up to modern standards. The essay "Participation and Knowledge: Problems of an Ontology of Cognition," for instance, was the sole English essay in an otherwise German volume. It required editing to bring it into standard English practice, especially regarding punctuation.

Transcribed Lectures

Three lectures have been transcribed and edited from audio tapes made available by Eleanor Godfrey, Director of the Media Resources Department at the Union Theological Seminary Library, Richmond, Virginia: "Expressions of Man's Self-Understanding in Philosophy and the Sciences," "Thing and Self" (1959), and "Religion, and Philosophy" (1963). Although they are now available through the seminary's collection of audio tapes, they have never been published.

These essays were first transcribed word for word from the audio tapes. From the manuscripts so created, they were edited for reading. Of great assistance in organizing the text were Tillich's handwritten lecture notes, made available in photocopy by Maria Grossmann, Librarian of the Andover-Harvard Theological Library, which houses the Paul Tillich Archives. These notes give outlines of the lectures and have been used to arrange the sectioning, paragraphing, and rubrics in each essay. Thus, insofar as the author's intentions are apparent in his lecture notes, they have been followed. Editing Tillich's lectures to put them into "idiomatic English without changing the Tillichian flavor" has been a traditional task of many of his editors and assistants.[2]

Translations

Three early essays have been translated from the original German for this volume: "Logos and Mythos of Technology" (1927), "The Technical City as Symbol" (1928), and "The Freedom of Science" (1932). The translator, John C. Modschielder, has previously published his translation of Tillich's "Christianity and Modern Society," *Political Expectation,* ed. and intro. James Luther Adams (New York: Harper & Row, 1971). These

---

[2]This was the instruction given to Clark Williamson, Tillich's assistant at the University of Chicago. Pauck, Wilhelm, and Marion, *Paul Tillich: His Life and Thought* (New York: Harper & Row, 1967) 236.

translations were made with a view to providing a readable English text that is faithful to the German original. Also, there has been an attempt to remain consistent with earlier translations of Tillich's work to provide for a continuity of concepts.

Documenting Sources

While the files at the Paul Tillich Archives provide documentation for many of Tillich's lectures, some of the essays listed in the Selected Bibliography at the end of this volume cannot be located as to the date of composition or place of address. Tillich's secretary at the University of Chicago, Eva Shane, was helpful, but knew of no appointment diary to document them. A call for audio tapes and information concerning these essays in the November 1984 newsletter of *The North American Paul Tillich Society* produced no result. The only certain dating possible for these undocumented manuscripts comes from the fact that Tillich did produce essays in German after 1933, but he produced no English works before this date. Therefore, while it is likely that some of these German language lecture notes were produced after to this date, it is certain that none of the English texts were produced before it.

PART I

The Situation
in Technical Society

CHAPTER 1

The World Situation

The Meaning of "World Situation"

To speak of a "world situation" is no longer, as it was even during the nineteenth century, a matter of daring anticipation or utopian vision. Two world wars within a quarter century reveal that "world" as an historical reality has come into being.

"World" in the historical sense connotes such an interrelation of all political groups constituting mankind that events occurring in one section have direct repercussions upon all other sections. "World" in this sense, anticipated by a steady increase in worldwide communication and traffic, by world economic and political relationships, has existed since the First World War. The process advanced with accelerating speed before and during the Second World War.

To be sure, such a "world" exists only in the formal sense of the universal interpretation of all nations. As yet there is no unity of spirit, of culture, of organization, of purpose. Moreover, even the formal unity of the world is more apparent in the West than in the East, and the analysis that follows is necessarily mainly from the perspective of the Occident. Nevertheless, the forces that are transforming civilization are dominant not only in Europe and the Americas. They have penetrated from the West to the East and, not conversely, have drawn Asia and Africa and Australasia also within a single revolutionary vortex. Therefore, it is not only possible but necessary to speak of a "world situation," to seek to discover the inner logic and meaning of that situation, and to ask what message Christianity has to offer it.

The Historical Development
of the World Situation

The present world situation is the outcome—directly in the West and indirectly elsewhere—of the rise, the triumph, and the crisis of what we may term "bourgeois society." This development has occurred in three distinguishable though overlapping phases. In the first, the new society struggled to establish itself over the remnants of a disintegrating feudal society—the period of bourgeois revolutions. In the second, mainly through the creation of a world mechanism of production and exchange, the new society came to triumphant power—the period of victorious bourgeoisie. In the third, mankind struggles to regain control over the self-destructive forces loosed by a regnant industrial society—the present crisis in civilization. The disintegration and transformation of bourgeois society is the dynamic center of the present world situation.

The Period of Bourgeois Revolutions

The first period was marked by great political, economic, and cultural revolutions in Western Europe and America. Feudalism and absolutism, both religious and political, were crushed. The bourgeois way of life became the determining, though not the only influential, factor in Western civilization.

The guiding principle of this revolutionary period was *belief in reason*. Reason did not mean the process of reasoning, but the power of truth and justice embodied in man as man. Man controlling nature and society was the ideal born in the humanisitic theory of the Renaissance, ripened under the patronage of enlightened authoritarianism, and brought to fulfillment through the bourgeois revolutions. Reason was the very principle of humanity that gives man dignity and liberates him from the slaveries of religious and political absolutisms. It is much more akin to the divine logos of the Stoics than to the manipulation of technical skills that won such triumphs in the second period of bourgeois society. The adoration of "Reason" as goddess in the French Revolution was a characteristic expression. The acknowledgment of every man as a rational being, capable of autonomy in his religious as well as his secular life, was the basis of the victorious struggle against the repressions of feudalism and every form of authoritarianism and tyranny.

In this struggle, out of which the modern world was born, one presupposition was always present, sometimes avowed, sometimes tacit. It was the belief that the liberation of reason in every person would lead to the realization of a universal humanity and to a system of harmony between individuals and society. Reason in each individual would be discovered to be in harmony with reason in every other individual. This principle of automatic harmony found expression in every realm of life. In the *economic* realm, it was believed that the welfare of all would be best served by the unrestrained pursuit by each individual of his own economic interests; the common good would be safeguarded by the "laws of the market" and their automatic functioning; this was the root-principle of the economy of laissez-faire. In the *political* realm, it was supposed that the political judgment of each citizen would lead automatically to right political decisions by a majority of citizens; community of interest would assure sound democratic procedures. In the *international* realm, the play of interest among the nations would result in a comparatively stable balance of power between sovereign states. In the sphere of *education,* the essential rationality of human nature would produce, through free self-expression by each individual, a harmonious community. In *religion,* personal interpretation of the Bible and individual religious experience would follow a sufficiently uniform course among all believers to assure moral and spiritual conformity and to create and maintain a religious community of individual worshipers, the church. Finally, this all-controlling idea found *philosophic* expression in various doctrines of preestablished harmony, those of Leibniz, Descartes, and their schools. The individual monad is a microcosm of the world. Ripening according to its own inner laws of logic, it develops in preestablished harmony with the whole of being.

This was the creed of the revolutionary movement in virtually all its intellectual and political leaders. Reality seemed to confirm it. Elements of automatic harmony could be discovered in every realm. The liberation of individual reason in economics and religion, in politics and education, did not bring on the disruptive consequences forecast by traditionalists and reactionaries. On the contrary, tremendous creativity was set free without the destruction of sufficient conformity to maintain national and religious communities. The enthusiastic belief in reason was vindicated by the prodigious achievements of mathematical science in the seventeenth century, by the development of autonomous national states after the disruptions of the Wars of Religion, by the establishment of natural laws in social and personal ethics. The law of harmony appeared to express the nature of reality. In the power of this belief, the new society overcame the resistance of feudalism and absolutism. In spite of all reactionary opposition, the nineteenth century may be regarded as the period of victorious bourgeoisie.

The Period of the Victorious Bourgeoisie

Reason was supposed to control nature, in man and beyond man, because nature and reason were held to be in essential harmony. But in the measure in which the bourgeois revolution succeeded, the revolutionary impetus disappeared, and the character of reason as the guiding principle was transformed. The new ruling class could and did compromise with the remnants of feudalism and absolutism. They sacrificed reason as the principle of truth and justice, and employed it mainly as a tool in the service of the technical society they were bent upon perfecting. "Technical reason" became the instrument of a new system of production and exchange.

Technical reason provides means for ends, but offers no guidance in the determination of ends. Reason in the first period had been concerned with ends beyond the existing order. Technical reason became concerned with means to stabilize the existing order. Revolutionary reason had been conservative with respect to means but "utopian" with respect to ends. Technical reason is conservative with respect to ends and revolutionary with respect to means. It can be used for any purposes dictated by the will, including those that deny reason in the sense of truth and justice. The transformation of *revolutionary reason* into *technical reason* was the decisive feature of the transition from the first to the second period of modern society.

This displacement of revolutionary reason by technical reason was accompanied by far-reaching changes in the structure of human society. Man became increasingly able to control physical nature. Through the tools placed at his disposal by technical reason, he created a worldwide mechanism of large-scale production and competitive economy that began to take shape as a kind of "second nature," a Frankenstein, above physical nature and subjecting man to itself. While he was increasingly able to control and manipulate physical nature, man became less and less able to control his "second nature." He was swallowed up by his own creation. Step by step the whole of human life was subordinated to the demands of the new worldwide economy. Men became units of working power. The profit of the few and the poverty of the many were driving forces of the system. Hidden and irresponsible powers controlled some parts of it, but no one the whole. The movements of the mechanism of production and consumption were irrational and incalculable. So it became for the masses a dark and incomprehensible fate, determining their destiny, lifting them today to a higher standard of life than they had ever known, throwing them down tomorrow into utter misery and the abyss of chronic unemployment. The decisive feature of the period of victorious bourgeoisie is *the loss of control by human reason over man's historical existence*. This situation became manifest in the two world wars and their psychological and sociological consequences. The self-destruction of bourgeois society and its elaborate scheme of automatic harmony is the characteristic of the present period of transition.

The Present Crisis in Civilization

Today the world stands in the third phase of modern history, though in varying degrees in different countries and continents. It has come to fullest expression in the industrial nations of continental Europe. In Anglo-Saxon lands, it has thus far achieved a fairly successful maintenance of the main features of the second period. In Russia and parts of Asia, it has come to power before the second stage had fully developed. These differences must be borne in mind. Their neglect would falsify the analysis and might lead to practical proposals that would be foredoomed to frustration. Nevertheless, it is possible to discern common structural trends that characterize contemporary world society and in its various types. The dynamics of bourgeois society that have precipitated the present world situation have been dominant not only in the industrial nations of the European continent with their unbalanced economies, but likewise in Britain, America, and some smaller European countries with their comparatively stable situations, and also in Russia and the East where resentment against the intrusion of dominating Western exploitation has led to a leap from the first to the third stage of modern social development, from a feudal and authoritarian society to a totalitarian order.

In the third period that determines our world situation, the foundation of bourgeois society has broken down: namely, the conviction of automatic harmony between individual interest and the general interest. It has become obvious that the principle was true only to a limited degree and under especially favorable circumstances. Its validity was dependent upon certain conditions—the continuing power of traditional values and institutions strong enough to counteract the disruptive consequences of the principle; the increasing strength of a liberal economy powerful enough to counteract the inner contradictions of the system through intensive and extensive expansion; the vestigial hold of feudal and absolutistic remnants powerful enough to allay the transmutation of all social life into a market-system. When these retarding and disguising factors disappeared, the principle of automatic harmony was revealed in all its patent insufficiency. Attempts to replace it by a planned economy began. "Rationalization" was invoked as a method of control over the "second nature."

Totalitarianism was the first step in this direction. One expression is the *Fascist systems*. They could achieve partial success because they understood the breakdown of the principle of automatic harmony and satisfied the demand for a planned organization of the life of the masses. In certain important respects, the Fascist systems mark an advance beyond bourgeois society. They have provided minimum security for all. They have reintroduced unassailable authorities and commanding obligations. For these purposes they have employed technical reason in the most effective manner. But the Fascist systems could not succeed ultimately because their basis was national, and thus they increased the disruption of mankind instead of uniting it according to the principle of reason. They destroyed any remnant of revolutionary reason and replaced it by an irrational will to power. Absolutism returned, but without the social, cultural, and religious traditions that furnished solid foundations for the earlier absolute systems.

The other radical expression of the trend toward a planned society is the *Soviet system*. It could succeed for the same reasons that brought partial success to the Fascist systems. And it achieved an even greater security for the masses. Moreover, it has retained, at least in principle, revolutionary reason as an ultimate critical principle. But it also was a return to absolutism without the traditional foundations. It has come under the control of bureaucracy that is inclined to replace revolutionary reason by technical reason after the pattern of the second phase of bourgeois society. Freedom for the individual is as completely lost as under the Fascist systems.

Both systems were reactions against the bourgeois faith in automatic harmony. Both are ambiguous: on the one hand, they attempt to bring the incalculable mechanism of world economy back under the control of man; on the other hand, they aggravate the self-destructive forces generated by the second stage of bourgeois society. Both seek to elevate technical reason to "planning reason"—the characteristic feature of the third period and the determining principle of our present world situation.

The logic of bourgeois society in its struggle for survival is expressed in the development of reason from "revolutionary reason" through "technical reason" to "planning reason." This development must be held clearly in mind in every analysis of the present situation, in every question and answer regarding the future. This development cannot be reversed. We cannot return to a half-feudal absolutism. Neither the spiritual nor the economic conditions for such a return are present. We cannot return to the principle of automatic harmony epitomized in laissez-faire liberalism in economics. The political and social conditions for reestablishing the status quo have been destroyed by the present world catastrophe. And faith in automatic harmony cannot be reestablished among the masses for whom it has meant oscillation between war, boom, depression, and war renewed through thirty years. We must go forward under the direction of planning reason toward an organization of society that avoids both totalitarian absolutism and liberal individualism. This is not an easy course to define or follow. Repelled by the inhuman brutalities of totalitarian planning, we are tempted to seek a return to a more or less concealed laissez-faire solution. Or, disillusioned by the catastrophic discredit of the philosophy of automatic harmony, we incline toward some kind of absolutism. Our task is to find a way between these extremes.

A biblical symbol may aid us in this attempt. When Hobbes developed his theory of the absolute state, he had recourse to the figure of "Leviathan," the all-embracing portent that, in the interest of the state, swallows all elements of independent existence, political and economic, cultural and religious. Struggle against the Leviathan of late-medieval authoritarianism was the genius of the bourgeois revolutions. But the revolutionaries did not foresee that Leviathan was able to assume another face, no less formidable though disguised behind the mask of liberalism: the all-embracing mechanism of capitalist economy, a "second nature," created by man but subjecting the masses of men to its demands and its incalculable oscillations. Since the First World War, the demonic face of this Leviathan has been unveiled. The battle against the destructive consequences of this mechanism has led to the totalitarian organization of national life, and Leviathan appears again with a third face combining features of the first and second faces. The struggle between Leviathan in its second phase and Leviathan in its third phase and the effort of individuals and groups to discover a way by which both of them may be brought into subjection furnish the basic structure of the present world situation. Christianity must give its message to a world in which Leviathan in its different aspects threatens all human existence to its very roots.

The World Situation Reflected in Cultural Life

The general character of the present world situation determines every aspect of mankind's existence. In each sphere of life, the underlying structure can be recognized as directly or indirectly controlling. In some realms, resistance against the general trend is stronger than in others, but none is independent of the determining factors. Although social and economic forces are predominant in our present world, the spiritual realm shows the traits of the "triple-faced Leviathan" as clearly as the economic sphere, and in certain respects more significantly. The mechanism of mass production and distribution has had profound effects not only on economic and political structures but also on the innermost center of *personal life,* and the character of all human *communities,* and on the aims and methods of *education.* We begin therefore with an examination of man's cultural and spiritual life, and return later to the economic and political factors that are there disclosed as more fundamental and determinative.

Changes in Personality Reflected in Portraiture

Personality and community in their interdependence are the very substance and basis of all social structures. The prophets of bourgeois society believed that victory over feudalism and authoritarianism would create both fully developed autonomous persons and true communities of those who had been emancipated to personal freedom; the principle of automatic harmony seemed to guarantee a harmonious society. But in no realm did the disintegrative influence of bourgeois society become more obvious than in that of personality and community. The "rational" individual is separated from every other individual. Society replaces community; cooperation replaces unity in a common reality.

We may take an illustration from art. The aesthetic realm always furnishes the most sensitive barometer of a spiritual climate. "Art indicates what the character of a spiritual situation is; it does this more immediately and directly than do science or philosophy. . . . Science is of greater importance in the formation of a spiritual situation, but art is the more important for its apprehension.''[1]

If we study portraits by Rembrandt, especially in his later period, we confront personalities who are like self-enclosed worlds—strong, lonely, tragic but unbroken, carrying the marks of their unique histories in every line of their faces, expressing the ideals of personality of a humanistic Protestantism. To compare these portraits with Giotto's pictures of St. Francis and his monks is to recognize the difference between two worlds. Giotto's Francis is the expression of a divine power by which man is possessed and elevated beyond his individual character and personal experiences. So are all other figures in Giotto's paintings. Between Giotto and Rembrandt are the portraits of Titian—individual expressions of humanity as such, representative of the greatness, beauty, and power of man. The transcendent reality to which Giotto subjects all individuals, their actions and emotions, has disappeared; but the unique individual, as in Rembrandt, has not yet appeared. The personality that found its highest portraiture in Rembrandt's picture is the personality of the early bourgeois spirit, still subject to absolute forces, still shaped by the Protestant conscience, but already standing by itself, independent alike of transcendent grace and humanity. In these painters, the development of the ideal of personality in the modern world finds classic expression.

If we take the long step to portraits painted since the middle of the nineteenth century, we are in still another world. Individuals with a highly developed intellectuality and strong will appear—the bearers of technical reason, the creators of large-scale world economy, of the great monopolies, the conquerors of the forces of nature, and the anonymous directors of the worldwide mechanism of capitalistic society. Personality has become at once the ruler and the servant of Leviathan. Will power and technical rationality are united, and thus the way is prepared for the Fascist type in which the last remnants of the classical and humanistic ideal of personality are completely lost.

In the time of Giotto, relation to transcendent reality gave meaning, center, and content to personal life. In Titian, belief in the divinity of the human and the humanity of the divine furnished the center of meaning. In Rembrandt, the experience of life with its tragedy and its ultimate hope determined personal existence. But the person of the period of triumphant

---

[1]Paul Tillich, *The Religious Situation* (New York: Meridian Books, 1956) 85.

bourgeoisie was dominated by purposes without ultimate meaning and by sensations and actions without spiritual center. It was a personality that could still use the traditions of the past for aesthetic enjoyment, but that was not shaped by them. This naturalistic personality was formed by the demands of modern economy and by neither divinity nor humanity, even if humanitarian and religious obligations were retained in the form of the moral or conventional standards of the bourgeois era.

The principle of harmony between reason and nature had promised the harmonious development of personal life if only ecclesiastical and political restrictions were removed. It was supposed that each man's personal center would organize all bodily and mental functions in a meaningful unity. The ideal of personality as the actualization by each educated individual of all human possibilities displaced the ideal of participation by every man, whether educated or not, in a common spiritual reality that transcends him and yet at the same time gives him a personal center. In this fashion, the majority of human beings, since they could not share in the realization of the individualist goal, were excluded from significant participation in the ideal. There were consigned to remnants of religious tradition, or to education in technical reason and conventional morals. But even in the priviledged strata of society, the situation was not greatly different. Technical intelligence replaced humanistic reason. Prophetic minds of the nineteenth century saw this transformation taking place, and they foresaw its destructive consequences. But they could not prevent it. Despite their protests, the technical depersonalization of man spread, not only in Europe and America but all over the world.

But man is fully rational only on the foundation of, and in interdependence with, nonrational factors. Therefore the predominance of technical reason evoked a reaction by the vital forces in man. They arose and made themselves manifest in both theory and practice. Whether called ''instinct'' or ''passion'' or ''libido'' or ''interest'' or ''urge'' or ''will to power'' or ''*elan vital*'' or ''unconscious ground,'' they cannot be denied. They make it impossible to transform man into a psychological mechanism with intelligence and adjustability. They revolt against control by merely utilitarian reason. The conventional veil concealing the dynamic center of living man has been torn aside. *Elan vital* displaced the rational center of early humanism.

However, the vitalistic protest against the mechanization of man is as ambiguous as reactions against Leviathan in other realms. These protests have changed its face, but not its being. Consciousness, discovering the unconscious, tries to bring it into servitude to its own purposes. Instead of repressing it, as early Victorian morals demanded, it elevates it into equality with consciousness. The "adjusted" personality becomes a more perfect instrument of an all-controlling will, surrendering itself with fanaticism to irrational and unconditioned purposes.

Changes in Structure of Communities

The development of the modern idea of personality in its main stages has had its parallels in the structure of all communities, natural communities such as the family and historical communities such as the state.

In the *first stage,* represented by the pictures of Giotto, every individual participates in a communal movement created by loyalty to a transcendent reality. It is an all-embracing community in which every individual, both peasant and prince, is borne forward by the same spiritual reality. In the life of the Renaissance, outstanding individuals are predominant. They are isolated, each in his own way representing general humanity, dealing with one another in the relations of a privileged society but no longer in terms of community. The person of Protestant humanism is a member of an active group united by common purposes—the defense of pure doctrine, the struggle against absolutism, the crusade for the establishment of the kingdom of God. This is a community, however, not on the basis of a common ground, of universal authority, but on the basis of common devotion to particular aims for which it is necessary to fight. The spiritual center of this community lies in the future.

In the *second period* of bourgeois society, not only a common spiritual ground but a common spiritual purpose was lost. In consequence, the different forms of community disintegrated. The family disintegrated into individuals, each of whom lives for himself in the service of the mechanism of society. Communities of workers were replaced by mass cooperation of a nonpersonal character. Patriarchal responsibility for the servant, his welfare and his loyalty, gave way to the relations of legal contract. Neighborhood as a form of community lost its meaning. The national community recovered reality only when attacked and lost it again when danger passed. Even the community of friendship was destroyed by the universal sway of competition. Bourgeois society in its second phase destroyed community because it destroyed any common foundation and any common purpose. The service of the mechanism of mass production is not a possible spiritual center for community. It separates individuals from one another in spiritual loneliness and competition. It turns them into atoms in the service of mechanical processes. It is not based on a common idea but on the controlling economic and psychological necessity that each man subject himself to the mechanism. Thus communities disintegrate into masses. Masses have neither common ground nor common purposes. They are driven in their objective existence by the incalculable movements of the mechanism of production, subjectively by the laws of mass psychology. This was the main sociological feature of the second period of bourgeois society. Many keen observers during the nineteenth century noted the dissolution of personality into atoms and community into masses, and they forecast the cultural and political self-destruction of society.

To be sure, the trends just described were never completely victorious. Prebourgeois groups and precapitalist attitudes survived. In Russia, the majority of the populace were hardly touched by the disintegration of community. In America, the Protestant humanist ideals of personality and community are still vital in large sections of the country. In Asia, the family system resisted bourgeois atomization. But all these forms are under continuous and advancing attack. The dissolution of the family, of neighborhood, of personal cooperation is rapidly progressing. Even more important is the fact that every attempt to halt the general process of mechanization was finally subjected to the mechanism against which it protested. For example, European youth movements sought escape by fleeing to nature and emotional communion. But they were caught in the totalitarian movements and transformed into instruments of its authoritarian machinery. To be sure, individuals in these groups no longer felt isolated and lonely. They were organized, and their every activity, thought, and emotion was planned and prescribed. Often they became not dissimilar to the "fighting orders" in the earlier opposite transition from feudalism to freedom. These groups that now embrace the whole younger generation in Fascist and Communist countries are "commanded" communities, logically a contradiction in terms, but in practice a very effective method for overcoming the feeling of solitude that was so prevalent in the second period, more effective than the invocation of solidarity in the labor movements of the nineteenth century. The new type of personality produced in these communities has its spiritual center completely beyond itself in the collectivity to which it belongs. The individual has become the self-dedicated instrument of the "second nature" in large-scale capitalism. Unconditional surrender to an unconditionally accepted purpose, resignation of any kind of autonomy, fanatical devotion are features of their existence. These are consciously dehumanized groups of human beings very different from the automatically dehumanized industrial masses of the nineteenth century.

Thus, in the *third stage* of the bourgeois development, the attempt has been made to reestablish community on the basis of antibourgeois doctrines through fighting groups fired by a fanatical will to a new order of life and forged into the unity that always characterizes the fighting period of any revolutionary movement. The question is whether a real community has been born in these groups, whether a new "we-consciousness" has arisen that can overcome the atomization of a mechanized society. The situation is as ambiguous as in all other realms. On the one hand, a great effort has been made to overcome the loneliness of the individual within an absolutely devoted community. On the other hand, the method employed in this attempt represents the most radical employment of mechanization in the service of the new idea. The struggle against the dehumanization produced by the mechanism of modern capitaliam has used even more fully mechanized methods and has thus carried through the process of dehumanization to its logical end.

Changes in Education

The disruption and transformation of personality and community were furthered, both consciously and unconsciously, by changes in the philosophy and methods of education.

Prior to the modern period, a principle aim of education had been the induction of persons into the living community and tradition of the church. It was significant that education originated within the church, was conducted mainly by the church, and was impregnated with the presuppositions and aims of Christian faith.

Reason as the principle of truth demands education for and through reason for everyone, and the massive achievements in educational theory and practice in Western civilization are due to this creative impulse. Humanistic education aimed to actualize humanity in each individual. World citizenship was the social goal and classical humanism the shaping tradition. Religion was recognized as one element in the development of the humanistic personality, but not its ground or center. This ideal had great power all through the *first period* of bourgeois society. It was set over against traditional ecclesiastical education, and it produced many notable representatives of Christian humanism.

But this humanistic ideal for education could not touch the masses. It requires favorable circumstances that society provides for only a few—a large measure of economic independence, outstanding intellectual abilities, rearing within a tradition of culture, et cetera. Consequently, education for the masses could not follow this pattern. Either it was neglected as in England or was adapted to a more technical pattern as in Germany.

In the *second period,* the humanistic ideal of education lost its hold and was employed more and more as a decoration necessary for social prestige or for professional advantage. Vocational education for particular purposes increasingly replaced humanistic education for a perfect humanity. In subservience to the demands of a technical reason, so-called realistic education based on the natural and technical sciences step by step supplanted education through the humanities. Meantime, technical education for the masses for the service of large-scale industry was extended and refined. "Adjustment" became more and more the principle of education, adjustment to the existing society. Everyone must receive public school education, everyone must learn those skills most useful for success in the mechanism of production, everyone must subject himself to the ideals and norms of the dominant system. For many, the main purpose of education became that degree of adjustment that prevents serious disturbance of the existing order by uncontrolled individual initiative or revolutionary group action. To be sure, this was often hidden to the educators as well as to those educated. Individual spontaneity was cultivated. Productivity was not suppressed but encouraged. Religious and humanistic traditions were appreciated and used. So it seemed to be a truly "liberal" education, faithful to the humanistic and Christian heritage. Actually, the cultural achievements of the past wove an idealistic veil over the nakedness of this education and hid the face of Leviathan who was its real master. They had lost their original significance, their power as the expression of human possibilities and ultimate realities. In the measure that education has been subjected to the mechanism of modern society, it has lost its relation to truth and justice and consequently any ultimate meaning. Thus it becomes a ready victim of various kinds of nonrational powers that seek to give it meaning.

The whole trend is clearly reflected in developments in specifically *religious education.* Religious education was originally an introduction into the tradition, the faith, and the sacramental experience of the Christian church. This was still true of the churches of the Reformation though emphasis upon individual experience had increased. In the early stages of the modern period, autonomous reason could use religion as an element in the full development of human personality. But the more radical types of bourgeois education excluded religious education or recognized religion simply as a subject of historical interest. Within the churches, religious education either sought to adapt itself to the demands of autonomous reason or cultivated seclusion from the dominant trends in the surrounding culture. If the method of adaptation was chosen, religious education tended to become more and more a means of confirming the ideals of bourgeois society with the authority of religious tradition. If seclusion was practiced, religious education became more and more unacceptable to the younger generation. Indeed it created powerful resistance against both religious education and religion itself and thus prepared fertile soil for totalitarian education to pseudoreligions.

But education without a determining center is impossible. Since the church with its beliefs and symbols was no longer the agent of educational indoctrination, the nation or local community increasingly took its place. States or cities took over responsibility for education. The nation was the community whose life must be interpreted by the teacher. Its history, constitution, and present needs were the realities to which the teacher must adapt the pupil. Many emotional elements such as language, home, landscape, friendships are tied up with it. The nation became the ideological center that demanded absolute devotion, though itself above criticism. Here likewise, the way was prepared for the third phase.

Vacillation in educational method between the ideal of autonomy and adjustment has been brought to an end in the *third period*. Adjustment as complete subjection increasingly swallowed the autonomous elements of liberal education. The breakdown of belief in reason had created intellectual insecurity and cynicism. Bourgeois conventions that, in the period of victorious bourgeoisie, gave an impression of rational harmony had lost their power. In the totalitarian schemes, education became an introduction to a fighting, and eventually ruling, group. Rational criticism is excluded. Knowledge for its own sake is discounted. Everything is related to the ultimate purpose of the group. Education for death, the demonic symbol created by National Socialism, expresses this final form of education in the service of Leviathan. Although there may be little danger that controlled education of this extreme type will prevail widely after the overthrow of

Fascism, it must be recognized that standardized communication through radio, movies, press, and fashions tends to create standardized men who are all too susceptible to propaganda for old or new totalitarian purposes.

The ambiguous character of totalitarian education is obvious. On the one hand, it leads beyond sterile adjustment to the mechanism of the industrial system. It overpasses the emptiness of such an aim. It creates enthusiasm, devotion, even fanaticism. On the other hand, it sacrifices personal life and individual creativity, the remaining elements of reason and harmony, more completely than has ever happened before.

The Christian answer to the educational problem must be given in unity with the answer to the problems of personality and community. Christianity achieves actuality in a community based upon the appearance of Ultimate Reality in a historic person, Jesus Christ. For Christian faith, this event is in a profound sense the center of history. The community that carries the spirit of Jesus Christ through the centuries is the "assembly of God," the church. But this church follows upon an age-long preparation—a general preparation in all religions and cultures throughout the world and a special preparation in an "elect people." Accordingly, we must recognize not only the manifest church but also a "latent" or "potential" church existing everywhere and at all times.

Ideally, education should be introduction into this church, the interpretation of its meaning and the communication of its power. Such education would embrace humanistic, scientific, and technical elements. But it would provide meaning and cohesion for them all. The more collectivistic periods of history were right in holding an aim for education equally valid for everyone and bearing directly or indirectly on everything. They were wrong in limiting free development of individual and social powers by the spiritual center toward which all education was oriented. The Christian answer to the present educational system must point men toward such a community as is sufficiently concrete and commanding to claim the hearts of individuals and masses and yet also sufficiently transcendent and universal to embrace all human ideals and possibilities.

The World Situation
Reflected in the Economic, Political,
and International Spheres

The Economic Realm

As already noted, it was the assumption of bourgeois civilization that, in the economic realm, the welfare of all would be best served by the unrestrained pursuit of each individual of his own interests; the common good would be safeguarded by the automatic functioning of the "laws of the market." This was the root principle of laissez-faire.

As a matter of fact, there was never a time when the economy of laissez-faire was in complete control. Since the beginning of the present century, a trend away from its rigorous application has been observable. State support and regulation more and more supplemented the operations of the free market. The necessity for such interference has become increasingly obvious since the First World War and especially in the days of the last great depression. Even in America, the insufficiency of liberal individualism for a large-scale economy under the dominance of rapid technical progress has become apparent. Economic crises become more frequent, more widespread, more disastrous. Chronic unemployment with its attendant misery and despair for large sections of the population, intolerable insecurity and fear for others, the dehumanizing effects of life bereft of meaning and hope for many—all these revealed the fundamental illness of the capitalist economy. At the same time, failure to maintain a sound balance between the potentialities of production and the demands of consumption, and the necessity of bolstering private enterprise to prevent total collapse argued to the same conclusion. A revolutionary situation emerged. In more critical moments when the threatened breakdown of large industries endangered the whole national economy, even the most ruthless individualists in big business sought state intervention. In these moments, they welcomed the "socialization of their losses," though in the next moment, when the immediate danger had passed, they vigorously opposed any attempt by the state to create conditions that might forestall a recurrence. The present phase of economic development is determined primarily by state interference with the self-destructive mechanisms of the capitalist economy.

But state intervention was in most cases an ambiguous device: on the one hand, it saved the monopolistic system from complete collapse; on the other hand, it produced resentment in those who were saved by it because it limited their free use of economic power.

State interference was a halfway measure that, in the long run, could not survive. In Fascist countries, its contradictions were solved by an amalgamation of the leading monopolies with the state, and the dictatorial administration of both of them, though without abolition of private ownership. In Russia, private ownership of industry was completely abolished and the entire economy is dominated by a bureaucracy interested in furthering production and in the prestige and power associated with it, but not in private profits. In the United States, on the other hand, state interference has induced a growing reaction against the managing bureaucracy and a strong trend back toward industrial autonomy. In Great Britain, public opinion oscillates between the two extremes and seeks a third way in terms of an all-embracing scheme of social security with the maintenance of capitalist ownership. In the meantime, the economies of all countries have been brought into complete subservience to centralized war administrations.

The basic question for the present situation is: Shall mankind return to the monopolistic economy from which our present economic, political, and psychological disintegration has resulted? Or shall mankind go forward to a unified economy that is neither totalitarianism nor a war expedient? If the former rulers are able to effect the first course against the demands of the masses for security, a reenactment of the history of recent decades leading to a final catastrophe can be forecast. On the other hand, if the masses are powerful enough to force their way forward against the vested strength of the traditional rulers, the question will arise as to how a rational organization of world economy can be developed without the creation of a mechanism as oppressive as the ''second nature'' created by capitalism. In summary, how can security and a decent standard of life for all be attained according to the infinite productive power of mankind, without the complete mechanization and dehumanization of man? This is the question to which Christianity must seek to bring an answer.

Christianity cannot offer technical advice for economic planning, but that is not necessary. According to leading economists, the economic problem can no longer be regarded merely as a problem of perfecting economic techniques. The technical aspects of planning for stability and efficiency have been explored in all directions, both theoretically and practically. The problem of an economic system able to give security of permanent full employment and certainty of decent livelihood for all lies much more largely in the realms of political and moral decisions. It is in the realms in which religious principles are decisive. Christianity can insist that the virtually infinite productive capacities of mankind shall be used for the advantage of everyone, instead of being restricted and wasted by the profit interests of a controlling class and the struggle for power between different groups within that class. Christianity should reveal and destroy the vicious circle of production of means as ends, which in turn become means without any ultimate end. It must liberate man from bondage to an incalculable and inhuman system of production that absorbs the creative powers of his soul by ruthless competition, fear, despair, and the sense of utter meaninglessness. Christianity must denounce equally a religious utopianism that talks about abolishing the profit motive by persuasion in order to evade necessary social transformation and a religious escapism that proclaims a transcendent security of eternal values in order to divert the masses from their present economic insecurity. At the same time Christianity must reject totalitarian solutions of the economic problem insofar as they destroy spontaneity in the relations between man and his work and deprive the individual of his basic rights as a person. Christianity must support plans for economic reorganization that promise to overcome the antithesis of absolutism and individualism, even if such plans imply a revolutionary transformation of the present social structure and the liquidation of large vested interests.

Politics

Politics and economics cannot be separated. They are interdependent. Democracy was the weapon with which the fighting bourgeoisie conquered absolutism. It was, however, a limited democracy. In England, up to the present century, it was limited by restrictions as to the right to vote and by an aristocratic and exclusive system of education for and election to political leadership. In France after the Great Revolution, it was limited by the device of a census designed to safeguard the bourgeois upper classes against participation in the control of the nation by the disinherited masses. In the United States, it was limited by the tradition of a two-party system that prevented the industrial classes from becoming an independent political power and, in the South, by a poll tax that prevented the masses from influencing policy. In imperial Germany, the power of conservative Prussia and the King-Emperior were effective checks upon the autonomy of the Reichstag. Alongside these limitations on democratic procedure, there were important outlets for the rising pressure of the masses—in America, the frontier and the inexhaustible resources of a continent; in France, the dominance of the petty-bourgeoisie and an incomplete industrialization; in Germany, a rapidly rising standard of life; in Britain, the colonial empire and shrewd adjustment by the ruling classes to the needs of the hour.

Today, the situation has changed, partly through dislocation in the factors that made effective democracy possible, partly under rising pressure from the masses who have become restive under the impact of recent political and economic catastrophes and demand full participation in democratic processes. In large sections of the world, democracy never existed. In many countries where it existed in varying degrees of strength, it has been destroyed. In still others, it has been saved by drastic modifications in original theory and practice. In all democratic countries, a marked antidemocratic trend is noticeable. There are three main expressions of this trend toward new forms of political life. In one, a single party attempts to gain totalitarian control over the entire nation, abolishing any democratic check upon its use of power—the Fascist type. In the second, aristocratic and monopolistic elements seek to strengthen their control by undermining democratic methods and a democratic faith—the reactionary type. In the third, a democratically established bureaucracy achieves more and more independence and creates the tools for a planned reorganization of society; the New Deal is representative of this type. By recourse to such measures democracy seems to be saved very much as capitalism was temporarily saved by recourse to state interference.

All these varied developments prove that the theory of liberalism has as limited possibilities in politics as in economics. It can work only under comparatively favorable conditions. Democracy presupposes a natural harmony between the different interests and, therefore, the likelihood of a satisfactory balance between them. When this balance is destroyed, democracy no longer works. More particularly, democracy is successful so long as the interests of different groups are harmonious to such a degree that the minority prefers acceptance of the majority decision to a revolutionary effort to overthrow it. When the point is reached where the minority no longer accepts the majority decision, democratic procedures fail. This may happen through the initiative of revolutionary groups from below or of reactionary groups from above or, in the case of Fascism, by an alliance of revolutionary and reactionary elements at the middle.

The great political question that emerges in the present situation is: Can we return to democratic institutions that have been partly abolished, by the development of democracy itself? Can we turn backward while facing the gigantic task of reconstructing a world in ruins with millions of human beings at the limit of a tolerable human existence? If it is not possible to go back, must we go forward to a centralized world bureaucracy? Would that not mean the end of democratic procedures everywhere? And would that, in turn, not involve the exclusion of the common people from the establishment of a world that is supposed to be their world?

In seeking answers to these questions, a first requisite is to recognize the ambiguity of the term *democracy*. *Democracy as a constitutional procedure* for the establishment of government is a political form that embraces a great variety of methods. It must be considered as a means to an end but not as an end in itself. It can be employed as long as it works successfully and no longer. *Democracy as a way of life* that does justice to the dignity of every human being is the basic principle of political ethics. But it may be that democracy in the latter sense can be realized only by a limitation or transformation of democracy in the first sense. Jefferson's prophecy that democratic procedures will work only as long as differences in power and property are not too great has been vindicated. New methods are demanded in order to save "the democratic way of life" in the ethical and religious sense. Such methods must effect a planned organization of society that is neither Fascist nor reactionary. Christianity must support them as it must support corresponding plans for social security and a higher standard of life. Christianity must support both, not by technical or legal suggestions, but primarily by the creation of a new community that can find expression in political forms. Christianity must not identify itself with any particular political form, whether feudalism or bureaucratic patriarchalism or democracy. It cannot sanction democratic forms that disguise the destruction of community and personality. It cannot accept the double-faced Leviathan whether he presents himself through democratic or authoritarian structures. Christianity must declare that, in the next period of history, those political forms are right that are able to produce and maintain a community in which chronic fear of a miserable and meaningless life for the masses is abolished, and in which every man participates creatively in the self-realization of the community, whether local, national, regional, or international.

International Relations

Thus the problem of international relations is raised. The present international situation shows one fact with unchallengeable finality; The division of the world into a larger number of states, each possessed of unlimited sovereignty and right of self-determination, does not effect what was expressed of it—a balance of power according to the principle of automatic harmony. The present international situation, not less than the economic and political situations, is the definitive refutation of that principle. This is true not only of continental Europe, where it is most obvious but also of the Americas and Asia and the Middle East. It is true of all sections of the world, just because today "world" is a historical reality.

Balance of power was the obvious principle for relations between nations at a time when the unity of the Holy Roman Empire had disintegrated and a number of independent sovereign states had appeared. Just as in economics and politics the former bases of unity were replaced by the theory of automatic harmony, so in the world scene the religious cohesions were replaced by the assumedly automatic harmonies of sovereign states. There is always a measure of natural balance of power in life, but the "balance of power" theory goes beyond this natural adjustment between all the forces of life. Moreover, it presupposed a second principle, that of national sovereignty. Logically the two principles are contradictory; only a powerful belief in preestablished harmony could assume their compatibility. This confidence was not wholly misplaced. As the frontier situation in America was the most favorable condition for liberal democracy, so the economic world-frontier situation of early capitalism was the most favorable condition for the balance of power. In a world with practically infinite spaces for external development and equally infinite possibilities for internal development, conflicts between states, though not avoidable, were not fatal in their consequences. Always some nations were not involved; wars between nations did not become global wars. World was still an idea but not yet a reality.

Today, world is a reality. This conflict between absolute national sovereignty and automatic harmony expressed through the balance of power has become manifest. The more internal and external extension by individual nations was blocked by world competition and the industrial development of backward and subject peoples, the sharper and more sanguine became international conflicts. The formation of the League of Nations was a recognition of the breakdown of natural harmonies in international relations. But the League of Nations, like state interference in economics and bureaucracy in domestic politics, was a halfway measure. It sought to limit sovereignty, just as state interference saved the principles of monopolistic production. And in similar fashion, it evoked resentment in some sovereign nations guaranteed by it, just as state interference evoked resentment in monopolist capitalists who were maintained by it.

In comparison with the ambiguity of the League of Nations, Fascism attempted a radical solution. It wiped out lesser sovereign states and created unity by conquest and economic consolidation. This destruction of sovereignty and balance of power by military occupation may produce a trend back to absolute sovereignty. Hate of the conquerors by the subjugated peoples is already leading to an increase of national fanaticism and self-reliance. It is ominous that in Asia enmity toward the white race drives in the same direction, toward intensified nationalism and exaggerated claims of absolute sovereignty. In the meantime, the necessity of achieving world unity tempts the victor nations to establish a centralized system of world domination under their control, but raises the question whether one group of nations can establish unity in the world without destroying creative freedom throughout the world. In still other quarters, there are efforts to find a "third way" in terms of "federation."

To the latter Christianity may lend its support as it must support the third way in economics and domestic politics. But Christianity must raise the question: What is the realistic basis of federation? Without a common ground in the substance of social life, federation cannot survive. Such a unifying basis may be found in the first instance in the obvious economic interdependence of all the nations. Indeed, the problem of international relations is much more likely to be solved by this emphasis than by a direct attack upon national prejudices and loyalties, which may well be aggravated rather than allayed by the war. But beyond the undermining of absolute sovereignty through stressing the economic unity of mankind, Christianity must stress the necessity of a common spirit within each federation of nations.

The World Situation
in the Intellectual Realm

From Philosophy to Natural Sciences

In the *first period* of modern history, the realm of knowledge and philosophy was the most important for discerning the deeper character of the age. Here belief in autonomous reason declared and justified itself to the mind of man. Reason was conceived as the organ of truth, in philosophy as well in psychology and sociology. The development of reason as the quest for truth was identified with the development of humanity. If every individual surrenders himself to the search for knowledge, truth will be discovered, and a "natural system" of thought and action will be established. Truth was conceived as the truth about life as a whole, embracing politics, ethics, aesthetics, religion. Although mathematics furnished a pattern of method, all realms of being and meaning were to be included in the construction of the "natural system of thought and life." The eighteenth century delighted to call itself the "philosophical century," not because it was productive of great systems but because it sought to bring every aspect of life within the sway of philosophy, in both theory and practice. Thus reason in the eighteenth century was revolutionary reason. It was not interested in describing what is merely because it is, but because it supplies materials for the reconstruction of society in conformity to what is natural and reasonable.

Very different was the outlook of the *nineteenth century*. The gargantuan mechanism of an industrial civilization was swelling to the height of its power and bringing every aspect of thought as well as life under its sway, thus radically transforming the guiding principles of the human mind as well as the actual conditions of human existence. Reacting against the revolutionary rationalism of the eighteenth century, the spirit of the times became skeptical, positivistic, and conservative in every respect with the single exception of technical science. The natural sciences furnished the pattern for all knowledge, and also for practical life and religion. Science itself became positivistic: reality must simply be accepted as it is; no rational criticism of it is permissible. The so-called fact and its adoration replaced the "meaning" and its interpretation. Statistics replaced norms. Material replaced nature. Logical possibilities replaced existential experience. The quest for truth became a method of foreseeing the future instead of creating it. Rational truth was replaced by instincts and pragmatic beliefs. And the instincts and beliefs were those of the ruling classes and their conventions. Philosophy was largely restricted to epistemology. It became the servant of technical progress, its scientific foundations and its economic control. Following the breakdown of belief in rational truth as the determining factor in life, "technical reason"—not aspiring to provide truth but merely to furnish means toward the realization of ends determined by instincts and will—became decisive throughout the world as far as the dominance of Western influences reaches.

The general trend in the first two periods of the modern development is clearly reflected in men's attempts to interpret themselves. It is the story of man's estrangement from himself and of his efforts to return to himself.

After he had divided human nature into two distinct realities after the manner of Descartes—the "thinking self" and the "extended self"—he detached his thought from each of these realities and made each of them objects alongside other objects to be analyzed and subjected to general laws as he might analyze and classify a stone or an amoeba. His physical mechanism, without spontaneity, and his psychological mechanism, without freedom, were separated from each other and then, one after the other, treated as elements in the universal mechanism of nature, in terms of either a physical mechanics or of mechanistic psychology assumed to underlie both. In this fashion, the living unity of all human existence became lost in the process of man's self-interpretation. Man had become a part of the abstract mechanism he himself had created for purposes of control. He had become a part of the machine into which he had transformed himself and his world in both theory and practice. In order to establish control of reality for mechanical ends, man had lost himself. This self-estrangement was the price he had to pay to modern science and economy.

To be sure, there were always reactions against the dominant tendency—old feudal and new mass revolts against the practical dehumanization of life, old idealistic and new vitalistic protests against the loss of spontaneity, of creativity, of concreteness in conceptions of man's being and of reality generally. But these reactions were suppressed as long as the bourgeois spirit was mounting in power and the contradictions of bourgeois civilization were not yet apparent. The tremendous success of natural and technical sciences doomed every theoretical protest against their universal applicability to futility.

The Aesthetic Realm

As we might expect, it was in the aesthetic realm that the same all-embracing tendencies found most sensitive and extreme manifestation. And, in accordance with a principle we noted earlier, it was in the field of the arts that the reaction from the dominance of a technical civilization and its consequences for personality first became evident.

Naturalism in literature and art accompanied the triumph of the mechanistic economy of large-scale production and its theoretical counterpart, the mechanization of all reality. Aesthetic naturalism, like scientific naturalism, started with the realm of objective reality. *Realism* was the depiction in word and color of a world under the domination of mechanism, the "second nature." But it revealed both the enmity between man and his creation and the gulf between man and man in the prevailing society. Inevitably there was a strong reaction against realism. It threatened the society that for decades had sought to cover its brutal reality with idealistic pretensions. Thus naturalism retreated into the realm of the subjective, trying to describe the impression reality makes upon the sensual subject. *Impressionism* is subjective naturalism that uses objective reality, with all its distortions and horrors, as material for aesthetic intuition. It is a method of escape, available only to those belonging directly or indirectly to the ruling groups, into a sphere of *l' art pour l' art* in which aesthetics becomes an end in itself and man's alienation from himself is forgotten through pure aesthetic enjoyment. Thus aesthetic naturalism had a double significance. On the one hand, it was an expression of the general development of the second period, supporting its dominant trend toward a mechanized world. On the other hand, it was also a disclosure of the self-alienation of man in this period, and thus has contributed to the revolutionary reactions of the succeeding epoch.

Naturalism in its two forms was the great creative style of nineteenth-century art and literature. To be sure, it was not the only one. Romantic and classical opposition were always present since bourgeois society was never all-embracing. But only those aesthetic works showed creativity and progress that either were in harmony with the general trend toward a mechanized naturalism or anticipated revolutionary opposition to it. Idealism in art and philosophy was cultivated by the middle-class creators of the "second nature" as a veil over the naturalistic face of Leviathan. When the evil was torn away by the contradictions of history and the rapid proletarianization of this group, they often became principal supporters of Fascism.

The development from the second to the *third* period is revealed in the realm of art by expressionism and surrealism. It is worthy to note that the artists and writers of the early twentieth century showed an almost prophetic sensitivity to the catastrophes soon to come. They turned away from naturalism in both its forms, either in the more mystical manner of expressionism or in the more demonic-fantastic fashion of surrealism. *Expressionism* has been well characterized as the warning of the earthquake that was approaching. In *surrealism,* the mechanisms of bourgeois society are used and cut into fragments at the same time; the real world disappears and objectivity is transformed into a phantasmagoria constructed out of pieces and fragments of the bourgeois reality. A panic-driven humanity reveals the doom of its world in its artistic and poetic creations.

The Rise of Existentialism

Since the close of the nineteenth century, the breakdown of mechanistic naturalism in all fields of knowledge has become apparent. History, psychology, biology, physics, and even mathematics entered a period of crisis with respect to their true foundations, their interrelations, and their meaning of life. A unifying truth was sought, a truth not merely theoretical but also practical. Philosophy itself helped to prepare the new situation. Against the imperious reign of technical reason yielding the detached impersonal knowledge of mechanistic naturalism, there arose the demand for knowledge concerned with life in which the very existence of the knower himself is involved. "Existential truth" was the goal. A truth that concerns us as living, deciding men has a character quite different from the truth that reason, whether humanistic reason or technical reason, was supposed to provide. It is not general truth to be accepted by everyone on the basis of his rational nature. It cannot be gained by detached analysis and verifiable hypothesis. It is particular truth claiming universal validity on the basis of its adequacy to the concrete situation. Existential truth in its many forms has one common trait: it has no criterion beyond fruitfulness for life. The dismissal of reason as guide to truth is the surrender of any objective standard of truth. Consequently the only basis of decision between contradictory claims to represent concrete truth is a pragmatic test: the power of an "existential truth" to make itself universal, if need be by force. Thus political power could become the standard of possession of truth.

Truth that concerns life, it was claimed, must originate in life. But, whose life? The "philosophies of existence" are as different from each other as the experiences out of which the various philosophers of existence interpret reality. It can be the ethical existence of the anxious and lonely individual concerned about eternity, as with Kierkegaard. It can be the revolutionary existence of the disinherited proletariat concerned about its future, as with Marx. It can be the existence of the dominating aristocracy concerned about its power over life, as with Nietzsche. It can be the existence of the vital intuitionist concerned about the fullness of experience, as with Bergson. It can be the existence of the experimenting pragmatist, as with James. It can be the faithful existence of the religious activist, as with apostles of the Social Gospel. In each of these definitions of existence, truth has a different content; but in each of them truth is a matter of fate and decision, not of detached observation or of ultimate rational principles. Nevertheless, it is claimed to be truth, possessing universal validity though not general necessity. It is supposed to be verifiable by subsequent experience, although not in the fashion of scientific experimentation.

The issue of existential truth has arisen and cannot be silenced. But it is ambiguous. On the one hand, it represents a protest against the mechanism of production to which reason as a principle of truth has been surrendered. On the other hand, through existential truth the mechanism, the "second nature," is greatly strengthened. For existential truth also surrenders reason and uses only technical rationality for its nonrational purposes. It dissolves the criterion of truth and with it the safeguard against irrational forces.

Truth in this sense concerns human existence as such, and not specialized knowledge except as the latter is dependent, directly or indirectly, upon decision about the nature and meaning of human existence. "Existential truth" need not interfere with methods of empirical research; it does interfere with the interpretation of the meaning of such research and its results. It does interfere with the foundations of knowledge, with man's understanding of himself and his situation in the world.

The issue, therefore, concerns not only philosophy but also all realms of knowledge. The steady progress of knowledge in the special sciences is not questioned, but their relation to other sciences, to truth as such, to the totality of life, to the meaning of existence, is questioned. It is the issue of the right relation between empirical and existential knowledge.

In practice, it is always different to draw a clear line between empirical and existential knowledge. The totalitarian systems have drawn a boundary in such fashion that everything with direct bearing upon technical processes, and therefore on the power it supplies over nature and man, is left outside of the question of existence. Technical science is not interfered with. Its task is merely to produce tools by which "existential truths" may be carried into reality. All other realms of life have lost their autonomy and are required to express the chosen existential truth. Thus, in the third period of modern society, technical reason is employed to execute the commands of an existential decision above which there is no rational criterion. The vitalistic interpretation with its irrationalism is radically opposed to the revolutionary interpretation with its cold use of reason for chosen ends—a basic contrast between Fascism and Communism. But in both cases, the idea of truth is grounded in a particular type of human existence that claims to have discovered an existential truth that is at the same time universal.

The abuses of existential thinking and the self-estranged position of reason demand an answer in which existential truth and ultimate truth are united. A very similar demand faced Christianity in its earliest period when Greek rationality, empty of all vitality and relevance for life, met a new existential truth springing from the experience and faith of the young Christian community. At this critical moment in its history, Christianity found an answer in its Logos doctrine. It pointed to a concrete event that it passionately proclaimed as both existential and universal truth for every man—the specific and concrete embodiment of the ultimate divine reason. "Jesus the Christ is the Logos." In this brief formula, early Christianity united, at least in principle, existential and rational truth.

The present world situation puts an essentially parallel problem before Christianity. It must give essentially the same answer, though in different terms and with different intellectual tools. Above all, Christianity must seek to develop the church toward an inclusive reality that unites different existential interpretations as far as they are compatible with each other and with Christian principles. The more the church succeeds in this, the more readily can it receive rational truth as an inherent part of the Christian faith. If rational truth, with its contributions to the different realms of knowledge, is excluded, Christian faith necessarily becomes sectarian and exclusive. If existential truth with its practical bearing on religious and ethical activity is excluded, Christian faith becomes relativistic and sterile. Only by a proper union of the two can the intellectual needs of our present world situation be met.

Christianity and the World Situation

Christianity is a faith and a movement far older than bourgeois society. In its nineteen centuries of history, it has had to come to terms with the most diverse cultures and philosophies. Inevitably it has adapted itself to the development of modern civilization in its three successive phases. But the relation of Christianity to any culture can never be adequately interpreted merely in terms of adaptation. By the very nature of its message, it must seek to transcend every particular historical situation, and history demonstrates that the church has in fact succeeded always in maintaining some measure of independence. Therefore, the role of Christianity today can be seen as one of both adaptation to, and transcendence over, the present world situation.

Destructive Effects of Modernity

Insofar as Christianity has adjusted itself to the character of modern society, it is able to bring only a very incomplete answer to its problems, for Christianity, as it has been drawn into the destructive contradictions of the present stage of history, is itself a part of the problem. In some measure this is true of the church in every age. But it is especially important in the present period because the latter period by nature has less affinity to a Christian order of life than former periods.

Indeed, in the later Middle Ages and at the Reformation, religion itself helped to prepare the soil for the growth of autonomy in all realms of life. Religion revolted against the totalitarian control exercised by the Roman church. Through the pre-Reformation and Reformation attacks upon Catholic authoritarianism, religion paved the way for the autonomous national state and the independence of science, economics, and the arts. Religion liberated personality and community from hierarchical control. Above all, religion freed itself from ecclesiastical bondage.

But in so doing, religion helped to create alongside itself a secular sphere that step by step invaded and mastered the religious sphere. Thus religion itself became secularized and was drawn into the conflicts and contradictions of the new society. This process can be clearly discerned in every major aspect of that society.

The growth of secular *arts* independent of the church not only impoverished the religious arts but secularized them. They became secular arts with a religious content instead of religious art with a universal content. We have noted this transformation in the development from Giotto through Titian and Rembrandt to the various schools of contemporary painting. Indeed from a religious perspective, expressionism may be interpreted as an attempt toward a new religious style and a new fusion of religion and art. The failure of this attempt proves that contemporary life cannot be expressed in a genuine religious style. Christianity cannot change this situation merely by ritual reforms, however useful they may be. A new unity of cult and art is necessary, and this can be effected only if the present separation of the secular realm from the religious realm is overcome. Religious art presupposes a religious reality embodying a transcendent source and a spiritual center. The totalitarian attempts to create such a reality on a limited and immanent basis have produced only a few fragments of quasi-religious art. Their sterility in this respect proves that they lack any ultimate and universal significance. But at least they have sensed the problem, while the problem of religious art as the expression of true religious reality has not yet been widely recognized within the Christian churches.

The emergence of autonomous *personalities* and *communities* has virtually destroyed true religious personality and community. With the supremacy of autonomous reason, the transcendent center of personal life was destroyed and personality was broken into divergent elements, the unity of which was partially maintained by the continuing hold of traditional beliefs or by conventional and technical demands. Within the religious sphere, personality fought a desperate struggle against dissolution. From Pascal's protests against the Cartesian mechanization of human existence to Kierkegaard's passionate affirmation of the "existential personality," the person in the crisis of decision about his eternal destiny, and Dostoevski's vivid contrast between Jesus' personal confrontation with God and the Inquisitor's secular arrogance, the battle to maintain true religious personality continued. But, for the most part, theology did not follow these prophets because its effect was mainly one of negative resistance. In this attempt some present-day theology has returned to antiquated forms of orthodoxy and produced a fighting type of religious personality great in its negations but weak in its affirmations. For example, Barth sought to save Christian personality from both secular disintegration and totalitarian mechanization, but did not produce a new type of personal life. His movement did not attempt to master the new Leviathan but rather retired before it, and thus left the field to the fanatical dynamics of the totalitarian "impersonal personality."

Religious community, prepared by the lay movements of the latter Middle Ages and carried to fulfillment by the Reformation and sectarianism, was another victim of the development. Religious community must be grounded upon objective beliefs and sacraments. It can be created for a short time by collective enthusiasm, but it cannot endure in this form. It requires "objectivity." And, since the rise of autonomous reason, there was no universally potent objectivity except the mechanical objectivity of a technical process. Therefore religious community was largely destroyed, as was religious personality, because a determining spiritual center was lacking. There was, and still is, a religiously colored society, but there is no true religious community. The general background of society resists the destructive influence of naturalism as long as the background persists. But when it has exhausted itself, the way is open for new totalitarian systems. Totalitarianism, especially in its early phases, produced fighting groups with an absolute faith, an unconditional devotion, and a dominating spiritual center. They are neither religious communities nor religious societies, but fanatical orders with quasi-religious features in which both personality and community are swallowed up.

Especially clear and important is the situation in the *intellectual realm*. The triumph of autonomous knowledge, particularly in the natural sciences, has pushed aside religious knowledge. Either it is repudiated altogether or it is relegated to a corner, or it is transformed by secular interpretations. The last fate is the most disastrous just because it appears to preserve the whole body of Christian truth. In reality it alters the meaning of all beliefs. It makes them a phase of secular knowledge, knowledge that deals only with *some* objects within the whole of reality or with *some* subjective processes mainly in the sphere of feeling. Religious ideas are drawn down to the level of physical or psychological objects. God comes to be thought of as one being alongside other beings, even though the highest. Christ is regarded merely as an historical person whose character and very existence are at the mercy of the conclusions of historical research or of human value judgments. Faith becomes one emotion among others, or a lower level of cognitive apprehension; it conveys probability but not certainty; its objects may exist or they may not. These transmutations bring religious knowledge into subjection to rational knowledge, and thus destroy its ultimate character. Oscillating between a doubtful objectivity and an unsubstantiated subjectivity, religious knowledge loses its authority. No longer does it express the presence in every reality of the transcendent source of being and meaning; rather it deals with particular realities, the existence and nature of which are matters either of argument or of irrational belief. But neither the way of argument nor the irrational way of vindicating religious knowledge is able to shake the grip of technical rationality, the former because it remains within the presuppositions of technical reason, the latter because irrationalism is only a negative denial of a false rationalism and is therefore unable to create anything new.

It is a well-known fact that this process of secularization has affected all of the great religions. Inasmuch as the influence of Western civilization has penetrated most sections of the world, religious faith has lost its power, and the danger of a naturalistic quasi-theology threatens all nations. The absence of a Christian theology able to express an ultimate reality and spiritual center in terms of religious belief has produced skepticism and cynicism regarding all questions of ultimate concern.

Totalitarianism has sensed this situation and has formulated doctrines and symbols supposed to express an ultimate reality. It has tried to indoctrinate its followers with an "existential truth." But this ultimate is not truly ultimate because it does not transcend relative interests and concerns. It tries to invest a particular loyalty with unconditional validity. On the one hand, the totalitarian "theologies" reveal the final result of the discredit of genuine religious truth by technical rationality. On the other hand, they disclose the powerful desire to break through this situation to new ultimate beliefs and loyalties.

The fate of religious knowledge is symptomatic of the fate of the churches. The Christian church should furnish the answers thrust forth by the present situation in the economic, political, and international orders. But the churches largely lack that power because they themselves have become instruments of state, nation, and economy. After the shattering of the authoritarian control of Roman Catholicism, national churches replaced the one church. They were supported either by the state or by the dominant groups in society—the former predominantly in Europe, the latter especially in America. In both situations, the churches largely surrendered their critical freedom. They tended to become agencies of either state or the ruling classes. Therefore they were unable to conquer the Leviathan of modern industry, or the liberal dissolution of community, or the nationalistic disruption of the world. In large measure, they became social agencies for the safeguarding of accepted moral standards. In this fashion, their influence was to support the governing classes and the existing social order, even when criticizing them within the general presuppositions of bourgeois culture. Only prophetic individuals and revolutionary groups attacked the system as such; the official churches did not follow. The latter exposed the evils of a class society; they sought to transcend the national divisions of mankind; they struggled against the disintegration of liberal individualism. But they did not recognize or understand the deeper nature of the system they tried to improve.

Inevitably, the totalitarian movements put themselves in the place of the church; they cannot be rightly understood apart from their semiecclesiastical pretensions. Since they offer an all-controlling idea, however demonic it may be, they are in fact serious competitors of the church. Their attacks on the Christian churches are thoroughly consistent. They can never tolerate a church within an absolute claim in competition with their own.

The problem for the church implicit in this situation is tremendous, especially for the Protestant churches, and most especially for liberal Protestantism. Protestant orthodoxy can hold aloof from the present world situation, at least to a considerable extent. Roman Catholicism can look forward to the moment when anti-Christian totalitarianism will be replaced by a revived Catholic totalitarianism. Liberal Protestantism can go neither way. It must, however, solve the problem of its relation to the present stage of civilization. It must not return to a position of servant to a social and cultural system whose contradictions have now become manifest. On the other hand it must not follow the totalitarian way in either its pagan or its Catholic form. Only if liberal Protestanism becomes truly ''catholic'' can it meet the needs of the hour.

Christian Acceptance
and Transcendence of Reason

Christianity has not only adapted itself to the contemporary world in its dominant aspects. In many respects and to varying degrees, Christianity has transcended modern culture. It has attempted to preserve its authentic message despite all ecclesiastical and secular distortions. Christianity is not only a part of the contemporary world; it is also a protest against it and an effort to transform it by the power of Christian faith. This is true in both the intellectual and the practical realms, with respect to both belief and life.

First of all, it must be emphasized that Christianity has accepted the reign of reason not only as a factor in the secular world to which it must seek adjustment, but also as an agency for its own regeneration. The acceptance and employment of reason as the principle of truth have dissolved certain orthodox ''stumbling blocks'' that had not been touched by the Reformation but rather had been more firmly anchored by the scholastic dogmatism into which Reformation thought hardened. Thus reason has enabled Christian theology to face fresh questions and seek new answers in the light of contemporary insights and problems. Historical criticism of the Bible has liberated Christian truth from legendary, superstitious, and mythical elements in the historic tradition. The honest radicalism of this work of Christian self-criticism is something new in church history and brought values never before recognized or accepted. Without it, Christianity could not have confronted the modern mind and made its message intelligible and relevant to that mind. Much the same can be said of more recent inquiries into the psychological and sociological roots and processes of Christian thought and acton.

All this, however, would not have sufficed to protect Christian truth from complete adaptation to the prevailing intellectual milieu. The Christian message itself had to be borne through the high tide of technical rationality. This has been done in three principal alternative ways that we may call the "preserving," the "mediating," and the "dialectical" types. Each type has many varieties. The first is represented by *traditional theology* in either strictly orthodox and fundamentalist form or in the form of moderate adaptation to the new influences, adaptation of structure but not of matter. It is due to this type of Christian interpretation that the treasures of the past have been preserved through a period when for many there was no possible way of comprehending them. The second type is represented by the so-called school of mediation from Schleiermacher, Hegel, and Ritschl though liberal theology to certain current formulations of ecumenical theology. These are distinguished from humanism by their refusal to adapt Christianity entirely to the demands of current vogues. They are distinguished from orthodoxy by their readiness to reexamine all theological issues in the light of the questions of our day. It is due to this type of Christian reinterpretation that theology has continued a living power in the church and the world. The third type is represented by Kierkegaard and his followers who, though themselves shaped by the modern world, are aware of the dangers of adaptation and mediation. The *dialectical approach* rejects the otherworldliness through which the first type seeks to preserve the Christian tradition. It breaks the protecting shell to reveal the relevance of its content to our time. But it does not intercept this content through the ideas of our period; thus it differs from the second type. Rather, it relates them to each other in radical criticism. In this sense, it is dialectical. It delights to declare no and yes in the same breath. It is due to this type of Christian interpretation that both the dangers of all adaptations to current thought and also the riches and profundities of tradition have again become visible within the churches. But the danger of the dialectical method has also appeared. When this type of theological thinking tried to become constructive, it simply relapsed into the mere reinteration of tradition. It became "neoorthodoxy."

Not only in the theoretical but also in the practical realm, Christianity has used reason as an instrument of self-regeneration. Reason has completed the religious emancipation of the layman that had been begun by the Reformation but had been halted among the orthodox Protestant churches. Following the abolition of the priest's rule, it has broken the minister's rule. The Enlightenment was in certain respects a Protestant lay movement. As such it produced new ideals of personality and community. In many parts of the world it destroyed the patriarchal form of community with all its implications for sex relations, for family, and for the workshop. Reason has accomplished much the same emancipation for Christian personality. It has opened it to receive the riches of humanism. It has released the suppressed levels of personal life. It has freed the individual from cruel religious absolutism.

However, Christianity would have been drawn wholly within bourgeois society if it had only used and had not also transcended reason in its practical application. Christian faith had to maintain true Christian life over against the demonic powers of the modern world. This, likewise, was accomplished in three alternative ways, analogous to the three types of theological reinterpretation—the pietistic or evangelical, the ethical, and the paradoxical types. *Pietism* in all its varieties has preserved the warmth, intensity, and creative power of personal relation to God. It has poured forth spiritual vitality in many directions. It is due to the evangelical tradition that elements of early Christian enthusiasm have never been wholly absent in the churches of the modern period. The *ethical* type, corresponding to the mediating school in theology, is the most influential in contemporary Christianity. It is not mere morals, as the mediating theology is not mere humanism. In it personal religion and ethical concern are so joined that religion is measured by ethical fruits and the ethical life receives its impulse from religion. It is due to this type of practical Christianity that the latter was able to penetrate different areas of cultural life and for a long time guard modern society from complete relapse into nationalistic paganism. But the inadequacies of the merely ethical form of Christian life became so obvious that a third time arose, corresponding to the dialectical school of theology. The *paradoxical* (or, in Kierkegaard's phrase, the "existential") type transcends both the ethical and the pietistic types. It makes religion the measure of ethics, rather than the reverse, stressing the paradoxical character of all individual Christian existence, denied and affirmed by God at the same time. For the same reason, it transcends the pietistic type, which is more interested in intensity of religious experience than in the paradoxical action of God.

Through this resistance of Christianity, both theoretical and practical, against the complete domination of technical reason and technical economy over human life, the church has succeeded in maintaining an authentic spirituality and transcendence. Despite its partial secularization, the church has profoundly influenced "Christian" nations and secular culture. Its very existence was and is a signpost pointing beyond the mechanism created by man's technical skill and now turned against man's freedom and fulfillment. Through preaching, education, and action, the churches have exerted a largely subconscious effect upon masses and individuals. This often unrecognized influence became strikingly visible in the resistance of the Christian masses to the attempts by pagan totalitarianisms to replace Christianity by tribal cults. Moreover, despite the adaptation of the churches to modern society, they have produced individuals who recognized, exposed, and attacked the system and all Christian subservience to it. The deeper meaning of the present world situation is not unknown to many individuals and groups within the churches. Indeed, against the nationalistic opposition to the religious and cultural unification of mankind, the Christian churches have created the ecumenical movement uniting Christians of all countries, Christian and non-Christian, enslaved and free. This movement is the only world unity left in the present demonic disruption of humanity.

Guideposts for the Christian Answer

It is not the province of this essay to attempt the Christian answer to the questions posed by an analysis of the present world situation. However, certain points that must guide and the answer may be indicated.

1. One thing is certain: The Christian message to the contemporary world will be a true, convincing, and transforming message only insofar as it is born out of the depths of our present world situation. No single thinker or theological movement can plumb the depths of the *world* situation. No merely theoretical group and no merely practical group, no one in America or Russia or China or Europe alone, can claim to comprehend the depths of the present *world* situation. These depths are simply not the depths of suffering or of profound insight or of proletarian revolution or of personal communion, but something of all of these, and more. The more a Christian group embraces elements from all these different aspects of the present world, the more adequately will it comprehend the true questions and formulate right answers. This means that the Christian church can speak authoritatively and effectively to our world today only as it is truly "ecumenical," that is, universal.

2. Next, the Christian answer must accept the modern development as an historic fact that cannot be evaded or reversed, and that, like every historic destiny, is ambiguous in its meaning and value. Our analysis has dealt primarily with the negative features of modern culture, its contradictions and aberrations that demand answers. The answers themselves must acknowledge and accept the positive contributions of the modern period. Here the principal point is the elevation of reason as the principle of truth above all forms of authoritarianism and obscurantism. This is a truly Christian issue even if it is fought out largely in humanistic terms. Christian faith that proclaims Christ as ''Logos'' cannot reject reason as the principle of truth and justice. The Christian answer must be framed with full recognition that the gains of the bourgeois period must not be lost from the future of mankind.

3. Furthermore, the Christian message must be illumined by the insight that the tragic self-destruction of our present world is the result not simply of the particular contradictions bred by that world but also of the contradictions that characterize human life always. History shows that, over and over again, the achievements of man, as though by a logic of tragedy, turn against man himself. This was true of the great creative achievement of sacramental faith as well as of the achievements of technical reason. Therefore the Christian message cannot anticipate a future situation devoid of tragedy even if the demonic forces in the present situation are conquered. The authentic Christian message is never utopian, whether through belief in progress or through faith in revolution.

4. Again, Christianity does not give its answer in terms of religious escapism. Rather it affirms that the influences of divine grace are never absent from each historical situation. It relates them directly or indirectly to the history of divine revelation and especially its central reality—Jesus Christ. It repudiates a tendency among many people, Christians and humanists, to withdraw from the struggles of our time. Christianity faces the future unafraid.

5. Lastly, the Christian answer must be at the same time both theoretical and practical. It will have reality only if it is the answer in action as well as in interpretation of men and women deeply involved in wrestling with the times. Despite the measure of their bondage to the present world situation, the Christian churches are the historical group through which the answer must be given.

CHAPTER 2

The Lost Dimension in Religion

Every observer of our Western civilization is aware of the fact that something has happened to religion. It especially strikes the observer of the American scene. Everywhere he finds symptoms of what one has called religious revival, or more modestly, the revival of interest in religion. He finds them in the churches with their rapidly increasing membership. He finds them in the mushroomlike growth of sects. He finds them on college campuses and in the theological faculties of universities. Most conspicuously, he finds them in the tremendous success of men like Billy Graham and Norman Vincent Peale who attract masses of people Sunday after Sunday, meeting after meeting. The facts cannot be denied, but how should they be interpreted? It is my intention to show that these facts must be seen as expressions of the predicament of Western man in the second half of the twentieth century. But I would even go a step further. I believe that the predicament of man in our period gives us also an important insight into the predicament of man generally—at all times and in all parts of the earth.

There are many analyses of man and society in our time. Most of them show important traits in the picture, but few of them succeed in giving a general key to our present situation. Although it is not easy to find such a key, I shall attempt it and, in so doing, will make an assertion that may be somewhat mystifying at first hearing. The decisive element in the predicament of Western man in our period is his loss of the dimension of depth. Of course, ''dimension of depth'' is a metaphor. It is taken from the spatial realm and applied to man's spiritual life. What does it mean?

It means that man has lost an answer to the question: What is the meaning of life? Where do we come from, where do we go? What shall we do, what should we become in the short stretch between birth and death? Such questions are not answered or even asked if the ''dimension of depth'' is lost. And this is precisely what has happened to man in our period of history. He has lost the courage to ask questions with an infinite serious-ness—as former generations did—and he has lost the courage to receive answers to questions, wherever they may come from.

Religion as Ultimate Concern

I suggest that we call the dimension of depth the religious dimension in man's nature. Being religious means asking passionately the question of the meaning of our existence and being willing to receive answers, even if the answers hurt. Such an idea of religion makes religion universally hu-man, but it certainly differs from what is usually called religion. It does not describe religion as the belief in the existence of gods or one God, and as a set of activities and institutions for the sake of relating oneself to these beings in thought, devotion and obedience. No one can deny that the re-ligions that have appeared in history are required in this sense. It is the state of being concerned about one's being and being universally.

There are many people who are ultimately concerned in this way who feel far removed, however, from religion in the narrower sense, and there-fore from every historical religion. It often happens that such people take the question of the meaning of their life infinitely seriously and reject any historical religion just for this reason. They feel that the concrete religions fail to express their profound concern adequately. They are religious while rejecting the religions. It is this experience that forces us to distinguish the meaning of religion as living in the dimension of depth from particular expressions of one's ultimate concern in the symbols and institutions of a concrete religion. If we now turn to the concrete analysis of the religious situation of our time, it is obvious that our key must be the basic meaning of religion and not any particular religion, not even Christianity. What does this key disclose about the predicament of man in our period?

The Loss of Ultimate Concern
in Industrial Society

If we define religion as the state of being grasped by an infinite concern we must say: Man in our time has lost such infinite concern. And the re-surgence of religion is nothing but a desperate and mostly futile attempt to regain what has been lost.

How did the dimension of depth come to be lost? Like any important event, it has many causes, but certainly not the one that one hears often mentioned from ministers' pulpits and evangelists' platforms, namely, that a widespread impiety of modern man is responsible. Modern man is neither more pious nor more impious than man in any other period. The loss of the dimension of depth is caused by the relation of man to his world and to himself in our period, the period in which nature is being subjected scientifically and technically to the control of man. In this period, life in the dimension of depth is replaced by life in the horizontal dimension. The driving forces of the industrial society of which we are a part go ahead horizontally and not vertically. In popular terms this is expressed in phrases like "better and better," "bigger and bigger," "more and more." One should not disparage the feeling that he is able to know and transform the world he encounters without a foreseeable limit. He can go ahead in all directions without a definite boundary.

A most expressive symbol of this attitude of going ahead in the horizontal dimension is the breaking through of the space that is controlled by the gravitational power of the earth into the world-space. It is interesting that one calls this world-space simply "space" and speaks, for instance, of space travel, as if every trip were not travel into space. Perhaps one feels that the true nature of space has been discovered only through our entering into indefinite world-space. In any case, the predominance of the horizontal dimension over the dimension of depth has been immensely increased by the opening up of the space beyond the space of the earth.

If we now ask what does man do and seek if he goes ahead in the horizontal dimension, the answer if difficult. Sometimes one is inclined to say that the mere movement ahead without an end, the intoxication with speeding forward without limits, is what satisfies him. But this answer is by no means sufficient. For on his way into space and time man changes the world he encounters. And the changes made by him change himself. He transforms everything he encounters into a tool; and in doing so he himself becomes a tool. But if he asks, a tool for what, there is no answer.

One does not need to look far beyond everyone's daily experience in order to find examples to describe this predicament. Indeed our daily life in office and home, in cars and airplanes, at parties and conferences, reading magazines and watching television, while looking at advertisements and hearing radio, are in themselves continuous examples of a life that has lost the dimension of depth. It runs ahead; every moment is filled with something that must be done or seen or said or planned. But no one can experience depth without stopping and becoming aware of himself. Only if he has moments in which he does not care about what comes next can he experience the meaning of this moment here and now and ask himself about the meaning of his life. As long as the preliminary, transitory concerns are not silenced, no matter how interesting and valuable and important they may be, the voice of the ultimate concern cannot be heard. This is the deepest root of the loss of the dimension of depth in our period—the loss of religion in its basic and universal meaning.

The Loss of Religious Symbols

If the dimension of depth is lost, the symbols in which life in this dimension has expressed itself must also disappear. I am speaking of the great symbols of the historical religions in our Western world, of Judaism and Christianity. The reason that the religious symbols become lost is not primarily scientific criticism, but it is a complete misunderstanding of their meaning; and only because of this misunderstanding was scientific critique able—and even justified—in attacking them. The first step toward the nonreligion of the Western world was made by religion itself. When it defended its great symbols not as symbols but as literal stories, it had already lost the battle. In doing so the theologians (and today many religious laymen) helped to transfer the powerful expressions of the dimension of depth into objects or happenings on the horizontal plane. There the symbols lose their power and meaning and become an easy prey to physical, biological, and historical attack.

If the symbol of creation that points to the divine ground of everything is transferred to the horizontal plane, it becomes a story of events in a removed past for which there is no evidence, but that contradicts every piece of scientific evidence. If the symbol of the fall of Man, which points to the tragic estrangement of man and his world from their true being, is transferred to the horizontal plane, it becomes a story of a human couple a few thousand years ago in what is now present-day Iraq. One of the most profound psychological descriptions of the general human predicament becomes an absurdity on the horizontal plane. If the symbols of Saviour and the salvation through him that point to the healing power in history and personal life are transferred to the horizontal plane, they become stories of a half-divine being coming from a heavenly place and returning to it. Obviously, in this form, they have no meaning whatsoever for people whose view of the universe is determined by scientific astronomy.

If the idea of God (and the symbols applied to him) that expresses man's ultimate concern is transferred to the horizontal plane, God becomes a being among others whose existence or nonexistence is a matter of inquiry. Nothing, perhaps, is more symptomatic of the loss of the dimension of depth than the permanent discussion about the existence or nonexistence of God— a discussion in which both sides are equally wrong, because the discussion itself is wrong and possible only after the loss of the dimension of depth.

The Loss of Self

When in this way man has deprived himself of the dimension of depth and the symbols expressing it, he then becomes a part of the horizontal plane. He loses his self and becomes a thing among things. He becomes an element in the process of manipulated production and manipulated consumption. This is now a matter of public knowledge. We have become aware of the degree to which everyone in our social structure is managed, even if one knows it and even if one belongs himself to the managing group. The influence of the gang mentality on adolescents, of the corporation's demands on the executives, of the conditioning of everyone by public communication, by propaganda and advertising under the guidance of motivation research, et cetera, have all been described in many books and articles.

Under these pressures, man can hardly escape the fate of becoming a thing among the things he produces, a bundle of conditioned reflexes without a free, deciding, and responsible self. The immense mechanism, set up by man to produce objects for use, transforms man himself into an object used by the same mechanism of production and consumption.

But man has not ceased to be man. He resists this fate anxiously, desperately, courageously. He asks the question, for what? And he realizes that there is no answer. He becomes aware of the emptiness that is covered by the continuous movement ahead and the production of means for ends that become means again without an ultimate end. Without knowing what has happened to him, he feels that he has lost the meaning of life, the dimension of depth.

Expressions of the Loss of Depth
in Art, Literature, and Philosophy

Out of this awareness the religious question arises and religious answers are received or reflected. Therefore, in order to describe the contemporary attitude toward religion, we must first point to the places where the awareness of the predicament of Western man in our period is most sharply expressed. These places are the great art, literature, and, partly at least, the philosophy of our time. It is both the subject matter and the style of these creations that show the passionate and often tragic struggle about the meaning of life in a period in which man has lost the dimension of depth. This art, literature, and philosophy is not religious in the narrower sense of the word; but it asks the religious question more radically and more profoundly than most directly religious expressions of our time.

It is the religious question that is asked when the novelist describes a man who tries in vain to reach the only place that could solve the problem of his life, or a man who disintegrates under the memory of a guilt that persecutes him, or a man who never had a real self and is pushed by his fate without resistance to death, or a man who experiences a profound disgust of everything he encounters.

It is the religious question that is asked when the poet opens up the horror and the fascination of the demonic regions of his soul, or if he leads us into the deserts and empty places of our being, or if he shows the physical and moral mud under the surface of life, or if he sings the song of transitoriness, giving words to the ever-present anxiety of our hearts.

It is the religious question that is asked when the playwright shows the illusion of a life in a ridiculous symbol, or if he lets the emptiness of a life's work end in self-destruction, or if he confronts us with the inescapable bondage to mutual hate and guilt, or if he leads us into the dark cellar of lost hopes and slow disintegration.

It is the religious question that is asked when the painter breaks the visible surface into pieces, then reunites them into a great picture that has little similarity with the world at which we normally look, but that expresses our anxiety and our courage to face reality.

It is the religious question that is asked when the architect, in creating office buildings or churches, removes the trimmings taken over from past styles because they cannot be considered an honest expression of our own period. He prefers the seeming poverty of a purpose-determined style to the deceptive richness of imitated styles of the past. He knows that he gives no final answer, but he does give an honest answer.

The philosophy of our time shows the same hidden religious traits. It is divided into two main schools of thought, the analytic and the existentialist. The former tries to analyze logical and linguistic forms that are always used and that underlie all scientific research. One may compare them with the painters who dissolve the natural forms of bodies into cubes, planes, and lines;

or with those architects who want the structural "bones" of their buildings to be conspiculously visible and not hidden by covering features. This self-restriction produces the almost monastic poverty and seriousness of this philosophy. It is religious—without any contact with religion in its method—by exercising the humility of "learned ignorance."

In contrast to this school, the existentialist philosophers have much to say about the problems of human existence. They bring into rational concepts what the writers and poets, the painters and architects, are expressing in their particular material. What they express is the human predicament in time and space, in anxiety and guilt and the feeling of meaninglessness. From Pascal in the seventeenth century to Heidegger and Sartre in our time, philosophers have emphasized the contrast between human dignity and human misery. And by doing so, they have raised the religious question. Some have tried to answer the question they have asked. But if they did so, they turned back to past traditions and offered to our time that which does not fit our time. Is it possible for our time to receive answers that are born out of our time?

Religious Answers That Confirm and Deny the Present Situation

Answers given today are in danger of strengthening the present situation and with it the questions to which they are supposed to be the answers. This refers to some of the previously mentioned major representatives of the so-called resurgence of religion, as for instance the evangelist Billy Graham and the counseling and healing minister Norman Vincent Peale. Against the validity of the answers given by the former, one must say that in spite of his personal integrity, his propagandistic methods and his primitive theological fundamentalism fall short of what is needed to give an answer to the religious question of our period. In spite of all his seriousness, he does not take the radical questions of our period seriously.

The effect that Norman Peale has on large groups of people is rooted in the fact that he confirms the situation he is supposed to help overcome. He heals people with the purpose of making them fit again for the demands of the competitive and conformist society in which we are living. He helps them to become adapted to the situation that is characterized by the loss of the dimension of depth. Therefore, his advice is valid on this level; but it is the validity of this level that is the true religious question of our time. And this question he neither raises nor answers.

In many cases the increase of church membership and interest in religious activities does not mean much more than the religious consecration of a state of things in which the religious dimension has been lost. It is the desire to participate in activities that are socially strongly approved and give a certain amount of internal and external security. This is not necessarily bad, but it certainly is not an answer to the religious question of our period.

Is there an answer? There is always an answer, but the answer may not be available to us. We may be too deeply steeped in the predicament out of which the question arises to be able to answer it. To acknowledge this is certainly a better way toward a real answer than to bar the way to it by deceptive answers. And it may be that in this attitude the real answer (within available limits) is given. The real answer to the question of how to regain the dimension of depth is not given by increased church membership or church attendance, nor by conversion or healing experiences. But it is given by the awareness that we have lost the decisive dimension of life, the dimension of depth, and that there is no easy way of getting it back. Such awareness is in itself a state of being grasped by that which is symbolized in the term, dimension of depth. He who realizes that he is separated from the ultimate source of meaning shows by this realization that he is not only separated but is also reunited. And this is just our situation. What we need above all—and partly have—is the radical realization of our predicament, without trying to cover it up by secular or religious ideologies. The revival of religious interest would be a creative power in our culture if it would develop into a movement of search for the lost dimension of depth.

This does not mean that the traditional religious symbols should be dismissed. They certainly have lost their meaning in the literalistic form into which they have been distorted, thus producing the critical reaction against them. But they have not lost their genuine meaning, namely, of answering the question that is implied in man's very existence in powerful, revealing, and saving symbols. If the resurgence of religion would produce a new understanding of the symbols of the past and their relevance for our situation instead of premature and deceptive answers, it would become a creative factor in our culture and a saving factor for many who live in estrangement, anxiety, and despair. The religious answer has always the character of "in spite of." In spite of the loss of dimension of depth, its power is present, and most present in those who are aware of the loss and are striving to regain it with ultimate seriousness.

PART II

The Structure and Meaning of Science and Technology

CHAPTER 3

The Logos and Mythos
of Technology[1]

With a suddenness and violence comparable to a natural catastrophe, modern technology came upon Western nations. And they bowed themselves before it without understanding what had happened. Gradually, however, a consciousness grew of a fate having fulfilled itself, that the West had gone a way that had led far beyond all the possibilities of humanity heretofore. And this way of the West somehow pulls the whole of humanity in its direction, even a reluctant Asia. Europe itself is being pulled along by an even younger, more quickly striding America. Questioning the meaning of technology opens up perspectives on the world that in turn require interpretation. But the interpretation of meaning is only possible on the basis of a view of being. To comprehend the logos of technology, its essence, its characteristic forms of being, its relation to other forms of being, that is thus our first and most important task. It shall be taken up in two steps: first, through an analysis of the essence of the technical structure; second, through the systematic location of technology within other realms of meaning. Only upon this basis can we then dare, in the second part, to give indications as to the existential meaning of technology—its place in the mythos of our life.

The Logos of Technology

To employ technology is to enlist means to an end. For this reason technology is present as an element whenever purposes are realized. Thus technology is universal. Technology is associated with τεύχειν to succeed. Where something is successful through the use of suitable means,

---

[1]Translated by John C. Modshielder, College of DuPage.

there is technology. And no area of reality can be named where there would be nothing technical to find. Τεχνάζει ἡ φύσιω—one could say, nature acts technically; more precisely translated, it acts cunningly. It makes use of surprising, indeed ingenious, means in order to achieve its goals, in order to bring life and gestalts (*Gestalten*) into existence in incomprehensible variety.[2] Nature acts technically when the carnivorous plant, comparable to the jaws of an excavating machine, closes itself at the slightest pressure of an insect, when the eye is a model for a photographic camera, when a bird is the model for an airplane, and when a dolphin is the model for a submarine. Nature cannot bring any new gestalt into existence without the use of new kinds of cunning, new kinds of technical forms. The riches of nature are not possible without the technical element. That is one of the great perceptions that Darwin gained from the era of early capitalistic technology. And what is valid for the individual is valid for the whole of nature; it has built a house on earth for organic life with fluctuation between light and darkness, heat and cold, dampness and dryness. And it lets organic life be interchanged, consumed, and produced—the prototype of production in consumption in the techniques of the economy.

And nature acts cunningly, acts technically, when it allows all the highly developed organisms to become stunted in their growth in order to bring to completion *one* organ in *one* being, the brain in human beings, thereby giving the spirit the possibility of coming into existence and beginning a new world age of a completely different kind—the age of technology. For in everything that nature does, it realizes itself, its own life. That which is means is also end insofar as it belongs to a life form; and that which is end is also means, insofar as the whole carries the individual. But it is different with the spirit: it separates what belongs together in the living process. It determines the end and it seeks out the means. And when the end is achieved, then the means become insignificant. And it creates objects that have no other meaning than that of the purpose for which they were created; it creates the technical gestalt and therewith technology in the narrowest sense.

---

[2]Translator's Note: The German root here, *Gestalt,* will be anglicized throughout this text. *Webster's Third New International Dictionary* defines *gestalt* as "a structure or configuration of physical, biological or psychological phenomena so integrated as to constitute a functional unit with properties not derivable from its parts in summation."

Developmental Technology

And yet another detour is necessary before we can turn to our actual problem. There is a kind of technology in which the spirit joins itself to a living gestalt—biological, spiritual, and social—not in order to destroy it and put it in the service of an alien purpose, but, on the contrary, to protect if from destruction, to preserve it, and above all to develop it. We call this enormous domain of technical action "developmental technology." For a plant, for an animal, and for the human body it is cultivation, nourishment, healing, and it encompasses all areas from agriculture to medical science. Considering the spiritual gestalt, it is healing and unbringing, from psychotherapy to pedagogy. And for the social organism it develops all the social functions: nutrition and defense as economics and strategy, commerce and communication as commercial technique and publicity, administration and protection as administrative technology, criminology, and hygiene and finally healing and upbringing as social service and social pedagogy. In all of this there is more than technology. But what most truly characterizes these realms is the technical element in them, the enlisting of means towards ends. In them, all that has developed itself in the life process is unfolded. To that extent they are very nearly like the technical action on the part of nature.

Actualizing Technology

There is, however, a second grouping that we want to designate as "actualizing technology," which is small and yet of highest significance. It gives the spirit the possibility of coming into existence. In music it is the instrument, in the graphic arts the material, and in science and poetry the book, insofar as it is not only a means of communication but also an objectification of the spirit that itself becomes transformed through this objectification. Here technology is directly interdependent with the spirit and gives it new forms of existence, as at present movies, with the help of a new technical practicality, are about to create a new art form. And it seems to me that the destiny of radio is locked into the same development.

Side by side with developmental and actualizing technology stands the third large grouping, technology in the narrowest sense, "transforming technology." It is primarily this we have in mind when we speak of technology. It has created the technical age to which we belong. From now on we turn our attention to it.

Transforming Technology

It is transforming. It creates systems determined only by the purpose they are to serve and uses material that is completely foreign to this purpose. It does not develop, rather it destroys living nexuses. It fells a tree and transforms it into a technical material: wood. It blasts rock formations and transforms them into a technical material: stone. It tears up the earth's surface with roads and canals. It presses resistant iron into whatever forms it pleases, suiting the spirit's purpose. Transforming technology creates the technical structure. The following are the distinguishing characteristics of its logical structure: fundamental is the fact that it is a purposive structure and only as such does it have a technical existence. A worn-out machine still exists, to be sure, but only as scrap, i.e., it has sunk back into the chemical sphere out of which technology had lifted it. A house no longer fit for use is good for salvage, or as a ruin creates a peculiar, charming aesthetic value through the loss of its purpose. With the loss of purpose, the technical form of being of a thing is lost.

Technological Rationality

This unconditional purposiveness results in the unconditional rationality of the technological structure. And this rationality expresses itself on three sides, first and fundamentally toward the truly technical side: the complete purposiveness of the whole and of the parts as they relate to one another; the exclusion of everything superfluous, the pressing on to a complete, inner necessity; the thorough engineering that constitutes the glory and ideal of technology, which gives the technical gestalt its inner beauty, as the overcoming of chance and arbitrariness in a personality is reflected in the spiritual beauty of that person's face.

This completeness, however, is possible only through unconditional devotion to natural laws. In the technical structue nature is raised beyond itself through the spirit, but nature is the means. And each of the slightest deviations from this order is avenged by nature through destruction. This objectification of natural law belongs to that which is staggering about the completely technical structure.

The third side of the rationality is economic. If the technical structure interposes itself into nature through the rationality of natural law, then it is through economic rationality that it interposes itself in society. Indeed, it belongs to both spheres. Whatever exceeds the economic possibilities or the social forces of production has no possibility of existence. And whatever does not correspond to the law of the economics of consumption has no technological consummation. One can observe that even the most perfect steam locomotive is wasteful in its consumption of coal, and this is felt to be a deficiency in the technical gestalt, as a lack of rationality. That is how closely both domains are connected, not only essentially but also empirically.

Now, of course, this threefold rationality of the technical gestalt does not mean that technology is created in a rational way. Rather, it shares in the peculiarity of all creations of the spirit—in its original conception—in being intuitive in its vision of the motivating principle of a gestalt. Also, the history of technology is the history of great intuitions. From the first wheel to the newest steam turbine, its great strides go from insight to insight. And in between lie the necessary and indispensable stretches of thorough reflective examination, without which a new insight would not be possible. Intuitive creation and complete rationality are not contradictory.

Systematics of Technology

More about the logical structure of the technical structure can only be ascertained in the context of a systematics of technology. Such a systematics is missing. We have a systematic botany, a systematic zoology, a grouping of its species and genera. We do not have the same in technology. Perhaps this is because it is more in flux, perhaps because its structures show that they have gone through more transitions, perhaps because the spirit of modern science is turned more toward genetic than to systematic problems. In any case, we need a systematics of technology. Science and life demand it in the same way.

To set up a systematics of the structures of technology, one could proceed from the fact that all technology is a further development of human organs. One could proceed from these and connect them with the corresponding technical gestalts. So, for instance, as one group, the organs for receiving and handling reality; as a second group, the organs for moving oneself about in reality; as a third group, the organs for secluding oneself and for working one's way into reality, to which would belong in the first place clothing and a dwelling. All this is conceived completely on the basis of that which is living. Conceived completely from a technical perspective, technology could be built up out of the simplest technical structures such a wheel, a lever, a screw, a prop, et cetera. Between technology and the human being stands a third principle of construction that bases itself on the relation of the two and is therefore especially to be understood sociologically. On the one side are the fixed structures for integration with the earth's surface, thereby altering its image: a house, a garden, a pathway. On the other side are the structures for fashioning the earth's surface that fall into two groups according to the relationship to human beings: the tool and the machine. The tool, which has grown organically together with human beings, gives all the production with tools the character of a vital expression, a personal signature that gave to handicraft, while it was still a reality, its greatness, now long disappeared.

And then there is the machine, the most characteristic and greatest creation of technology. The mechanical sets in where a tool can no longer be used by hand but attended and operated. Therein lies on the one side the detachment from the vital process that takes place in machines and on the other side a last remnant of connection. Without the attending (the preserving and healing), and without the domination (the operating and putting into service), the machine cannot be. It is a particular gestalt, even if not an original one that has come forth directly from the life process. Thus its gestalt is a derived one, but one that is distinct and impressive. It has a relatively individual existence that compels each one who has to deal with it to feel one's way into it, to listen obediently to it. It has an individual existence—and the more complicated it is, the more so—that cannot be figured out completely, that can have an uncanny, even a demonic effect. And not infrequently a relationship is developed between the machine and its operator that is akin to the relationship to a living being. Here technology has succeeded to the highest extent: pure purposive gestalt has again become particular gestalt, even though a conditioned one.

Through the machine's having an individual existence, technical production is independent of the vital productive power of human beings. In that way the machine becomes a symbol of unbounded possibility, unlimited in relation to all production with tools and any other projected possibility, limited only by the limits of raw materials and naturally stored up energies. This unlimited character of the machine and its being a particular gestalt is the reason for its revolutionary significance for society.

Secondly, to a consideration of the logos of technology also belongs its position in relation to the remaining domains of the spirit. They may be briefly indicated, on the one side in relation to science and art, on the other side in relation to the economy.

Technology and Science

Technology is the great, constantly convincing experiment for the truth of science on which it rests. And it is thereby at the same time a continuation of science. It is a Greek inheritance when pure science is more highly valued than the technical, for the Greeks knowingly sought to flee from existence and wanted to devote themselves to pure, unchangeable being. This is the pathos of their knowledge. But the West since the Renaissance, since Leonardo, wants to shape existence, at first magically, then technically, and this is the pathos of *its* knowledge. It is in accord with this pathos to give preference to the technical sciences, but then of course in the broadest sense of technology, as previously indicated. But perhaps it is the case that we are presently struggling with a third form of scientific attitude in which essence and existence, insight and gestalt, are united around an active historical realism whose fulfillment, of course, lies yet in the future, but which, once fulfilled, would include pure and technical science within it.

Technology and Art

The reflection on technology and art will be carried out in three steps. The inner beauty of the thoroughly engineered technical structure has already been discussed. This becomes clear in comparison to something poorly engineered of the same kind: the locomotive of an express train over against the first machine of this kind, the modern automobile over against the oldest exemplar. This is neither the beauty of art nor the beauty of nature, as would be a railway station in the fog or a train in the night. Instead it is its own category of beauty, namely, a technical one, that finally must be valued as such.

The second step is the joining of technology and art. The most significant examples are architecture and clothing. In both cases it is a matter of purposive structures that must be appropriate at the same time to the totality of life and, therefore, that must be an expression in material and form of this totality of life that they serve. That is why a house is no dwelling machine but rather an ambiguous structure in which rational purposes have to be united with the inner strength of symbols for the life of the inhabitant, for example, for the inhabitant's delimitation from unlimited space and at the same time for being included in space through significant proportions. Of course, this side has to recede the less individual elbowroom there is, but it does not completely recede since all human beings and all human beings of our time have something in common in their feelings for life. But this is certain: if, currently, houses, furniture, and clothing are still being produced upon which past styles are imprinted as ornamentation or patterning, then this is a lie and inartistic, and it has to be demanded that the spirit of technical rationality tear down the facades and give honest and thereby aesthetically valuable expression to the fact of their origin from machines. A lot of technical beauty is holy, so to speak, over against that untruthfulness that nowadays still floods the market.

And third: pure art. Is it purposeless? Certainly it is purposeless in the technical sense. But is it altogether free from purpose? Again let it be pointed out that instead of the irresponsible arts, free from purpose, we long for an art that is integrated into the context of life, as was ancient art that gave expression to the meaning of life in a magical and cultic way. This, too, lies in the future. Should this be achieved, however, then all three of the form-giving steps would be included in a last unconditioned purpose, and the antithesis of technology and art would become synthesized, as it once was in each tool of the primitive.

The incentive of technology is production. Every technology is driven by economic necessity. To be sure, [it is driven] not just by that; it has its own impulse, that of a purely technical creative will. But only seldom does this manifest itself purely, as perhaps in the invention of flying. Ordinarily it is embedded in economic impulses. And no economy has ever given such impulses as has the capitalistic one. It gave technology the possibility of subduing the earth. And yet capitalism is also a hindrance to technology. Actually, even more than that, it has obscured technology by the shadows of its own corruption. In innumerable cases, it has hindered rational improvement or new creation in the interest of power groups. It hinders the machine from taking over completely that for which it is there, namely, the mechanical, and thereby hinders the liberation of countless people from the curse of mechanical work—freed for servicing and controlling work. It forces the machine to use its boundless possibilities for the production of goods that in no way have any inner necessity, that artificially generate needs for the sake of profits and then for the sake of profits satisfy those needs badly. Within the machine sleeps neutral possibility. The economy awakens it to bad actuality. The possibility of the machine could also be awakened to good actuality. The machine is neutral. With this observation, almost everything with which technology has been reproached in terms of ravaging the spirit and society falls aside. Technology is neutral. It offers the means.

One thing, to be sure, is true: in its possibilities lies its power to experiment. Temptation is always present where possibilities arise. And our temptation is technical possibility. That we have fallen into temptation is expressed in the fact that we tolerate this economy that misuses technology.

The Mythos of Technology

This section pertains to the few indications we want to make concerning the mythos of technology, to its place in the ultimate meaning of our life. We no longer have a mythos that expresses itself in symbols as past times had. We cannot determine a place for technology as they did. We can only contemplate the matter itself and interpret it and hope that in the interpretation something resonates from the hidden, symbol-less mythos that sustains our time and gives it meaning.

It is the innermost pathos, the innermost mood of the true technician that he knows that through him a new gestalt comes into existence. His invention is an original finding, an initial composition. The technician carries on the process that pervades all of nature, the creation of gestalts in which the depth of being comes into existence. What was hidden in the womb of creative possibilities becomes reality through him. Of course, the technician is not a creator in the unconditioned sense. No primal gestalts are created by him. But this is in accord with our creaturely existence. And this also accords with it, namely, that the technician's creations grow old, grow yet older than the work of the symbol-creating spirit. And yet he knows that even in his creations is something that does not grow old, that continues to operate in each new technical gestalt, that participates in the eternity of each true gestalt.

All technology is not merely composition but also a domination of gestalts and through them a domination of nature. The words of the ancient myth, "subdue the earth," are fulfilled by technology, more fulfilled than magicians and fairy tale tellers ever dreamt. In presentiment of such possibilities of technology the eighth Psalm sings; "You have made him little less than a god, you have crowned him with glory and splendor, made him lord over the work of your hands, set all things under his feet."[3]

Through the domination of nature, human being is liberated from the mechanical function unworthy of every living being. The machine can take over what is purely mechanical, and nowadays it has already taken endless

---

[3]Jerusalem Bible.

burdens from human shoulders. Only a few workers, servicing or operating (but not mechanized), are seen today in the biggest factories in which the work of hundreds of thousands is done by a machine.

And technology can free one from the unrelenting stress of bodily pain, from the stifling oppression of the daily evils of the natural process, from the defenselessness with which the earliest human beings were abandoned to nature. What is self-evident to us was an unimaginable miracle to previous times.

And technology can liberate from the bounds that space and time set to the human community. Without it the great idea of all eschatological hope—the idea of *one* humanity—could never be realized.

And technology liberates from the sinister, the demonic in things, from their sancrosanctity, from the fear that hinders and oppresses the lives of the primitives. Whatever is technically formed is de-demonized.

But of course, it is also emptied; it has lost something of its fullness of life. It is dominated, and therewith power has taken the place of the eros that binds being with being. It is the power of rationality before which things must bow themselves. But because they must, therefore they do speak to us only as rational, they cut us off from the living current that streams through all beings, they allow in us only the forces that are turned toward rationality, they tempt us through boundless possibility, and we succumb to the temptation and lose our meaning and our necessity. We draw something new and ever again something new out of the "realm of possibility," and the process of technology passes over us, and nobody knows where it will take us. And because of that many long to be back in the time when there was no such possibility, and they become in spirit—and here and there also in fact—machine smashers. They want to undo what has happened. But this is not the way of the spirit. It goes forward. It does not pursue the phantoms of romanticism. Technology has transformed the world, and this transformed world is our world, and no other. Upon it we must build; and more than hitherto we must incorporate technology into the ultimate meaning of life, knowing well that if technology is godlike, if it is creative, if it is liberating, it is still also demonic, enslaving, and destructive. It is ambiguous, as is everything that is; not more ambiguous than pure spirit, not more ambiguous than nature, but as ambiguous as they are.

It also—liberating technology—must be liberated. Its mythos must also flow into the great mythos of the groaning of all living creatures and the yearning for a new being in which spirit and nature are reconciled.

CHAPTER 4

The Freedom of Science[1]

The Concept of Free Science

"Free science" says no more than scientific science. Science is free or it is not at all. The freedom of science does not mean *actual* presuppositionlessness; there is no such thing. For as radically as one might want to call into question everything given, the direction of the question, the form of the question, the sense of the question contain an abundance of presuppositions. Rather the freedom of science means *fundamental* presuppositionlessness, the right to call into question every presupposition that has come to be seen as unquestioned. The great advances of science are accomplished in this way. It goes its way through "fundamental crises," through inquiry into that which was previously the presupposition of the question. If this way is barred to science, if presuppositions are forced upon it that it may no longer call into question, then it ceases to be science. Because of this, a confessionally bound theology or a politically bound political science can certainly have a scientific form, but they are not science. For them, science is a tool, not a principle, as the old theology in all honesty acknowledged, and as the political dogmaticians of Fascism and Bolshevism should likewise acknowledge. Whoever has sworn a modernist's or Fascist's or Marxist's oath, and to the extent that he is thereby restricted from questioning, he stands basically outside of science. Science is liberal, or it isn't science. Illiberal science is "wooden iron."[2] And inasmuch as the freedom to call into question every one of its presuppositions is the most radical human impossibility, science and scientific liberality belong to human beings in general, to humanity in the strictest

---

[1]Translated by John C. Modschiedler, College of Dupage.

[2]Here, Tillich is using an oxymoron.

sense. Science, liberality, and humanity not only belong together, but are basically one and the same.

Science and Orthodoxy:
Religious, Political, Intellectual

The question that is of pressing importance at the present time can therefore only be as follows: To what extent can the great communities of a religious and political nature allow for science? The official obeisance they all give to science does not prove that they really allow for it or that they intend to allow for it as soon as they have achieved power. One cannot, on the one hand, hurl every thinkable invective at liberalism and, on the other hand, kowtow to science.

The conflict begins with the choice of those who are supposed to do and teach science on behalf of the state. And this conflict does not first appear in dictatorships with dogmatic foundations but already in liberalism itself no matter how far-reachingly it has been carried out. From the natural sciences to the human sciences all the way to philosophy, the necessary presuppositions of all inquiry that are operative in science itself are making themselves felt in growing measure and are determining the selection, namely, of the candidates of the younger generation, as can be seen from the university's practice in terms of tenured faculty as well as in terms of the vocations. Even in the most ideal case this cannot be avoided, for it lies in the essence of the matter itself and does not mean any curtailment of the freedom of science. Besides, it has the advantage of forcing deeper intellectual competition, and thereby eventually a balancing in the variety of researchers occurs, and thus it serves the richness of scientific life.

But this ideal situation is not real because not only the unavoidable presuppositions internal to science but also those factors external to science are decisive for the selection process. Here also the ideal situation is to be presupposed: that personal connections or nepotism of any kind whatsoever plays no role. However, in liberalism as in dictatorships, it remains of crucial importance for the actual political and confessional posture for the selection of the succeeding generation. Even the most rigorous liberal guides himself instinctively by such norms, namely, those in the sciences that are more strongly defined by a world view. In the nineteenth century, amidst liberalism and the idolization of science, bourgeois class interests succeeded in bringing about a very strictly political selection—mostly without the consciousness that the allegedly purely scientific evaluation was also determined by the ideology of classes and confessional instincts. Consequently, decisive questions, namely, in the human sciences, but also in the natural sciences, could not gain acceptance. They contradicted the interests of the ruling parties and were not allowed. One need only think of the fate of the purely scientific problems raised by Marx and by socialism at the universities. This frame of mind prevails as an aftereffect to this day, so that if a scientifically outstanding scholar were influenced by Marx methodologically or materially, his appointment would be fought as political, whereas the appointment at the same time of a dozen professors of opposing tendency causes no political offense in any way at all. Seldom has the restrictive power of class interests and confessional instincts shown itself more clearly in the midst of free science. Nevertheless, it is better for science that it undertakes this unconscious and unwanted self-imposed restriction of its freedom than that it allow itself and its fundamentally scientific attitude to be violated through any oath of *ism*. The freedom of scientific research is only possible under the simultaneous condition of the freedom of scientific expression. For only as such can the community of research come about in which science lives. A restriction of the freedom of scientific expression therefore also puts an end to science as such; of course, only then when the expression itself is science. If the presentation of scientific results in unscientific form—for example, as a confession, a manifesto, a political speech, as agitation, et cetera—is hindered, then the free expression of opinion in general is thereby restricted certainly, but not scientific freedom. The first rule of conduct of every professor must be, therefore, that in the scientific utterances for which he is responsible, under no circumstances, neither in an oral report nor in a written statement, should the strict methodological attitude be relinquished that characterizes a statement as scientific. If he does abandon the scientific stance, then he cannot claim the protection of scientific freedom for his remarks. In any case, as places of scientific research and education, institutions of higher education must ward off every interference in the freedom of scientific expression with the passion of a struggle over existence or nonexistence. If a society believes that science—through education toward impartiality, self-critique, and humanitarianism, and then also for the building of the state—is indispensable, then if science questions society's dogmatic foundations, religious and political, then society cannot break science's back by prohibiting questions and denying freedom of expression. Society must place its trust in the creative powers of the scientific perspective, in the inner power of intellectual honesty, and must protect institutions of higher education from the attacks of the powers outside science whether in academic or nonacademic garb. And professors and their agencies (rector, senate, departments, association of university professors) should lead this battle without any compromise. For each scientific question is inextricably linked with every other one. A compromise, such as the acceptance of a prohibition even in only one area or one problem, therefore means the destruction of the possibility of science itself.

Science and Heteronomy

If one no longer believes in the value of the scientific perspective and scientific education for building society, then one would turn the universities into technical schools with prescribed, censored, and controlled presentation of material. There are very strong tendencies from the confessional as well as and particularly from the political side that are going in this direction. And large groups of young people feel that they are no longer in a position to question their submission to the situation itself, as well as to question the uncertainty that is necessarily connected with scientific questioning. They flee to authority and heteronomy and want to subjugate at least parts of science to extraneous authorities. They no longer risk allowing their own presuppositions to be questioned, be they religious, social, or national presuppositions. This, however, means the end of science. As the last instance of honesty and sincerity there should then be demanded only this: that they not hide their inhumanity and illiberality behind the still continually luminous name of science. For science is free or it is not.

CHAPTER 5

Participation and Knowledge: Problems of an Ontology of Cognition

Basic Considerations

The Polarity of Individualization and Participation

An adequate investigation of the numerous and difficult problems connected with the question of cognitive participation would require a much longer and more complete analysis than is possible here. This, therefore, must be considered merely an initial approach to the problems of an ontology of cognition.

The most adequate starting point of ontological inquiry would seem to be the possibility of the ontological question itself. Whatever we may say about the nature and structure of being, whether openly in ontological terms or disguised in antiontological terms, we must answer this question: How is it possible to ask about being at all? What is the structure of being that makes asking possible? The first, though incomplete, answer is: Being, insofar as it is an object of asking presupposes the subject-object structure of reality. Being, when we view it in the light of the question of being, exhibits the structural polarity of subject and object. But his polarity is the cognitive side of an all-embracing polarity—that of self and world. Asking is an activity of an ego-self; it is a process going on in a world to which the ego-self belongs and to which it is related as "its world." This highly dialectical polarity includes other polar elements, of which individualization and participation are one pair.

Individualization points to that which is self-centered, which, in other words, is particular. As self-centered it resists being merged into the universal. The degree to which something is self-centered determines its capacity to maintain its own identity in an infinite variety of relations. One of these relations is cognition.

Participation literally means "taking part," but there is an ambiguity in the meaning of the word. It can mean "sharing," as in having shares in an enterprise, or it can mean "having in common," in the sense of the Platonic Μέσεξις of the individual in the universal, or it can mean "becoming a part," as of a political movement. In all three cases participation points to an element of identity in that which is different or of a togetherness of that which is separated. Whether it is the identity of the same enterprise, or the identity of the same universal or the identity of the same whole, of which one is a part, in each case participation implies identity. But it is an identity that is in polar correlation with the most radical separation—that of self-relatedness. Knowledge, in common with all other kinds of participation, has the polar interdependence of identity and difference and this on the level of the most complete kind of separation, the separation of the self-centered ego-self from everything else.

The Tension between Separation and Participation in the Cognitive Act

There are classes of finite beings that are related to each other in terms of replacing each other in time or of resisting each other in space, or of producing each other causally, or of inhering in each other substantially. There are other kinds of finite beings that are related to each other in terms of encounter. Man, who belongs to this class of finite beings, encounters other beings as other beings. About twenty years ago I tried to elaborate an ontology of encounter on the assumption that it is possible to derive the subject-object relation from the phenomena, while it is impossible to make forms of encounter like love or knowledge understandable by starting either with pure objectivity or pure subjectivity or by starting, as Spinoza and Schelling did, with a preceding identity. What precedes is not identity but polarity, and, in the actual process of life, encounter. The *contra* root in encounter, like the *gegen* in *begegnen,* points to a notion that is also contained in *ob-jectum,* in that which is thrown opposite to him who has it as an object. But in addition, encounter has the connotation of coming from both sides, of meeting in a common situation, of participation in this situation by becoming a part of it. Cognition is such an encounter and such a participation in a common situation. Subject and object meet in the situation of knowledge. Both are parts of the situation.

But to be able to encounter cognitively, subject and object must be open for each other. The knower and the known must receive each other. Openness is a metaphor taken from the spatial realm, but often it is applied to psychological and spiritual phenomena. Its presupposition is the potentiality of taking something into one's totality or of being taken into some other's totality. When Leibniz rejected the openness of the monads, he had to make of each of them a world, a closed, all-embracing totality that cannot receive anything because there is nothing to be received that is not already present. Therefore no monad can have a direct knowledge of any other monad. This doctrine of Leibniz demonstrates in its absurd radicalism the significance of open "doors and windows" for the sake of cognition.

But knowledge is not only dependent on openness to encounter and participation. It also depends on separation, self-containment, and detachment. If this were not the case, the structure of that which is known would be invaded and destroyed by the dynamics of the knower. There is no knowledge where there is no separation. Man can have knowledge because he has a world and is, in this respect, separated from his environment. Environmental theories of man do not take into account that in order to have a theory, namely something that claims to be universally valid, man must have transcended his environment and have a world. A being that is environmentally determined cannot fulfill the conditions of knowledge that we have called self-containment and detachment. A being that is determined by its environment is not a complete self, and therefore it is incapable of free self-containment. Nor is it capable of complete detachment, for it is essentially a part of its environment.

The unity of separation and participation in every cognitive act is implicitly discussed in the old question of whether the equal recognizes the equal or the unequal the unequal. Empedocles, following Parmenides, says that with the fire in us we recognize fire, with the love in us love, and the hate in us hate, et cetera. Anaxagoras, following Heraclitus, says that the warm is recognized by the cold, and that for this very reason, the only pure and unadulterated substance is able to recognize all things: πάντα ἔγνω νοῦς.

The arguments given by both sides for either the necessity of participation or the necessity of separation in every cognitive act are valid as far as they go. It is important to note that the scientific type of thought favors the side of separation, while the metaphysical side favors the side of participation. This leads to the question of whether the different levels of the real in the cognitive encounter favor different relations between the element of participation and the element of separation. We shall now turn to a consideration of this question. On the basis of the preceding discussion the general answer is obvious: If subject and object are participants in the cognitive situation, the situation as a whole changes with the different forms of cognitive encounter.

Cognitive Attitudes and Levels of Being

Participation, Detachment,
and the Phenomenological Intuition

Without accepting the basic assumption of Husserl's phenomenology, that is, the bracketing of existence, I believe that the Platonic tradition in all its variations is right in asking a question that empiricism never can answer, namely, the question of the structural presuppositions of experience. It is the constitution of the subject as subject, and correspondingly of the object as object, that is the subject matter of the phenomenological question. The way in which phenomenology has reformulated this question has been very impressive; it has changed the philosophical climate since 1900 in many respects. However, it has lost much of its standing, partly by exaggerations as in Max Scheler's attempt to make bishops and angels into objects of a necessary phenomenological intuition, partly by the impossibility of avoiding existential decisions in the choice of examples of intuition, and partly by confusions between empirical and phenomenological statements. But there is an irreducible though indefinite minimum of structural presuppositions of every cognitive encounter that is a genuine subject matter of phenomenological research. The evidence of their presence is apparent in the necessity of applying them even in the act attacking their validity. I believe that the logical, categorical, and ontological principles, in short, everything that constitutes the structure of a cognitive encounter or, as previously formulated, the structure of asking questions, belong to his kind of being.

In this respect, participation seems to be absolutely predominant over separation. The subject is a part of the process in which it not only encounters the object, but also encounters its own encountering. The seeming lack of detachment has made the phenomenological intuition suspect. It seems that no verification is possible, that the intuiting subject produces what it wants to see. Since the time of Plato and Aristotle there has been lack of agreement about the first principles, and Husserl's ideal of philosophy as a strict science has broken down in all his pupils (as Mr. Husserl once confessed to me with great sorrow).

Participation, Detachment, and Controlling Knowledge

Max Scheler, in the volume *Versuche zu einer Soziologie des Wissens,* distinguishes between three types of knowledge: *Heilwissen, Bildungswissen, Herrschaftswissen,* which may be roughly translated as saving knowledge, educational knowledge, controlling knowledge. By eliminating educational knowledge that does not constitute a special cognitive type, and by enlarging the realm of saving knowledge so that it encompasses what is called today existential knowledge, we can establish a scale on the one pole of which we have controlling knowledge, on the other pole existential knowledge. Between these poles, which correspond to the elements of separation and participation, lie different combinations of controlling and existential knowledge of reality.

Controlling knowledge is represented by the mathematical sciences and all other scientific endeavors insofar as they follow their method. The term *controlling* points to the ultimate connection between scientific discovery and technical application, a connection that reaches into the depths of the method itself, into analysis, experiment, and hypothesis, and that is also anticipated by Anaxagoras when he says that the completely separated νοῦς controls every movement of the things around it. The question therefore is whether there is not participation as well as separation in controlling knowledge. I find it at two points: The first, already discussed, is the categorical structure that is present in every subject-object encounter. But there is another point of participation in scientific knowledge indicated by such terms as *the given, perception, information, vernehmen,* and its derivative *Vernuft.* In all of these the metaphor of "give and take" is used in order to describe the cognitive act. Knowing means taking in what is given through the senses; but it is taken in thoroughly, as what it really is, as the syllables *per-* and *ver-* (and the *piras* in *empiria*) indicate. This reception of the really Real forms and informs that which does the receiving, the cognitive self. The phenomenon of scientific curiosity is profounder than the word *curiosity* seems to admit. It is the desire to participate in that which is real and which, by its reality, exerts an infinite attraction on the being who is able to encounter reality as reality. Participation in that which has the power of being the really Real gives fulfillment to him who participates in it. Scientific curiosity, the desire to know for the sake of knowing, which Aristotle attributes to every man, highlights the limits of the term *controlling knowledge;* and it points to the fact that there is an element of participation even at the scientific pole.

Participation and Understanding

The words used for the phenomena of understanding also demonstrate an awareness of the element of participation. Under-standing itself uses the metaphor of "standing under" the object. *Ver-stehen* uses a similar image. *Comprehendere* uses the metaphor of grasping and bringing together. A strong emphasis on "being with" is manifested in all of these words.

Understanding is usually used to denote the physical and linguistic grasp of the meaning of a word or a sentence, or of a nonverbal expression. To learn a language means to participate increasingly in the meanings of a special system of linguistic expression. But beyond this, two cognitive problems of understanding arise, one dealing with the knowledge of personal life processes in oneself and in others, and the other dealing with the knowledge of the spiritual (*geistigen*) expressions of life processes. Roughly speaking, the first is the problem of empathy, the second the problem of interpretation.

One of the consequences of the predominance of the principle of separation in modern theories of knowledge has been that man has tried to describe his understanding of others as an inference from his understanding of himself. This presupposes that the individual participates first in himself and then, indirectly, in others. Actually both the understanding of oneself and the understanding of others are secondary phenomena. The primary phenomenon is the understanding of the situation of encounter in which both oneself and others participate, but not as separated subject and object. The infant experiences friendliness or anger with a situation before he objectifies the participants in this encounter as the father and himself. Participation precedes objectification. If the state of objectification is reached, the other person may become an object of controlling knowledge. He can be tested, calculated, and handled, be it by a test-psychologist in America, or by a propagandist in a totalitarian country, or by a diplomatic husband or wife in any country. He has become an object of controlling knowledge. The communion of existential understanding, of understanding by participation, has been broken.

The same duality of levels can be observed in the act of self-knowledge. In modern psychological terminology, empathetic participation in one's own being is often called "insight." Both syllables of this word emphasize cognitive participation. The meaning of depth psychology is completely misunderstood if insight is interpreted as the knowledge and self-application of psychotherapeutic theories. The healing power of such a knowledge must rightly be denied. Insight is healing knowledge because it is the conscious participation in situations, processes, and strivings of present and past that have been covered, repressed, forgotten. Self-knowledge participates and becomes insight not in an externally remembered past, but an internally reactivated one. Every analyst knows that scientific knowledge of the psychological processes involved makes reactivation, insight, and healing almost impossible. The difference of the cognitive levels is obvious.

But it seems that in these cognitive attitudes the element of separation, and with it, of objectivity and verifying criteria, is lost. Insight can become a word for fanatical self-assurance, and understanding of the other person can become a matter of wishful thinking or romantic idealization. This difficulty can be solved only by a description of the "right" participation. Here the cognitive criterion coincides with the ethical criterion: true knowledge of the other person is possible only to the degree in which the relation to him is neither blinding passion nor beautifying wish nor distorting hate but rather a criticizing and accepting ἀγάτη that is detached and involved at the same time. Likewise a true knowledge of oneself is possible only to the degree in which ideologies and rationalizations about oneself have been removed by the ἀγάτη towards oneself.

These statements about insight and participation may help to overcome a rather old misunderstanding of the Socratic doctrine that knowledge creates virtue. If knowledge had to be understood in terms of controlling knowledge, the Socratic assertion would be absurd. But since knowledge means existential knowledge, namely one's cognitive participation in that which is essentially human, the Socratic assertion is true. For the act that produces such a participation is virtue itself and includes all other virtues.

Now we must look at interpretative knowledge. The syllable *inter* in interpretation points to the fact that one must be "between" in order to understand. One must participate in the spiritual process that is expressed in a text. One can distinguish between philological and existential interpretations, but not by representing them as two different methods. They are the two poles in every genuine interpretation. It was a very unfortunate state of things when Protestant exegesis was carried on as an indifferent philology to which a devotional trimming was added. The concept of cognitive participation must be used as a weapon against such a situation, of which one could find many examples in philosophy and literature as well. Philological interpretation must follow the strictest hermeneutic rules. But it must always remember that it is meaningful only to the degree in which the creation of the past is taken to the present creativity of the interpreter or speaks more generally to the interpretative potentialities of the present period. Again the polarity of separation and participation is effective. The philological element of an interpretative act is directed towards the unchangeable past of the text that is *ob-jectum* in the full sense of the word. It must be kept pure and must be literally explained as perfectly as possible. But the text is understood only if an encounter with the past has taken place, if the past has become an integral part of the present in the interpreting mind, be it in terms of rejection or of acceptance. This is true of every new generation with respect to the documents of the past, and it is even true of the author himself, when he returns to his own work. A new union of understanding between the present and the past state of the author is needed, as every autobiography shows. This has a further significant implication: If refutes the doctrine that the past is completely and unchangeably finished. Creative understanding transforms the past insofar as potential meanings implied in a text of the past become actual meanings in its present interpretation. Then the past with respect to its meaning has been changed. As an example, I could refer to the history of the meaning of classical Greek culture from its own time up to the present day. Every succeeding period is irrevocably separated from classical Greece. But by participation each period knows and by knowing it transforms what is given in the unchangeable expressions of the Greek past. It changes their meaning beyond what they meant for the Greeks themselves, which was, as it is for us, an ambiguous combination of potential and actually experienced meanings.

I have not dealt with special sciences, since in most of them different ways of cognitive encounters come together. What I have said about understanding and about the relation of participation and separation is valid for historical knowledge in all its ramifications. A discussion of biology, of psychology, anthropology, and sociology would reveal the same situation. It would also show that many methodological prejudices, which are rampant in these disciplines, could be destroyed by a careful and discriminating analysis of cognitive participation. It would show to what degree the reality of man and society is cognitively bypassed or distorted by methods in which understanding is reduced to causal, genetic, or even functional explanation to the exclusion of the creative understanding in terms of existential knowledge.

Knowledge and Commitment

The last type of cognitive encounter to be considered is characterized by a definitive predominance of participation, namely, by a total, person-centered participation that one might call cognitive commitment.

Symbolic for this kind of knowledge is the Greek word γνῶϛιϛ in its later development. In the New Testament period, it had three meanings: mystical union, sexual intercourse, and a knowledge that is not ἐτιϛτήμη. It is obvious that in this terminology γνῶϛιϛ represents the side of participation. The cognitive commitment is—according to the word γνῶϛιϛ—analogous to erotic and mystical surrender. Nevertheless it remains knowledge and in the system of the later ancient period it is united with refined logical and epistemological analyses.

However, the problem of cognitive commitment is much larger. It refers to everything that is called religious knowledge and to the methodological explanation of it that is called theology. If religion is defined—as I think it should be—as the experience of ultimate concern, the cognitive element within the whole of this experience participates in its nature as ultimate concern. The concept of participation is a necessary and effective tool for the understanding of the cognitive element in religion and its relation to the cognitive act generally. It is not qualitatively different from knowledge in all other realms, insofar as it unites separation and participation, although it does so in a special way. Only if, through a kind of methodological imperialism, we make controlling knowledge the pattern of all knowledge, do existential knowledge and cognitive commitment become meaningless concepts. But it is not only in religion that one had to resist such imperialism.

Participation within cognitive commitment means being grasped on a level of one's own reality and of reality generally that is not determined by the subject-object structure of finitude, but that underlies this structure. Commitment in this dimension does not mean the surrender of oneself as subject to an object, even the highest object, as popular theism demands. It means rather the participation of the whole personality in that which transcends objectivity as well as subjectivity. Religion has expressed this in innumerable symbols, all of which have in common the fact that they must be interpreted in negative as well as positive terms: they imply the negation of what they affirm and the affirmation of what they negate. This is a necessary consequence of the act of transcending the subject-object scheme in religious knowledge.

But now the question must be answered: How is knowledge possible if its presupposition, the subject-object structure of reality, is transcended? What is left of the element of separation, objectivity, verification in this kind of encounter? The answer is that knowledge is an ontic relation and that, therefore, it is subject to the categories of being, above all to time. It is the time difference between the moment of uniting participation and separating objectification that makes religious, and—in some degree—all knowledge possible. This does not mean that a former participation is remembered and made an object of cognition. But it does mean that the moment is present in the cognitive moment and vice versa. Participation still persists in the moment of cognitive separation; the cognitive encounter includes moments of predominant participation, which I have called the perceptive moments, as well as moments of predominant separation, which I have called the cognitive moments. They alternate and establish in their totality a cognitive encounter. This is the situation in all realms, and it is the structure that makes religious knowledge possible.

I cannot deal more fully with the knowledge of commitment generally and with religious knowledge in particular. The point I want to make is this: the concept of cognitive participation removes the barrier between the different forms of cognitive encounter and, above all, it rolls up the iron curtain that now separates religious and controlling knowledge.

It was a fascinating and surprising journey through the history of philosophy when I tried to discover the way in which the different philosophies have dealt with the ontological principles of participation and separation. They all knew the problem and decided in favor of the predominance of one or the other principle. But none of them could eliminate the opposite principle completely. The unity of participation and separation in the cognitive situation will always remain a fundamental problem of philosophy, and the astonishing reality of knowledge will always remain an occasion for that cognitive task that we call the "ontology of knowledge."

PART III

Science, Technology, and Human Self-Interpretation

CHAPTER 6

How Has Science in the Last Century Changed Man's View of Himself?

The formulation of our problem raises questions about the exact meaning of some of its terms. Since I suppose that this was intended, I take the liberty of deciding how I shall understand them. Referring first to the word *science,* I take it to mean every cognitive approach to reality that is methodologically disciplined. This implies not only the natural and much of the social sciences, but also elements of history and philosophy. Related to this question is that of the relation of the sciences to their practical application in all realms of human culture. I believe that in the context of our question the effect of the science-created technical world cannot—and certainly should not—be ignored. A third question refers to the meaning of the phrase "man's view of himself." One asks, which man's view? I suggest: all those who have been influenced directly in their view of man by the sciences themselves and all those who have been influenced indirectly in their view of man by the technical application of the sciences. This includes people in all social classes, nations and cultures; but it does not include all men, not even a majority. Finally I must refer to the qualifying words of the title "in the last century." The year 1861 and even a few decades before or after it have only limited significance within the total impact of science of man's self-interpretation in Western history. Nevertheless, I intend to mention several of the most important contributions to such impact in the last one hundred years, though within the frame of the total picture.

The Change of Man's View of Himself under the Impact of the Technical Application of Science

I intend to reverse the logical sequence that would start with science as such and then go on to its technical application. It seems to me that the more widespread and more powerful impact of science on man's view of himself stems from the technical world, created by science as a world above the given world.

The Change in Man's Telos

Man's view of himself is summed up in an answer to the question of the meaning of his being, his *telos,* the Greek word for the inner aim of a life process. I shall use the word *telos* because it prevents us from being confused by the connotations of *purpose,* which stands for an aim, external to him who has it. Telos is the inner aim of any being, it is its *entelecheis*—that towards which it drives by its given nature—as every tree, from the stage of its being in a seed, drives towards developing that power of being that impresses us whenever we look at a tree. What is the inner aim, the telos, of man was the question of Western philosophy and theology since their beginnings. And three fundamentally different answers have been given. All three are still with us, but only the third one is a genuine creation of the last five hundred years, the period of Western history in which the impact of science becomes predominant.

The Classical-Humanist Definition of Telos

The first conscious definition of man's telos is the classical Greek one: Man's inner aim is the actualization of his potentialities and the conquest of those distortions of his nature that are caused by his bondage to error and passions. This definition of man's telos was alive not only from Heraclitus and Socrates to the Stoics and Epicureans but it is still alive in all those who could be called "humanists" in the modern world. Science, for this view of man, is one amongst many other human potentialities. It supports the idea of the general development of the humanist out of the bondage of his autonomy under demonic and superstitious forms of religion. But it does not determine this change.

The Transcendental-Religious Definition of Telos

The second conscious definition of man's telos is the late ancient and early Christian one: Man's inner aim is the elevation from the universe of finitude and guilt to the reunion with ultimate reality, the transcendent ground and abyss of everything that is. Here science was kept in narrow limits. Especially physics was deemed to be dangerous, not because of its critical power, but because it ties the mind to the material world. The supranatural invaded the natural (as Huxley has described). What we call the medieval view of man is the attempted amalgamation of the two definitions of the telos, the transcendental and the humanist one. It was done most successfully by Thomas Aquinas, yet the supranatural prevailed. Science was admitted in a subordinate position, but developed undercover towards a new birth.

The Scientific-Technical Definition of Telos

Since the Renaissance and Reformation a third definition of man's telos developed: Man's inner aim is the active subjection and transformation of nature and man. The roots of this view of man lie in the two other views, but after an important change has taken place in both of them. Renaissance humanism is in its very depth an active humanism and one that is politically and technically oriented. And Reformation piety, especially in its Calvinistic and Evangelistic forms, aims at the subjection of world and mankind to the kingdom of God. On this new ground the third definition of telos in the Western culture developed: rational man, the active center of his world, analyzing, controlling, and changing it according to his purposes. Obviously, under the determination by this telos, science necessarily received a predominant place, and this place became more elevated the more the theoretical and practical success confirmed the claim of science to domination. The two older definitions of man's telos, classical humanism and religious transcendentialism, were pushed aside. In most cases this did not happen intentionally; but the power of the world of technical means, including the means to increase them indefinitely, drove the mind into the horizontal direction to the neglect not only of the vertical elevation, symbolizing the religious aim, but also the circular enlargement symbolizing the classical aim.

Consequences of the Scientific-Technical Telos

Necessarily, this view of man had many consequences for more particular problems of human nature. One of them is the subordination of all other functions of man's mind to calculating reason. If the means-ends relation prevails, calculation is its primary tool. Reason is reduced to it; it loses its larger meaning that included the moral and the aesthetic function.

But more important are the inner problems of the science and technique determined description of man's telos. All means are by definition means for an end. But what is the end, if the production of means is the inner aim of man's being? Is this not the surrender of a telos altogether? One can answer: the production of tools serves man's happiness. It glorifies man's infinite possibilities. It liberates him increasingly from merely mechanical functions, avoidable evils, the power of nature over him. It makes life easier and longer for the masses of people. All this is true. But happiness was an accompanying element in the two older teloi, also called *eudaimony* or blessedness. Happiness may accompany the fulfillment of a telos, but it does not constitute it. And this means that the subjection of nature and man by man is a telos that negates a telos. The dominant view of man in the present period is characterized by the inner contradiction of an end that is the endless production of means without an end.

There is an indirect proof of this analysis; the universal outcry against this lack of a telos in the gown of a telos. The manifestation of this outcry is the so-called existentialist art, literature, and philosophy. In the expressions of emptiness, meaninglessness, and life-anxiety, the loss of a convincing telos becomes conscious. Neither science nor its technical application are able to give a telos, a definition of the inner aim of man's being. This situation is especially noticeable in Asiatic countries like Japan where the most urgent question is that of a telos. The old answers are disappearing; the new ones come in terms of the present Western telos, and the result is a split consciousness, indifference, and disintegration.

The Change of Man's View of Himself under the Impact of Science Itself

Although our subject is not religion and science, I want to say something about their relation, because the change in man's view of himself is often attributed to the scientific criticism (including historical criticism) of religious doctrines, e.g., the Christian doctrine of man. If we look at the last hundred years, one could point to three important scientific events: the theory of evolution, the rediscovery of the unconscious, and reductive behaviorism.

Evolution and the Distinction between Religion and Science

The first one, just about a hundred years ago, in the work of Darwin, came as a shock to the traditional theological view of man. It seemed to transform man into a meaningless product of a meaningless universe depriving him of the greatness and dignity that was presupposed in the religious as well as in the humanistic view of man. The shock vanished when it became understood that the genesis of a being does not determine its character and that the evolutionary process is more adequate to the symbol of creation than casual interferences of a highest being in the process of life. The view of man as creature and as that creature that is aware of its creatureliness was not changed but deepened by the theory of evolution. One learned again what earlier generations under the impact of Galilean and Newtonian physics and astronomy had to learn: that the dimension of ultimate concern about the meaning of existence, i.e., religion, should not be confused with the dimension of methodological cognition of finite reality, i.e., science.

The Rediscovery of Unconscious "Ideology"

The second change in the view of man happened in the last half century under the impact of the scientific rediscovery of the old philosophical concept of the unconscious. The shock produced by the way in which this was done, primarily in the work of Freud, was caused first by its ethical implications, especially the assumed emphasis on sex, second by Freud's antireligious bias, and third—above all—by the resistance of a moralistic society (moralistic even if immoral) against the discovery of its underground motives. Summed up in one word, it was the discovery of the "ideological" character of conscious actions that made for the change in man's view of himself in the first half of the twentieth century. It is worth noticing that the same analysis was done half a century before by the early Marx, and further, that the pessimistic valuation of moral man, expressed in the concept of ideology, agreed with the existentialist view of man. The result of this silent agreement was the tremendous impact of the psychoanalytic discoveries on existentialist literature, art and philosophy in all their forms, and that today the existentialist view of man is being taken into psychotherapy as its philosophical foundation. It is also important to notice that the change in man's view of himself, produced in this way, became a support for the religious valuation of man's predicament (while the humanistic view of man was strongly defensive against it).

Behaviorism and Objectification

The third way in which scientific impact changed the view of man was reductionist behaviorism. Its theoretical foundation is the doctrine of the conditioned reflexes; its practical application is social and psychological engineering. But its ground lies even deeper. It is the temptation of science to transform everything encountered, including man, into an object that is nothing other than an object. Obviously, every scientific inquiry has an object opposite the inquiring subject. And the more deprived a being is of subjectivity, namely, spontaneous reactions, the more precisely can it be analyzed. This situation has often produced a half-conscious attitude, often a fully conscious philosophy, according to which nothing is other than a mere object or—in another terminology—a thing that is something altogether conditioned (*bedingt* in German). The universe, including man, is a sum of things to be described and manipulated. The logical object has become an ontological object and has drawn the ontological subject to itself. Novels like the half-ironical, half-serious *Brave New World* by A. Huxley and the deadly serious *Walden II* by B. F. Skinner have shown consequences of this process that already have appeared in our actual social situation. Yet the most pertinent question (Who controls psychological conditioning and social engineering?) has not been answered except by the horrifying shadow of "Big Brother" in Orwell's *1984*. But this question is the decisive one. It shows that there is at least one point in which subjectivity cannot be annihilated, namely, in those who annihilate. Science cannot reduce into mere objects the bearers of science and its application. And this exception undercuts any view of man that is based on reductive behaviorism.

May I conclude with the hope that the ever-increasing protest against the dehumanization of man in the latest stages, not of science and technology, but of scientism and technicism may soon become more than a protest, but a support for a view of man that takes into consideration all dimensions of the multidimensional unity that man is.

CHAPTER 7

The Decline and the Validity
of the Idea of Progress

I

My subject is the idea of progress, which I will examine from the point of view that it is valid, that it has declined very much in its importance, and that in a new form it might be revived. Therefore, my title is "The Decline and the Validity of the Idea of Progress."

Let us, first, examine some basic considerations about the concepts involved. This is where my semantic critics are right. Every discussion today in philosophy and theology demands a semantic clearing up of the concepts that are used, because we are living in Babylon after the tower has been destroyed, and the languages of man have been disturbed and dispersed all over the world. This is the situation one faces today in reading theological and philosophical books. Therefore, I must guide you through some burdensome logical, semantic, and historical journeys.

The Concept and the Idea of Progress

Now, first, there is a difference between the concept of progress and the idea of progress. The concept of progress is an abstraction, based on the description of a group of facts, of objects of observation that may well be verified of falsified; but the idea of progress is an interpretation of existence as a whole, which means first of all our own experience. Thus, it is a matter of decision. It is an answer everybody has to give about the meaning of his life. Progress as an idea is a symbol for an attitude toward our existence. As so often in history, a concept open to logical and empirical description and analysis has become a symbol, and in the case of progress this is particularly true—the concept has become a symbol. What is extracted from a special realm of facts has become an expression of a general attitude toward life. Therefore, we must look at progress both as concept and as symbol. Since observation always precedes interpretation, I will give most attention to progress as a concept, because most of the confusions about progress as a symbol come from a limited and wrong analysis of progress as a concept.

Obviously progress is a universal experience that everybody has. The word is derived from *greassus,* which means step; progress means stepping ahead from a less satisfactory situation to a more satisfactory situation. Imagine a lecture like this about progress, yet denying the idea of progress; someone might attempt this. But even such a person in denying the idea of progress works for progress; that is, he wants the less informed of his listeners to be better informed at the end of his lecture. In this sense, even if he speaks against the idea of progress, he accepts the concept of progress. He is implicitly progressivistic. I call this kind of thinking about progress "progressivism," which is implied in every action. Everybody who acts, acts in order to change a state of things in the direction of a better state of things. He wants to make progress. This is the most simple, the most fundamental, and actually the least contradictory way of understanding progress—the progressivism implied in every action. Nobody can get away from this. Yet this simple sense of progress is far from progress as the universal way of life, and as the law of human history. Therefore, we ask how could the idea have arisen that human history and, even preceding it, the history of all life, the history of the universe, has a progressivistic character—is progress from something lower to something higher? How could this idea develop? What are the motives behind it?

Now I must first guide you on the thorny path—especially so for Americans—of historical reminder. I hope it is a reminder because I presume that all of you know what I am referring to, but if not, be patient with me because the historical question gives the basis for the understanding of what today seems natural to us. The idea of this country is that it represents a new beginning in the history of mankind. This is true in many respects. But the new beginning is never fully new. It is always a result of preceding events, and if I may comment on my experience on two continents, I would say that Europe is endangered by its past and by all the curses coming from the past. America, on the other hand, is endangered by going ahead without looking back at the creative forces that have determined the whole of Western culture. So I wish to direct your thoughts in the first part of this paper to the past. You will discover how relevant this is to our present understanding of such an idea of progress.

Let us first consider the religious background of the idea of progress. The fundamental factor in this respect is prophetic religion as expressed in the Old Testament and in many forms ever since in the Christian church as well as in Judaism and Islam. It involves the idea that God has elected a nation and, later on in Christianity, people from all over the world, that he has promised something related to the future, and that in spite of all resistance on the part of the people, he will fulfill his promise. There is the vision of progress toward the future in this idea. The belief of the prophets that Yahweh, the God of Israel, will establish his heavenly rule of his kingdom over all the world is the primary basis of an interpretation of history as the place where the divine reveals itself in progress toward an end. Now this idea has always been important in the development of Christianity. There was, for example, a man whose name should be remembered, Joachim de Fiore, an abbot in Southern Italy in the twelfth century, who expressed this idea of progress in the doctrine that there were three stages in history, the stage of the Father in the Old Testament, the stage of the Son (the last thousand years of church history), and the coming of a third stage of the Divine Spirit in which there will be no more church since everyone will be taught directly by the Spirit. In this last stage, too, there will be equality and there will be no more marriage: history will have come to an end.

Now this half-fantastic, half-realistic idea had many consequences for the whole subsequent church history, and also for this country. The idea of the third stage was taken on by the radical evangelicals in the time of the Reformation, which underlies most of this country's religion, and is seen in the idea of a revolutionary or progressivistic realization of the kingdom of God in Calvinism. It became the religious basis deep-rooted in every Western man. If you don't believe it, go to Asia—to India or Japan. I had the privilege of being in Japan for ten weeks talking every day with Buddhist priests and scholars. There is nothing like this. "The religions of the East are of the past," I was told, "not of the future." For the religious people of the East, one wants to return to the Eternal from which one came directly, not caring for history, going out of history at some time of one's life into the desert, if possible. If you contrast this with the Western religious feeling of progressive activity, then you see what the difference is.

However, this was only the religious basis for the idea of progress. Now we come to the secular motives, and the secular elaboration of the idea of progress, which, of course, starts with the Renaissance. The man of the Renaissance is something new, not only as compared with the Middle Ages but also as compared with the late ancient world. The most important impact of the ancient world on Renaissance man was made by Stoic philosophy, but it was transformed Stoicism. It was not the Stoicism of resignation, as it was under the Roman empire in the later Greek world, but it was the Stoicism of action. The Romans—some of the Roman emperors even—were partly mediators in this direction. However, the man of the Renaissance does not feel he is dependent on fate as the Stoics did. Rather, he feels—as expressed in painting—that when the destiny of man is compared with a sailboat, driven by the winds of contingency, man stands at the rudder and directs it. Of course, he knows that destiny gives the winds, but nevertheless, man directs destiny. This conception is unheard of in all Greek culture and is a presupposition of the idea of progress in the modern world. Out of this arose the great Renaissance utopian writings, that is, the anticipation of a reality—*outopos*—that has "no place" in history, but that is nevertheless being expected. Such utopias have been written ever since, into the twentieth century. It was the idea of the third stage of history, the stage of reason in bourgeois society, the stage of the classless society in the working-class movements. It was a secularized idea of the third stage, the religious foundations of which we saw. But it was not only ideas that produced this passion for purpose, it was also the social reality, the activities of bourgeois society at this time, such as the colonial extension of Europe in all directions; space extension, which has remained an element in the idea of progress up to the space exploration we are doing today; and technical extension—continuous progress in controlling nature and putting it into the service of man. All this has been based on the boundary lines of science that we have trespassed year by year since the beginning of the Renaissance up until today.

But there was another element of great importance in the idea of progress, namely the vision of nature as a progressive process from the atom to the molecule, to the cell, to the developed organism, and finally to man. This is evolution, progress in largeness of elements united in one being, with centeredness and, therefore, power being in the individual. And this line, then, was drawn beyond nature through humanity, from primitive to civilized man, to us the representatives of the age of reason in which the potentialities of creation have come to their fulfillment.

When I tell you this, you yourself can feel how overwhelmingly impressive it is, and how virtually impossible it was to escape this idea as a symbol of faith. Progress became in the nineteenth century not only a conscious doctrine but also an unconscious dogma. When I came to this country in 1933 and spoke with students of theology, and criticized certain ideas of God, of Christ, of the Spirit, of the church, or of sin or salvation, it didn't touch them very much; but when I criticized the idea of progress, they said to me, "In what then can we believe? What do you do with our real faith?" And these were students of theology. It means that all the Christian dogmas had been transformed in the unconscious of these people (which my questions brought out) into a faith in progress. But then something happened! This dogma was shaken in the twentieth century, as foreseen by some prophetic minds in the nineteenth, first in Europe, then in America.

In Europe one of the greatest expressions of the shaking of this faith was Nietzsche's prophecy of—what unfortunately today has become a fashionable phrase—the death of God. This doesn't mean primitive, materialistic atheism; Nietzsche was far from this. But it meant the undercutting of the value-systems, Christian as well as secular, and the view of the human predicament as something in conflict, in destruction, in estrangement from true humanity. Nietzsche was one of the predecessors of what today is called "existentialist" literature. The trend was further supported by the historical pessimism of men like Spengler, who wrote two important volumes on *The Decline of the West* in which much historical imagination was connected with much true prophecy. In the year 1916 he prophesied the coming of the period of the dictators, and in the early thirties the Communist and the Fascist dictators were a reality. The First World War and then the rise of what he prophesied of the totalitarian powers—this was the end of the belief in progress as an idea in Europe. In America it started somehow with the great economic crisis in the thirties. In Germany it started with the beginning of the Hitler period and the experience that history can fall back and that a rebarbarization can happen in any moment even in the highest culture. Then came the Second World War, the cold war, and the atomic crisis. And with all this there came in this country the end of the crusading optimism of the first third of the century. Instead, opposite utopias appeared in literature—negative utopias—like Huxley's *Brave New World,* or Orwell's *1984.* In many other novels and treaties the future is painted in terms of negative utopianism, in terms not of fulfillment but of dehumanization. The same can be seen in the existentialist style in the arts—whether you call it expressionist, cubist, or abstract—wherein the expression of the demonic in the underground of the individual or the group moves away from the figures and faces of human beings toward the abstract elements in the underground of reality. In philosophy there is a withdrawal into a merely formal analysis of the possibility of thinking without going into a reality itself with one's thinking. This was the end of a phase in the idea of progress, but the active motive of all our behavior cannot die, nor can the lure of future possibilities.

Today we need a new inquiry into the validity and the limits of the idea of progress. There are symptoms of reconsideration: for instance, in philosophy now there is an attempt finally to use the sharpened instruments of logical analysis to go into the real problems of human existence; and in the arts at least an attempt to use the elementary forms discovered in the last fifty years to express in a new way reality as manifestly encountered. There are other elements too: the extension of national independence; the real fight about the racial problem; and the increasing awareness, even among conservative theologians, that our attitude toward the non-Christian religions has to be one of dialogue—even the present Pope used that term. But, of course, these are symptoms and not yet fulfillments, and the threat of a relapse into the predominant pessimism (if you use that word, which shouldn't be used by a philosopher) is always in danger.

We must now contribute to this reappraisal by going through a serious and perhaps painstaking analysis of the concept of progress as it appears in the different realms of life. After this somewhat dramatic historical section, I ask you to follow me through an analytic section, through an analysis of all the things one does oneself, especially in academic surroundings.

II

The tremendous force of the progressivistic idea was rooted, firstly, in observations about particular instances of progress in technical and scientific matters. But this observation was inadequate, and what is needed now is to show the nonprogressive elements in reality and culture, and to demonstrate in some way how they are related to the progressive elements. There is a general principle for all this that one can follow through more fully when one thinks about these ideas. The general principle is: where there is freedom to contradict fulfillment, there the rule of progress is broken. Freedom to contradict one's fulfillment breaks the rule of progress.

This freedom is nothing else but another word for the moral act, which we perform every day innumerable times. There is no progress with respect to the moral act because there is no morality without free decisions, without the awareness of the power to turn with one's centered self in the one or the other direction. It means that every individual starts anew and has to make decisions for himself, whether he be on the lowest or highest level of culture or education. The German rebarbarization was looked at with great astonishment by a world that was adhering to the faith in progress. But there it was. In one of the most highly civilized nations, decisions were made by individuals and followed by many that contradicted anything we consider to be human nature and human fulfillment. This was a tremendous shock. And here is the first answer to the whole problem of progress. Every newborn infant has, when it comes to a certain point of self-awareness, the possibility of stopping progress by contradicting fulfillment in man's essential nature.

There is something else in what we usually call progress in the ethical realm, namely, coming to maturity—maturation. The child matures, and in this respect, there is progress. There is as in nature a progression from the seed to the fruit of the tree, or to the fully grown tree, but this element of maturity belongs to the individual first, and he may at any moment break out of it. We know how much this happens, even in people whom we consider to be mature, and we know many who never become mature. There is something like maturing also in social groups. It means deeper understanding of man's essential nature in individual and social relations. This is not moral progress but it is cultural progress in the moral realm. It is cultural because it sees better what human nature is, but it doesn't make people better. If we had attained the full idea now of the social interrelation between the races in this country, we would be on a higher, on a more mature level; we would have deeper insight into human nature and into the content of the moral demand, but we would not have better human beings, because the goodness or nongoodness of a human being appears on all levels of culture and insight. So we can say—and this is very important for our whole consideration of this idea and for our whole culture today with respect to the free moral decisions of individuals—there are always new beginnings in the individual and sometimes in the group, but the contents can mature and grow from one generation to another. This is the difference between civilized ethics and primitive ethics, but do not believe that on the level of primitive ethics people were worse than we are. In the smallest decisions you make in your classes, or in your homes, or wherever it may be, there is the same problem of ethical decision that is found in the crudeness of the cavemen; you are not better than they. You may be better than one of them, but one of them may be better than you. The distinction between moral decision and progress in moral content is fundamental for our judging the whole of past history.

When we look at education, we arrive at the same result. Education leads to higher cultural levels, to progress and maturity, to a production of habits of good behavior. As a consequence, education can be a kind of second nature in each of you, useful for society, but, when it comes to moral freedom, you are still able to become rebarbarized, even if not as openly as it was in Germany, in your personal relation to another person, to your children, your husband, your wife, or your friends. You can again start on a level that is that of freedom to contradict what you ought to be. When we add to the ordinary educational process, as we have it in a college or university, when we add to it education psychotherapy, psychoanalysis, counseling, and all these things that are so important, what can they do? They can heal you from disturbances, they can help you to become free, but when you have been set free, let us say by successful analysis, you still have to decide. This is not moral progress; it is progress in healing, but the moral decision remains free, and now has become really free by medical or psychoanalytical help.

Besides moral freedom, the freedom of contradicting every possible instance of progress, there is a second element where there is no progress, namely, the freedom of spiritual creativity—creation in culture.

Let us look at the different cultural functions. There are the arts. Is there progress in the arts? There is progress in the technical use of materials, in the better mixing of colors, and in things like that, but is there progress in the arts? Has Homer ever been surpassed by anyone? Has Shakespeare ever been surpassed by anyone? Is an early Greek frieze worse than a classical sculpture, or is a classical worse than a modern expressionist? No. There is maturity of styles; there are good and bad representatives of style, but you cannot compare artistic styles in terms of progress. A style starts, often very modestly and preliminarily. It grows, it becomes mature, it produces its greatest expressions, then it decays. But there is no progress from one style to another. There is no progress from the Gothic to the Classical style. (And this needs to be said against our Gothic church buildings—we shouldn't pretend that we can go back to the Gothic style, after our modern stylistic feelings and developmental possibilities have become so different.) So, creativity in the arts admits of maturity, admits "great moments"—*kairoi*—right times, decisive times, turning points, all this, but it does not admit progress from one style to another.

The same is true in the realm of knowledge. If you look at philosophy, you see an analytic element in our great philosophers as well as a visionary element. Take Aristotle, for example, who unites both of them so clearly. In every kind of knowledge a philosophical element is present. You can also speak of a logical and empirical element in knowledge that is detached and necessary, and an existentialist and inspirational element that is involved. Both are there, and the very fact that in all great philosophers there was this visionary, involved, inspirational element makes it impossible to speak about progress in the history of philosophy except in those elements that are connected with a sharpened logical analysis or a tremendous increase in empirical knowledge. I have never found a philosopher who I could say progressed over Parmenides the Eleatic of the sixth century, B.C. Of course, there is much more empirical knowledge, there is much more refined analysis, but the vision of this man, and of Heraclitus, his polar friend and opposite, cannot be surpassed. There is no qualitative progress from Heraclitus to Whitehead.

And there is no progress in humanity, that is, in the formation of the individual person. I was struck by this once when I saw a photograph of an old Sumerian sculpture, perhaps of a priestess, and looking at it said to myself, "Look at the sculptures and paintings of great representatives of humanity in the following history of three or four thousand years." I found no progress at all. I found differences, but I didn't find progress. This means that even justice as well as humanity are not matters of progress except in technical elements. If I think, for instance, of democracy there is progress in largeness of the number of people involved, and progress in maturity in some respects, but there was justice in the state of Athens, justice in old Israel, in Rome, in the Middle Ages, and there is justice in modern democracy. The progress is quantitative, but the quality of the ideas of humanity and justice has not progressed.

Now I come to the most difficult problem—progress in religion. Of couse, it is simple if you follow the conservative or fundamentalist idea that there is one true religion and many false ones. Then, needless to say, there is no progress. But even if you hold this view, you have a difficulty, namely, the Old Testament—what about that? Isn't there something then like progress—progressive revelation? So the problem appears even in Christianity. There is development, there is progress. Even in church history there is supposed to be progress according to the Gospel of John where Jesus is reported to have said that the Spirit will introduce you into all truth. This is progress. Furthermore, there are Christian theologies that expect new revelations even beyond Jesus the Christ. This, of course, would be post-Christian religion. Now if we look at this, we encounter great difficulties. On the one hand, Christianity claims that there is no possible progress beyond what is given in Jesus the Christ; on the other hand, there is great progress in world history in many respects—in knowledge as well as other areas. How shall we deal with this problem?

Here is where religion might provide the standpoint from which we might understand the whole problem better. I would say that we must replace the idea of progress by two other concepts: the concept of maturing, and the concept of "the decisive moment." What we need is an understanding of history in which there are two things, rather than a single, continuous line of progress. (I hope that what I have said about all the other realms—the ethical, the cultural, the artistic, the scientific, the philosophical, the religious—showed this clearly.) "Great moments" or, if you want to accept the term I like very much, taken from the New Testament or from classical Greek, the term *kairos,* the right time, fulfilled time, time in which something decisive happens, is not the same as *chronos,* chronological time, which is watch time, but it means the qualitative time in which "something happens." I would say, therefore, that in history we have two processes, not progress as a universal event, but the maturing of potentialities, the maturing of a style, for instance, or the maturing in the education of a human being. It is not progress beyond this human being. He or she may give something to his or her children, but children must decide again on their own. There is no progress; they must start anew. Two things then we can see in history. One is the process of maturing in terms of potentialities; the other is the great moments, the *kairoi,* in history in which something new happens. However, that new thing that happens is not in a progressive line with the other new things before and after it. This is only true in the technical and scientific realm so far as the logical elements are implied, but it is not so in the realm of spiritual creativity and of the moral act.

My description and analysis of progress has been more careful than is usual, but I believe that the service an academic lecturer can give is to show his listeners where the problems lie, and to steer them away from the popular talk about such weighty problems. This I have tried to do, and now perhaps we will have some of the fruits of this. When progress is elevated into a symbol or idea, as I said in the beginning, then it can take on two forms. The one is the idea of endless progress, without limits, in which one moves further and further along, and things get better and better. The other is the utopian form, which is historically much more important; namely, that at some point in time man's essential nature will be fulfilled. What is possible for man will then exist. Now, what happens with these two? In the first type, progress runs ahead without aim, unless progress itself is taken to be the aim, but there is no goal at the end of the progression. Thus, it is simply a matter of going ahead, and of course, if my analysis before was right, this is possible to a certain extent in the technical and scientific realms. But it is not possible in the realm where vision and inspiration play a role. The other type, the utopian, has produced all the tremendous passions in history, for it is the principle of revolution. However, after the revolution is successful, the great disappointment follows, and this disappointment produces cynicism and sometimes complete withdrawal from history. We have it in some forms of Christianity—we have it strongly in Lutheranism and in the Greek Orthodox Church; we have it less in Calvinism and Evangelical radicalism, which underlie this country; and we have it in an anti-Christian ways as a result of the terrible experiences of suffering in Asiatic religions, especially in Buddhism with its withdrawal from history.

Now the question is, is there a way of avoiding the utopianism that sees the fulfillment of history around the corner, that says, only one step more and we will be in the classless society; only one step more and we will be an educated nation; only one step more and all our youngsters will reach full humanity, or all our social groups will stand for true justice. If only all men of good will—that means we—stand together, everything will be all right. All this is utopianism. In my long life I have experienced the breakdown of the utopianism of the Western intelligentsia both in Europe and America and the tremendous cynicism and despair that followed it and, finally, the emptiness of not being ultimately concerned about anything. Therefore, I think that we must put something else in place of these two types of progressivism. Endless progress may be symbolized by running ahead indefinitely into an empty space. We will do that, but it is not the meaning of life; nor are better and better gadgets the meaning of life. What is the meaning of life then? Perhaps it is something else. Perhaps there are great moments in history. There is in these great moments not total fulfillment but there is the victory over a particular power of destruction, a victory over a demonic power that was creative and now has become destructive. This is a possibility, but don't expect that it *must* happen. It might not happen; that is a continuous threat hanging over development in history. But there *may* be a *kairos*.

After the First World War in Germany, we believed, just because of the defeat of Germany, that there was a *kairos,* a great moment, in which something new could be created. In this sense we were progressive, but we did not believe that it was necessary that this would happen. Inevitable progress should not be sought by us, for there is no such thing. Of course, what we hoped for then was completely destroyed by the Hitler movement. Out of these experiences we came to see that there is a possibility of victory over a particular demonic power—a particular force of destruction—or to put it simply, there is a possibility of solving a particular problem, as for instance, the race problem in our time. But even if this does happen, it doesn't mean inevitable progress. We must fight for it, and we may be defeated, but even if not, new demonic powers will arise.

There is a wonderful symbolism in the last book of the Bible, in the idea of the thousand years' rule of Christ in history. In these thousand years, which is a symbolic number, of course, the demonic forces will be banned—put into chains in the underworld. This is all symbolism. But they are not annihilated, and they may come to the surface again, as they will in the final struggle. When we thought about our problems after the First World War, we used this symbol—not in its literal sense, of course—as expressing the awareness that you can ban a particular demonic force. Hitler was banned, but the powers behind Hitler, the demonic forces in mankind and in every individual are not definitely annihilated; they are banned for a moment, and they may return again. So instead of a progressivistic, utopian, or empty vision of history, let us think of the great moments for which we must keep ourselves open, and in which the struggle of the divine and the demonic in history may be decided for one moment for the divine against the demonic, though there is no guarantee that this will happen. On the contrary, in the view of the Bible, especially the book of Revelation, the growth of the divine powers in history is contradicted by a growth of the demonic powers.

So in every moment the fight is going on, and the only thing we can say is this: If there is a new beginning, let us mature in it; if there is a new beginning in world history as we have it now in this country and beyond this country, let us follow it and develop to its maturity. But let us not look at history in the sense of progress that will be going on and finally come to an end that is wonderful and fulfilling. There is no such thing in history, because man is free, free to contradict his own essential nature and his own fulfillment. As a Christian theologian I would say that fulfillment is going on in every moment here and now beyond history, not some time in the future, but here and now above ourselves. When I have to apply this to a meeting like this, then I would say it might well be that in such a meeting in the inner movements of some of us, something might happen that is elevated out of time into eternity. This then is a nonutopian and a true fulfillment of the meaning of history and of our own individual life.

CHAPTER 8

Expressions of Man's Self-Understanding in Philosophy and the Sciences[1]

Recapitulation and Introduction

Style as Self-Interpretation

Ladies and gentlemen, in my last lecture I spoke about expressions of man's self-understanding in literature and the arts. I concentrated on the different styles in the development first of all of the visual arts and then also on the development of novel and drama. The style of modern art and modern literature reveals something about the way in which man understands himself. And so I tried to go back to earlier periods and tried to show how they gave indications to their interpretation of man in their period.

And I especially emphasized the representation of man in the visual arts with respect to his body, his face, the posture, and the group relations in our period.

The Two Poles

In doing so, I discovered two poles. On the one hand we observe that man disappears; the humanity of man is more and more extinguished, is cut into pieces, and finally he disappears completely. But at the same time we found in these artistic expressions that there is a protest against this disappearance of man, a protest that goes very deep in our time and that tries to save man from becoming a piece of nature, or a thing, or a mere object, or from disappearing completely. This fight between man being extinguished and man protesting against his extinction was the main content of

---

[1]This was the second of six Lowell Lectures delivered at Harvard Divinity School in 1959.

my first lecture. And I tried to show this in all artistic expressions of the twentieth century and especially in the ever-present style that characterizes the great artistic creations of our century.

The Aesthetic Expression of the Situation

In saying so, I say at the same time that we should not see in this artistic description of man, or interpretation of man, only the negative element. And I want to emphasize this especially, since many people feel modern drama, modern lyrical poetry, modern novels, modern visual arts are completely negativistic, or as the more popular term says, "pessimistic." Now this certainly is not true. I would say that the artists who dare to show the disruptiveness of our time are artists who have a great courage, and by showing this great courage are at the same time in our time and above our time. And this should not be forgotten. We should not forget that if an artist creates a drama, a play in the theatre like *The Ice Man Cometh* or *Death of a Salesman,* he certainly is in the situation of our time, in its desperate situation, in its predicament of disruptedness and negativity, in the feeling that man has lost himself in the world of things that he has created. But at the same time, by creating this play he raises the protesting voice, and this protesting voice elevates him above the situation against which he protests. And therefore I hope that your judgment about modern art and modern literature and modern plays and so on will be guided by this consideration. A great artistic creation, the subject matter of which is the negativity of man's predicament, is both in it and above it. It is not only negative; it is also positive. And it is very important to know this in order to understand modern artistic expressions at all.

The Analogous Situation in Philosophy and the Sciences: The Struggle about Man

Artistic Style and the Philosophical Element in Science

But now I come to the analogous situation in philosophy and the sciences. And again I say what we see here is the struggle about man. Has man completely become a thing, or has man saved himself as man? This is the same problem in the arts and in sciences and philosophy. We can compare what I call the *style* in the arts and the *philosophical element* in the sciences. Every science has openly or hiddenly a philosophical background, a philosophical presupposition. And this philosophical element within it is exactly the same thing as the style in the arts. In the arts the ultimate question is answered by the style of an artistic expression, and in the sciences the ultimate question is answered by the philosophical implications of a scientific statement. This should be acknowledged by all scientists. They should rise above that kind of unconscious primitivism that we call "scientism," namely, a philosophy that denies that it is a philosophy. They should realize that in their negation of philosophy they have a philosophy. And if they acknowledge this, then they could transform their primitive philosophy into a conscious and sophisticated philosophy as most great scientists in the past have done.

Symbols of Iliad and Odyssey

In order to describe in this lecture the fight about man in sciences and philosophy, I want to use a beautiful symbol that has been used by the German philosopher of romanticism at the beginning of the nineteenth century, Schelling, from whom I have learned more than from any other philosopher. He speaks about the Iliad and the Odyssey of the human mind: the human mind separating itself from the infinite from which it comes and going into the finite world, and then the Iliad, trying to return, with the Odyssey trying to return from this point of removal and the many difficulties encountered, like Odysseus in returning to Ithaca. This is a beautiful symbol for the human mind going out from the home from which it comes, becoming removed from this home more and more, becoming estranged from what it essentially is and then coming to a point where it desires to return to the place from which it came. And then occur the infinite difficulties of this return like the adventures and suffering of Odysseus. In Schelling the point of return is romantic philosophy and romantic art, as sometimes for German classical philosophers it is they themselves and their philosophies. Now certainly this was a great mistake. After him and after the fulfiller of German classical philosophy Hegel, a removal, a going away from man's home in himself, took place that was more radical than anything that happened before. As with all prophets, Schelling was right in his prophecy but he was wrong when he gave a special time in which his prophecy was to be fulfilled, namely, his own time. Actually it is as in all prophecies; there is never a point in history in which prophecy is fulfilled. There is always movement ahead and something for which we have to wait. If Schelling's Odyssey return of man's mind to himself had been fulfilled in his time, history would have been fulfilled and would have come to an end.

Cognitive Separation: Subject and Object

Now, what I want to show is man's estrangement from himself in the realm of knowledge, and then the desire, and the way, and the failure to return. What is man's estrangement from himself in the realm of knowledge? Every act of knowing has something in it that you all will see immediately if you think about it, namely, the separation of the thinking subject from the object that the subject wants to know, the detachment of the knower from the known. This detachment is the opposite of participation. All life processes have both detachment and participation. In all love—and the innermost part of life is love—there is both detachment and participation.

In the act of knowledge, the element of detachment becomes overwhelming. The subject separates itself from the object in order to know it. And in this way a "second world," so to speak, is created by man, the world of known objects, what we call the "objective" world. It is not the world as we encounter it, as we encounter it in every moment in which we look at it. But is a world that is constructed by man's cognitive power, by his ability to observe, and to abstract, and to create concepts, and to create laws. It is very interesting that modern physicists are very much aware of the fact that their most abstract concepts are their own creations. The electron is a valid concept. You can destroy mankind and perhaps the whole earth with the knowledge that is given to us by the discovery of the electron. But the electron the physicists know is not an object, a thing beside other things. So we must distinguish, even in physics where the detached attitude is most outspoken, a valid concept from an object, from a thing.

And so it is generally. The world of objects is a construct of man's mind, nevertheless a valid construct. You can do something with it; you can produce and destroy with it. But it is not an assembly of objects. Men ask the questions, and things answer the questions men have asked. All answers given by things to men are answers that have one side of men themselves in them, namely man's way of asking the question.

Cognitive Objectification
and the Objectification of Self

This is the situation. But this situation is not seen by most popular interpretations of the scientific approach to our world. One does not distinguish between the validity of the concept and its objectifying character. And since this so, since one believes that science has transformed our whole world into a mass of moving objects that one can calculate and manage, something happened to man himself: man himself became an object amongst the other objects. And in a very special way he who has created these objects now is seen as one amongst them. But of course, man is a very complex object. Man has many levels. And so a further step has been taken. Man has been divided up into these levels and has been found within them in the objective world. He has become partly a physical object, a chemical object, a biological object, a psychological object, a sociological object. In all these levels of being, parts of man have been found and have been described. And this is in the realm of knowledge what I would call man having lost himself in the world created by him because he has forgotten that this world *was* created by him. This situation has three consequences.

First, many people tried to reduce all the other levels to one level— usually to the basic level, the physical—and reduce man himself to a combination of atoms or electrons. This was the attitude of the second half of the nineteenth century, but there are still people (although scientifically obsolete) who see men in this way.

The second consequence of this loss of man in this world of objects was that the unity of man was lost. If he now asks the question "What is man?" then one answers: "He is a combination of atoms," or "He is a combination of processes of chemical kind," or "He is a biological phenomenon," or "He is a process of psychological movements," or "He is a product of the sociological environment." All these answers are given. But all these realms are discovered and objectified by man himself. Where then is the unity left that has produced all this, the unity that we call "man"? In a comparatively simple way, this was foreshadowed in the philosophy of Descartes, the man who rightly has been called the father of modern philosophy, who divided man into a conscious subject on the one hand and to a body that is subject to mechanical necessity. And all his followers tried to find the unity between these two parts. And in spite of all the great attempts, nobody could find it. Because after you have cut a living being into pieces you never can bring him together again. Either the unity precedes the parts, then you can understand both the unity and the parts, or the parts precede the unity, and then you never can return to the unity. You have lost man as the united reality who has produced the world in which he is now lost.

And what above all is lost is the centered self that makes it possible for us to have language, to make tools, to make decisions, to deliberate, and even to come in conflict with ourselves—which no other being can. This is the third consequence and perhaps the most disastrous of all. It means that everything that is human in man is now lost.

The Odyssey of Return

Now against this situation the Odyssey starts, the attempt to return. And here philosophy and empirical research work together. I want to name on this point the name of Einstein, who certainly can be considered the greatest of the scientists in the twentieth century, and one of the few greats in all world history. He was aware of how much philosophical foundations lie behind his attempts to enter into the mystery of matter. And only because he was aware of this, he remained a representative of humanity in all his expressions.

The Fight about Man in the Cognitive Field

Reduction of Man to Knowing Subject

Now let's go into special problems. There is one problem, the most difficult, but I want at least to mention it because you will often find the references to it: man reduced in Descartes to a knowing subject, to a logical subject. He remains completely detached from everything he tries to know. The only thing that is allowed to him by being a knowing subject is to have emotions. But these emotional elements in him must be completely repressed in every cognitive attempt. Where there is emotion, truth cannot be reached.

Now let us look at this for a moment. This means that where man participates in what he wants to know, there he cannot know. This is not true. We will see it is not even true in physics, certainly not true in psychology. It is certainly not true in the social sciences. It is certainly not true in history. If we make man's cognitive ego a really detached subject, then some elements, some abstract elements, can be known. But the reality itself is lost. The consequence of this attitude is a thing that happens often in philosophy today, namely, that man is deprived of language.

Now then let me say a few words about this. In the semantic and analytic philosophy of today, the whole of language is reduced to mathematical science that can be calculated. Man, in this way, in his knowing function, is made into something that equals a mechanical brain. But no mechanical brain ever has made another mechanical brain. The creation of it and the putting into it of that which one wants to get out has to be done by a brain that is more than mechanical, more than mere calculus, mere calculation of mathematical science. Nevertheless, this is now a very strong trend in philosophy, and I feel it is very like those pictures of which I spoke in my last lecture in which the human face has disappeared. Here the human language is reduced to science. But every language has not only logical meaning, it also has power expressing something of the person who speaks, of the encounter of the culture with the world, and this power is lost. Man is deprived of his language.

The Existentialist Protest

Now on this point philosophical protest starts. A return has started in philosophy. We call this return today "existentialism." And within it one little thing is clearly expressed by one of the leaders of this philosophy, Heidegger. He asks, what does it mean if Descartes says "I think, so I am?" What does this "I am" mean? Who has such being? And then he says if we try to find this out, then we discover that this is not simply an epistemological subject who knows in detachment, but an existing reality. Or, in other terms, he who thinks does exist, and you cannot separate his existence from his thinking. And he exists as that in which the reality becomes conscious of itself. He exists as a finite being with all the anxiety of finitude. He exists as he who runs ahead towards his own death. And all this is not only emotional; all this is at the same time the description of what we are and of what we can understand only because we *are* it, we participate in it, and we are not detached from it. I spoke of the fact that in some philosophy we are deprived of the power of language. Let me quote a word of Heidegger against it. For him language is the "house of being," as he says, being habitat, so to speak, in the human language. When it makes itself manifest it makes itself manifest through the word. And here one hears strains of both the oldest Greek thinkers and the Christian doctrine of the word.

So the protest is expressed, and the follower of Heidegger, Sartre, tries to do the same thing: to save man from being an object by emphasizing his freedom, his absolute freedom to make of himself what he wants to make of himself. This is the protest of Heidegger, Sartre, and the other existentialists. But when Odysseus started his return trip the storms came and kept him and it took him ten years before he could go home. Now it may take more than ten years—perhaps it may take all history—in order to go home.

When Heidegger and Sartre tried to save man from being an object, in this way then they themselves fell victim to the storms of the Odyssey. Their freedom is a freedom of arbitrariness. It is a protesting freedom, but it is not a freedom that makes you really free because it is without ultimate norms, without criteria, without context. And so it could happen that the freedom of Heidegger became a freedom to become a Nazi, and that the freedom of Sartre is the freedom that he expresses in his great novels (not great as novels, but very interesting and revealing), like *The Age of Reason,* where the hero who keeps himself free from everything falls victim to the first moment in which an impulse grasps him. Now this is one of the examples of man attempting to return to himself and falling victim on this way. This is a hard way, and a way perhaps never-ending.

Conditioned Reflex and Gestalt

Let me go to biology as another representation of science. There is the struggle about the concept of conditioned reflex. You know this famous theory, which you don't need to read in any biological book. Read about it in Huxley's novel *Brave New World,* or read about it in the stories of the concentration camps in Germany, and then you know what conditioned reflex means as a social factor and not only as an abstract theory. It means that you can condition man by an adequate reflexive into everything you want him to be and to do. And here we have an example of how intimately the theory and reality of life are related to each other: these two things, the poetic anticipation of the *Brave New World* and the reality of the attempt made in the dictatorial countries. Both are the inner consequences of making man into an object, and this is done in biology by the theory of conditioned reflexes—which is true insofar as a living being is not in the spontaneous life process but in conditioned situations, laboratory situations, or sickness situations. The living being in its living freedom has spontaneity and is a gestalt, a structure that reacts as a whole and that cannot be dissolved into conditioned reflexes.

So the fight has started against this theory. The theory of gestalt, the theory of spontaneity, of creativity has tried to do so. But again, there is always a warning against these protests. In the moment in which you make out of them—out of these concepts of gestalt, or spontaneity—a mythological factor that you introduce into these life processes, then you are a victim of the storms of the Odyssey. You have lost against what you attack.

Another fight now in physics itself is the fight between determinacy and indeterminacy. We are in this moment somehow in a great moment in these talks. It is a new concept that has come up and that is a great problem, the concept produced by Niels Bohr, "complementarity." That means you can have statements that cannot be united in logically consistent terms, but the observation forces us to accept both concepts. Now if we do so, then we must say our relationship to nature is such that we are forced to accept complementary concepts that cannot be reduced to one. This is a great step, and we cannot apply it to many other things. The old, fruitless discussion between determinism and indeterminism, between freedom and destiny can be solved, but not solved if we accept the principle of complementariness. It can be solved but we are not at home yet because one question remains, namely, the question of an ultimate unity that is the reality itself.

The Social-Scientific Interpretation of Human Being

And so, difficulty after difficulty comes up. Let me go to social science for a moment. In the Marxist theory of economic materialism, that we all are determined by our economic situation in every moment and everything else depends on this, this theory has been given up. But if you look at the state of scientific anthropology and ethnology we find that another magic concept has replaced this concept, namely, the concept "culture." Everything is dependent on the culture, and nobody asks upon what the culture is dependent. And in this way you can again produce man out of something that he has produced without asking how he was able to produce it.

Now this situation—the protest, the negation, and the falling back all the time—is analogous to what I have said about the situation in the arts. And it is not only the same as the situation in the arts; it is also identical to what we have in reality. Let us look at this for a moment. What is developing today has been called "mass man," the man who wants security, who does not dare anymore, who does not want to be outstanding, who has no ambition to go the top, but who wants a twenty-five-year contract in which his old age pension is guaranteed by the corporation for which he works. The advertisement and its consequence of making man into an object, the motivation research that tells the researcher what he has to do in order to transform man into an inhabitant of Huxley's brave new world, namely, to react exactly as faceless man wants him to react, all these phenomena are phenomena of man becoming an object. Now this means the social reality is threatening us—as threatening as in the Eastern world that is now mostly under Communist rule—to become mass men, to become manageable objects by a small group of individuals who manage us. This is the actual situation, and against this the people who react against scientific objectification also want to react.

Now we can say our human predicament is an expression of these tendencies fighting with each other. When I speak of man's self-understanding in science and philosophy, then I speak about this situation. It is a situation of a tremendous drama. And if we can look through what is given to us in newspapers and magazines and speeches and books then we will see this drama and we will see something that according to our feeling may horrify us or may inspire us, namely, the fact that we ourselves belong to this situation as parts. We are in it and we ourselves are what is going on at the platform of our present-day world situation.

And now I come to a last word about the philosophical situation. What existentialism tried to do was to fight against the faceless man, against the man without a countenance, without a face, without that which makes him man. In fighting, existentialism had to undergo all the same problems, all the same relapses that I have described in the sciences, and there is no safe way out. And here I ask you to understand one side of existentialism. It seems to be negativistic, pessimistic. Of course, its concepts are finitude and the inner-awareness of finitude, anxiety. Its concepts are estrangement of man from himself and from his world and the inner-expression of this, the feeling of guilt. Its concepts are meaninglessness and doubt, the futile attempt to find symbols for the meaning of life. But in this seemingly negativistic form, the existentialist philosophers try to do something extremely positive. They try to show that man in his very nature does exist and is not a describable object amongst other objects. Neither economically nor sociologically can we be described as an object amongst other objects. There is always something left, and that which is left is the centered self. But if these philosophers and novelists and others describe the situation of man, then they can describe and find this attitude only in terms of the desperation of a group of human beings who struggle for their centered self, who are in anxiety, in a state of guilt and meaninglessness.

Now we can ask: Isn't there something else? Certainly. It is possible to go beyond this, and what I said about the artist I say now about the philosopher. To describe the human misery as Pascal, the first existentialist, has said in the seventeenth century is at the same time to describe the human greatness. Man's greatness and man's misery: this is what one has to put against our present situation of being and becoming more and more an object amongst objects; a man who is patternized according to that pattern that is necessary for him in order to survive in our society against the man who is described in sciences and philosophy as a mere subject, empty, or a mere object moving as a particle of the mass according to the laws of this mass. So take these descriptions of man's existential situation not as devaluations of man, but as the way of regaining man in a period in which the historical situation itself, supported and produced by sciences with some kinds of philosophy, is itself devaluated.

Now let me give the last example for it. I use the words *mass man*. What is a mass? A mass is a combination of particles in which no particle moves according to its own law but all of them move according to the law of the mass to which they belong. This is the metaphor when we speak of mass men. Now it is clear what this means. If you are in a situation in which you move as individuals, you are not a particle of the mass. But if a whole culture tries to bring you into a situation in which you can move only as a particle of a mass—otherwise you are destroyed—then you are a mass man. And all the hopeful elements of man's Odyssey in our time, in all the sciences, as I tried to show, and in the existentialist way of philosophizing are the other possibility. It is not so that we already are in the brave new world. It is not so that we already are only particles of the mass to which we belong, but it is threatening in every movement. And the discussion of this dramatic conflict between this reality and this tendency in science and philosophy, and then the opposite reality, the protest against it, the failures of this protest, the relapses, the new beginning, this whole dramatic scene is what we see if we look at man's attempt to understand himself today in the sciences and in philosophy.

PART IV

Dehumanization
in Technical Society

CHAPTER 9

Thing and Self[1]

Introduction

I divide this constructive section into three subjects. The one we discussed last time, namely, "Surface and Depths." The second I intend to discuss today under the title "Thing and Self," and the third I want to discuss next month under the title "Estrangement and Return." I believe that these three are in a definite way related in three realms in which we have collected the material before Christmas.[2] The problem of "surface and depths" was mostly founded in our findings in the visual arts and literature. The problem of today, "thing and self," is mostly based on what is going on in the sciences and philosophy. And the problem of the last lecture a month from today will be dependent upon what we have elaborated in relationship to religion and theology.

So, today the question is "thing and self." This was prepared last time in our analysis of "surface and depth." In this analysis of these two fundamental concepts, I referred above all to the way of knowing persons. I referred to what is called with the valid term, "depth psychology." And I referred to the dimension of depth that is absolute in itself, the depths toward the absolute, towards the ultimate. In this analysis we discovered something, namely, that below the unconscious and conscious level there is a depth that is deeper than both of them, so that depth psychology does not point to the ultimate depth, the depths of the unconscious. But we discovered that below the unconscious there is something more fundamental

---

[1]Delivered at Harvard Divinity School in 1959 as the fifth Lowell Lecture.

[2]Tillich is referring to the first three lectures in the series concerned with the "self-understanding of man" in literature and the arts, in science and philosophy, and in religion and theology.

and more real, because it is the centered self: the self that decides, that deliberates, that cannot be grasped in its very center by a philosophy of consciousness or by a philosophy of the unconscious. It surpasses both of them. It has an element that neither of them can reach, the element of freedom, of deliberation, of decision.

From this, however, follows a second problem. And this second problem is the self itself. Much of present-day self-interpretation of human nature is dependent on the problem of the self. In order to go into it, the most useful way seems to me to be that we immediately name the contrast. According to the title of this lecture, I give to what is opposite the self the preliminary name *thing,* a thing. Now the problem of self and thing was already implicit in what we discussed in the second lecture before Christmas time, namely, the cognitive estrangement of man, which I compared at that time with the Iliad of Homer: the going out from the home, man going out from himself, creating a world and losing himself in this world of objects. And then the Odyssey: man's attempt to return to himself in philosophy and the sciences and in history. And all these attempts continue, counterbalanced by forces that are not yet able to conquer, just as Odysseus was.

The Thing and the Dimensions of Life

Self-Objectification and Loss of Unity

Now, what I want today is to go into the problem—man losing himself in the world of his own creation, and man trying to return to himself and being inhibited in doing so. But I don't want to describe it from outside. I want to go into the problem itself as it is discussed and try to show the direction in which I believe it should go.

The basic idea, namely, man's self lost in his own production, in the production that he calls the world of objects, has two sides: he became an object amongst the world of objects produced by his own cognitive approach, losing the power in which he produced it, namely, his own centered selfhood, his own subjectivity. And the other side, as we found, was that man was divided into different spheres within this world. He lost not only his self, his subjectivity, he lost also his unity. And taking both sides together, he became deprived of his centered self, in theory as well as in practice.

And then we found that in many scientific and philosophical developments of the middle of the twentieth century, there was a protest against this self-loss. There were attempts to find himself again, and there was failure after failure—solutions that were premature and that broke down. What I do today is nothing else than another attempt, and it might well be that it runs into the same barriers as the others and may fail in the same way as they failed. But only if we attempt after failure can we go ahead at all.

Logical and Existential Objects

What is the opposite of a centered self? I called it a *thing,* but using this word doesn't mean very much. We must go deeper into its meaning. And the first answer that describes the character of what is opposite to a self is that it is a mere object. What does this mean semantically? *Objectum,* being cast against, is the literal translation, and in this much, other language is implied. There is the *ob-jectum,* that which is cast against me, the observer, the subject. It is outside of myself. I look at it. I do not participate in it. Nevertheless, there is one connection with me: it is present to me. And this is also implied in the word *objectum* in German, *Gegenstand,* which stands opposite to me, at which I look. All the finite world has the character that it is a totality of objects at which subjects are looking. This is the universal character of everything. Therefore, everything can become an object for somebody, perhaps for something. In this moment, I am an object for you (you look at me), and you for me (I look at you). But there is a difference. This fact does not mean that I transform you into mere objects. Maybe I could desire to do so, and certainly I *would* desire to do so if I were a dictator in a totalitarian government, or if I were an experimenter in a laboratory of conditioned reflexes. But I do not want to do this even if I could.

This leads to the distinction between logical objects and existential objects. Everything, even God, can become a logical object. I can speak about him as I can speak about everything. But now let me make a statement that is the innermost center of my whole philosophy of the universe and of life: although everything in the world can become a logical object, nothing in nature, not even an atom, is only or merely an existential object. Everything in nature shows resistance against becoming a mere object. But there is a power that may be able to transform it into an object that is only an object, into an existential object. This power is man. The existential object, in difference from the logical object, is a product of man, and sometimes is he himself.

Natural Objects

Ordinarily, one calls the existential object a thing. If we follow this usage (which is not absolutely necessary, but I think expedient and very near to the feeling of language), then one must say there are no things that are only things in nature. This has great consequences. Our effort to speak about man then is not to contrast him simply with nature and to say he is a self, nature is not. This method is wrong and makes man (who, after all, has a body) completely incomprehensible. There are not things in nature that are merely things. Man alone can make things that are nothing else. He can make them out of what is given in nature: inorganic, organic structures, and even man. He can transform (and has tried to transform, theoretically and practically) the encountered world into a whole of mere things. But it is interesting to observe that even the material of any technical composite, for instance, is not only a thing. There are atom structures, molecular structures, and other structures used.

The Thing and Centeredness

Man can deprive everything, including himself, of subjectivity, of centered selfhood, although from an ultimate view, he is encountering limits. But here is underlined the statement that in nature itself there is nothing without centeredness. Because there is centeredness, there is not only thinghood. We can find this still in the Greek word *physis,* derived from *furein,* growing. That which grows must have an identity in change. That is a characteristic of every growth.

Dimensions of Life

In this sense, everything is centered, and the differences in the levels of nature are differences in centeredness, from the structure of the atom to the self-conscious man. I like to call these differences "dimensions." This is, of course, a metaphorical use of the word *dimension.* In man, all dimensions of life are actual. In the atom all dimensions of life are potential. And in the levels between atom and man they are partially potential, partially actual. In view of this immanence of all dimensions within each other, one can repeat what I said in the beginning: there are no mere objects in nature. Everything in nature resists the fate of losing its centeredness. It wants to maintain its centeredness. And in man's forces are needs to destroy the centeredness of the microcosmic realities. But man is able to do so.

Now, what is this being, man, in the view of this interpretation of life in terms of dimensions. We may distinguish in a popular way (which is not altogether wrong, but rather expedient) the inorganic, the organic, and the spiritual dimensions of reality. Thereby the word *spiritual,* as I often say it in these and other lectures, must be written with a small *s* and means the creative functions of man's spiritual character. If you prefer to use the words *mind* or *mental,* as many in English-speaking countries do, then do so. I prefer the classical word *spiritual,* which we have in all old languages, Hebrew, Greek, Latin, and still today in French, Italian, German. Only in English is it written always with a capital *S,* and means something religious and therefore cannot be used anymore for the description of man. This is a great mistake and almost a catastrophic event that the word *spirit* with a small *s* has been lost in English, and I belong to those who try to reestablish it.

But however we call it, we can distinguish the different dimensions of centeredness as the centeredness of structure, the centeredness of spontaneity in the organic life, and the centeredness of freedom in man: structure, spontaneity, freedom. I believe all doctrines of man that do not take into consideration the reality of nature as a whole, of the universe as a whole, are not able to say something meaningful about man in his unique form of centeredness. Only on the basis of the universal character of reality—to be centered—will centeredness be understood.

Mind and Body

On this basis, problems can be solved that will be discussed as long as there is a philosophical interest in discussing problems, and that at the end of the last century had come to a complete dead end. But in the twentieth century this dead end has to a certain extent been overcome, broken through. I mean the mind-body problem. In the moment in which we use the metaphor of "dimension" and not the metaphor of "level," or "stratum," we can say that all dimensions are present in man. In the inorganic, the spiritual is present. In the spiritual, the inorganic is present, and both in the organic. I could say with most of the progressive biologists and neurologists that man's spiritual dimension is present in every cell of his body. This is, of course, a monistic interpretation of man, which also implies the opposite, that in every spiritual act of man, the function of every cell is noticeable. You cannot separate them. They are one and the same reality.

Of course, for somebody who comes from traditional theology, this is a bold statement, because it seems to undercut the doctrine of the immortality of the soul. But I have consolation for this heretic's attitude, namely, that the

Bible (the New Testament and even stronger, perhaps, the Old Testament) was equally heretical, as it often was in opposition to traditional Christianity. The Old Testament doctrine of man is monistic. And the symbol of the monistic character of the New Testament of man, of man's eternal destiny, is not the continuation of an immortal soul after death, but the symbol of the resurrection of the body. That means (if you take away the literalistic absurdity) the participation of man in his totality in what Christianity calls "eternal life," beyond the temporal process of past and future. And here I am extremely grateful in my theological work to modern biology that it presses in the direction of a monistic doctrine of man, as does the psychology of the unconscious, especially if it is a little bit skeptical about the word *unconscious,* and means more the totality of man in all his dimensions. This was the first problem that can be solved in terms of a present-day self-interpretation of man. There are a few other problems.

Language and Tool

What makes man *man?* What differentiates historical man whom we encounter from the realm of animal life, for instance. And here something really wonderful has developed in modern philosophy, namely, interest in language and symbols. The answer is that neither the one nor the other is possible without language. Language alone makes man a completely centered self, and language alone gives man the possibility to transform parts of the nature that he encounters into things. And from this it follows that an interpretation of language is perhaps the decisive way of entering (at least we feel today) into the interpretation of man.

Connotative and Communicative Functions of Language

The first function of language is the connotative, pointing to something universal. In doing so, language is freed from the given situation through the universal validity of its concepts. And if you are free from the nightmare of the traditional discussion of the freedom of the will and want to deal with the problem of freedom, then the best way is to speak about language, because in language man's fundamental freedom is manifest. Everybody who fights against the idea of freedom in man, and does so with the help of universals, refutes himself, because in using language he shows his freedom from the given situation. Animals (who never reach language, even if they imitate human sounds) are completely bound to the actual and acting situation in which they find themselves. They are in the bondage of all nature. This bondage makes their special character, their perfection. They cannot destroy themselves in the way that man can. Man, by being able to dissolve the encountered world into a system of universals, is free from bondage to the concrete situation. If he comes to a river, perhaps he is thirsty like an animal. He may drink. But this is all that an animal can do. Man can ask the question ''is the water pure?'' or ''can I reach the other side by a bridge?'' and such questions are expressions of the fundamental character of human freedom. But of course, this freedom separates man from the situation in which he found himself. Now he is the subject and that which he encounters becomes object. The self is not involved any longer (in the sense of ''bondage'') in its surroundings. It stands logically opposite the world of objects, can handle the objects, can do something with them. Now, one must think of this fact if one deals with human being and with human freedom. This is a tremendous fact, and out of this fact all other consequences follow.

The other side of language is the communicative function, and here again language creates the self, the subjectivity, the centered self. No self would exist at all if we were not continuously encountering other selves. Man would run ahead in all directions. He would be without limit. He would not be rejected by himself. He would not find himself to himself. He would be a distorted animal, but not a completely formed self. The imagination of a being who has never encountered another human being is the imagination of an imperfect, distorted, physical power, even if anatomically he would be a man. But it is not a self. And here again, the language with which we address each other includes the acceptance of the other one as a self, and the answer from the other one makes us a self. Here language becomes the bearer of the all-embracing moral commandment, namely, to acknowledge the other one as a person, which presupposes that he acknowledge me as a person. This means language is a bearer of the ethical universals. The birth of a self without language would be impossible.

Tool as Tool

This brings me to a third point. Out of this double function of language follows its possibility to produce things, to dissolve the encountered reality into elements, to become analytic, and by analysis to destroy the given centers and make things out of them. I believe that present-day analytical philosophy is intimately related to the understanding of man as a thing—first as creating things, and then as becoming a thing himself. Here we encounter the trend under which we all are suffering, namely, that this power of man to produce things has led more and more to man becoming a thing himself in theory as well as in practice. But this leads to another characteristic of man in the confrontation of self and thing, namely, the meaning of the tool. Only man is able to have tools as tools. Of course, there are spontaneous self-realizations by animals in time and space, like the nest of a bird. There are occasional uses of objects as means, as tools by animals in special situations. But there is no product that is by definition a tool—a knife, a hammer that is always a knife and a hammer—that is conceived of in terms of a universal. Only man creates tools that by definition remain tools.

Making tools is like language, an act of freedom from the immediately given, and therefore tool and language, language power and technical power, belong together. From the paradise story where they are united (man gives names to the animals and cultivates the garden) to the way in which Socrates works with the craftsmen of Athens and in dealing with them produces his concepts, language and toolmaking belong to each other.

Man and Thing

The Reduction of the Self to Its Elements

The tool is the way in which things are actually produced. And therefore we come to the result that technical things are the things that are the proper type of all things. Only in the technical realm does the thing as a quality of being come to its fulfillment. It never does so anywhere in nature. Now it happens that man himself becomes a thing in this sense, theoretically and practically. The analysis of the elements that constitute him and of their interrelations reduce the self to a process of elements without a center. And that is the way in which man is made into a thing. We have discussed this in our second lecture in the different sciences, in biology and psychology, and we have found in all these ways man ceases to be to what he essentially is—the completely centered self—and we have seen the reaction against it.

Social Forms of "Thingification"

I want to come now to the actual social way in which man becomes a tool for men, for something that is not man himself. We have it in slavery to a great extent. We have it in the free market where the threat of hunger can bring man into a situation of being a mere object. We have it in the collectivistic systems where the central authorities try—with the help of force embodied symbolically in the concentration camps—to transform men into processes that are dependent on directions from outside and that have lost their independent selves. I believe it is a great glory of man that in many cases they did not succeed, that man was able to resist the attempt to be made into a thing. And the question of our period of history is: Will our period generally, universally, be able to resist the transformation of man into a thing? Will the theoretical protest against the stimulus and response mechanisms, against the chemical mechanisms succeed? These mechanisms are all true, but in the moment in which they are considered the only ones, they are not only false, but they are the basis for all those problematic activities in the twentieth century for which we have drawn the consequences. I referred in one of these lectures to books like *Brave New World* and *1984*. These books are questions. They are symbols of negative utopias. In the nineteenth century, since the Renaissance, we have had positive utopias. They are negative utopias, utopias that are based on man having become a thing.

Mass Society

Now let me close with a few words about a phenomenon that sticks together, so to speak, all the problems, namely, the phenomenon of mass society. Mass in physics is a quantity of matter, and the unity of a mass is the unity of particles that are kept together by cohesive forces and that move together by physical laws. Therefore, we can define a mass as a moving quantity of matter consisting of particles that all share in the same movement. Now this does not exhaust the physical concept, but it determines its metaphorical use for mass society.

What then is a mass society? What is a mass in a sociological sense? A mass is a unity of human individuals kept together by some forms of social cohesion, driven by laws of movement whereby the individual character of the particles is irrelevant for the movement itself. This is decisive for all mass movements. Mass societies are societies whose cohesion has the character of such united movements of all particles whose human differences are irrelevant for the movement. We can experience momentary anticipations of this state by occasional situations in which the individual characteristics become irrelevant. There is the call "fire" in the theatre, or in situations of mass suggestion as we have experienced them for a purpose, or the gang reaction in a school class, or hate reactions in the outbreak of war, or fear reactions against nonconformism or against the real or imagined enemy. The decisive point is that the mass movement contains a mass that moves, contains individuals who in this movement have surrendered their individual reaction. Now these events we all know, and against our will we have all sometimes participated (at least, I am not ashamed to confess that I did, although I always was ashamed afterward). But these examples are momentary and passing when the occasion has gone. But in mass societies, having lasting social cohesion over long periods of time, their basic characteristics are identical to those I have described. But there are differences. In the shocklike mass reaction, the individual expression may go completely in order to be restored shortly after it. In a mass society, the resistance is not completely destroyed, but it is continually undercut, undermined. The movements of the individuals in our society, insofar as it is a mass society, determine the behavior of the individual more than his spontaneous reaction. He is being pressed into a particle of the whole.

Now it is very interesting to follow through this analogy to physical mass movements with the help of the basic categories in which physical nature moves and reacts. Take the categories of "quantity" and "quality." The incalculable and uncontrollable character of quality is removed for the sake of calculable quantity. See our applied statistics and the tremendous role they play in all judgments, even the highest moral and spiritual judgments. The attempt to reduce quality to quantity characterizes in all realms of life the movement toward becoming a particle of a mass and to be subjected to the mechanisms. We have the same problem with the category of cause and effect. The effect in nature is creatively independent, to a certain extent, from the cause. But there is a causality that removes the creative difference between cause and effect and transforms actually the effect into a cause. Nothing new is in the effect over and against the cause. The reduction of the effect to the cause plays a tremendous role, for instance, in psychology. If everything spiritual is derived from the libido basis by sublimation, then nothing is in the effect that is not already in the cause. Or, if in social psychology everything spiritual is derived from social tendencies, desires, attitudes, behaviors—instead of acknowledging its own dimensional character—then the cause has swallowed the effect. The whole theory of projection is based on this swallowing of the effect into the cause. And, of course, against this, one tries to save the newness of the effect over against the cause. This is a problem everywhere in the doctrine of man and the doctrine of culture. You can also apply the same thing to the category of substance and accidents. *Persona* is a substance, that means something that stands upon itself. It can be dissolved into accidents where the center is lost by sociological determinism, by philosophies of processes. And the same is true of time and space. Is time qualitative? Has it elements of the newness of creation in itself or is it simply the calculable time process? The same can be said of space. Is space simply what is called today when we speak of "space travel," the empty space where nothing comes in the meaningless movement? Or has space a qualitative character, namely, the space on which we stand, on which we have our roots, which has something to do with our being and is qualitatively different from any other space? Here you have in terms of categories the transformation of self into a thing. And these categories are so revealing because they are not only abstractions; they have immediate experiential reality for all of us. We know what it means to have qualitative time or to have only watch time; to have roots somewhere, physically, geographically, sociologically, spiritually, or running ahead in space from one rootless to another rootless point. We know what it means to have an effect in ourselves that is not simply a result of the causes that have determined our self up to now, but in which we start something new.

Now I am near to my end, but let me ask the question: Is there a possibility of resisting the dynamics of our society in which language and tool have become means to deprive the creative self of its selfhood? Is there a point beyond this situation? I cannot help but speak in half-philosophical, half-theological terms, and certainly in metaphoric or symbolic terms, saying that the finite center cannot maintain its centeredness over and against the continuous temptation to be transformed into a thing without resting in an ultimate center. Without an ultimate center of meaning and being, no finite center can resist the destructive power that comes from that which self itself has created, namely, the world of things in theory and practice. If you call this "religion," all right. But the reality itself is that towards which all religion aims, namely, to have symbols in which the individual self in its finitude, in its greatness, and in its situation of being tremendously in danger is rooted ultimately, even if it is not rooted in space and time any longer.

CHAPTER 10

The Person in a Technical Society

Existentialism

It is my understanding of the movement that is called Existentialism and that is at least one hundred years old and that it rebels in the name of personality against the depersonalizing forces of technical society. For the sake of my special subject as well as in the spirit of this volume, I want to begin with some references to the early history of Existentialism.[1] This history, going on since the middle of the nineteenth century, has determined the fate of the twentieth century in all spheres of human existence. The immense tragedy of our political as well as the creative chaos of our spiritual situation is foreshadowed and deeply influenced by the Existentialist rebels of the nineteenth century. Moreover, the tradition out of which this book is written and out of which he to whom it is dedicated has worked, is rooted in the protest of the lonely prophets of the nineteenth century against the threatening destruction of humanity and personality by technical society.[2] Finally, it is my conviction that the new beginning of which this volume is supposed to be a symbol should be and I hope will be a continuation of this tradition under new conditions and with new means. But the aim should be what it was in the preceding movements of protest: a fight for humanity, which includes both community and personality, against the dehumanizing power of modern society.

Kierkegaard and Existentialism

It is usual to refer to Kierkegaard as the instigator of Existentialism. For the theologians especially this is the natural start. Historically, how-

---

[1]This essay originally appeared in the volume *Christian Faith and Social Action,* ed. John A. Hutchison (New York: Charles Scribner's Sons, 1953) 135-53.

[2]This work was dedicated to Reinhold Niebuhr.

ever, this is incorrect, since people like Pascal, Schelling, and othes had raised the Existentialist protest before Kierkegaard. They had done it for the same reason and with the same purpose as Kierkegaard: to resist a world in which everything was transformed into a thing, a means, an object of scientific calculation, psychological and political management. Kierkegaard saw that, in spite of many romantic elements in Hegel and in spite of his doctrine of freedom as the purpose of history, *this* was the meaning of his attempt to subject all reality to a system of logical forms: the existing individual was swallowed; the deciding personality was eliminated. The world process, playing with the individual, gave him the feeling that he was deciding for himself, while the process, governed by dialectical necessity, had already decided about him. Kierkegaard's metaphor of the ''leap'' embodying his protest against Hegel's logically determined world process is the idealistic mirror of the realities of the modern world. This was its greatness and this was the reason why the revolt against our world found its most successful expression in the protest against this mirror. Kierkegaard made his protest on the basis of classical Protestantism. But classical Protestantism had ceased to be an immediate reality. It has been lost and had to be regained. How? By being put in its place in the whole of the dialectical process, answered Hegel. By being reached through the leap of faith, answered Kierkegaard. Hegel's answer makes classical Protestantism a useful element within the frame of technical society; Kierkegaard's answer asks the individual to break away from this society in order to save his existence as a person. Therefore Kierkegaard's loneliness, therefore the pathological traits in his dealing with marriage, vocation, and church, therefore the lack of any effect in his own time. All this is understandable if the existing person can only be saved by a leap. Our own period, in which Kierkegaard has shaped philosophy as well as theology in the existentialist direction, has shown this clearly. Philosophical existentialism demands the leap of the individual out of his given cultural and intellectual situation into the acceptance of a sacred tradition formulated hundreds of years ago. The leap liberates, but does it not enslave again? The personalities of Sartre's novels have absolute freedom, but it is actually the freedom of falling under the compulsion of the internal or external situation of the moment. And the neoorthodox Christian subjects himself through the leap of faith to traditional ecclesiastical dogmas, He is free in the moment of his leap. But his leap into freedom involves the sacrifice of his freedom. The power of technical society is manifest in this conflict between rational necessity and the leap of freedom. The person is lost if rational necessity prevails. He tried to save himself by the leap that, however, leads to new forms of servitude, natural of supranatural ones. Only if we face realistically this situation can we realize the seriousness of the problem: "The person in a technical society."

Marx as Existentialist

While Hegel provided the idealistic mirror of technical society, Marx gave its realistic description. This accounts for his ambiguous relation to Hegel, his opposition to him, insofar as the idealistic side is concerned, his dependence on him, with respect to the dialectical analysis of present-day society. Marx saw much more clearly than Kierkegaard that it is not a system of thought but the reality of modern society that is responsible for the reduction of the person to a commodity. His famous descriptions of the dehumanizing effects of economy in the industrial age center around the proletariat, but they are meant for all groups of society. Everyone, insofar as he is drawn into the all-embracing mechanism of production and consumption, is enslaved to it, loses his character as person, and becomes a thing. Marx did not think it is the technical method of production as such that destroys personal freedom, but that the social structure of the class society is responsible for it. He believed in possibilities of humanizing the technical process, but he did not believe that this could happen within the frame of the class society. Therefore he became a political rebel against the social and economic structure of bourgeois society and a tremendous historical force, not only in the countries that became "Marxist"—at least in pretense—but also in those that avoided a radical transformation by fulfilling demands of the Marxist movements within the framework of bourgeois society. This latter fact should not be forgotten by those who are still interested in an unprejudiced, scientific criticism of Marx. The way in which Marx envisages the salvation of the person in technical society unites in a highly ambiguous way dialectical necessity with political decision. Marx, the sociologist, follows Hegel's method of structural analysis and derives from it not what Hegel did, a systematic glorification of the present, but a necessary, calculable development into a glorious future. At the same time he appeals to the action of the proletariat, especially the vanguard that consists of proletarians and people from other groups who have joined them. Appeal is senseless without the presupposition that it can be accepted or rejected. He did not believe that the "person" in the proletariat was extinguished to such a degree that political appeals would be meaningless. This view is supported by the two concepts that characterize Marx's view of man, the concept of "dehumanization" and the concept of "real humanism." Both presuppose that man can be distorted by social conditions in such a way that his humanity is lost, and both presuppose that there will be a state of things in which his community is reestablished. Both show that Marx is concerned with the loss and the salvation of the "person" in the technical society as he experienced it.

But again, as in the case of Kierkegaard, the power of this society became manifest as soon as the question was: how can one break away from it? The answer seems to be easy: through the dialectical process and the revolution it will bring about. But social dialectics and revolution occur through human beings, and this introduces alternatives that are as difficult as those we found in Kierkegaard's doctrine of the leap. If those in a state of complete depersonalization are carried by the dialectical process into the "realm of freedom," how can they use it without radical transformation from thing to person? But if they are still persons they introduce an incalculable element into the situation. The proletarians may not see their real interest, or their enemies may be unexpectedly strong, or groups may become active who do not fit the simple class scheme, or the proletarians may carry through their demands to such a degree that they cease to be proletarians in the genuine sense of the word. All this has actually happened and has produced two contradictory reactions. The one is the reaction by what is called today "the free world," namely, the attempt to save the person within the frame of the bourgeois-capitalistic society by methods of reforms (whatever they may be called). The other is the reaction by what is called today Communism, namely, the attempt to save the person in a future state of history by removing in the present those personal elements that might endanger the future. This has led to the establishment of the communist system in which all technical refinements are used to eliminate the risks involved in personal resistance against the system. A type of technical society has been created in which the person of the present is completely sacrificed for the sake of the expected person of the future. A movement that started with a passionate fight against depersonalization has turned into one of the greatest powers of depersonalization in all history.

Nietzsche's Protest

The fight of Existentialism against the dangers of the technical society was done, at the same time, on a third front, on that front that determines more than the two others the present fight against depersonalization. It was in the name of life that Nietzsche fought against the "nihilism" of the technical culture. Many followed him in all spheres of spiritual creativity. He and the movement of which he is the most conspicuous symbol saw more sharply than Kierkegaard and Marx the deepest roots of the dehumanizing and depersonalizing implications of modern society. Technical society—this is the message of all adherents of the "philosophy of life" (whether philosophers or poets or writers or artists)—destroys the creative power of life. Man becomes, according to Nietzsche, a cog in the all-embracing machine of production and consumption. This self, whose center is the will to realize it has nothing to will any more, and, therefore, it wills the "nothing." Only a new beginning of the will that wills itself can save life from a complete disintegration. This will (misleadingly called by Nietzsche the "will to power") is the self-affirmation of life as life against everything that transforms it into an object, a thing, a tool. Only a small group of people are the bearers of this new beginning, persons acting in the sense of heroic self-affirmation. They are the saviors of personal existence, through whom the power of life will reappear. On this basis the philosophers of life denounce the technical mass civilization, the egalitarian ideals, the subjection to the system of values that are accepted in this civilization, including the Christian values insofar as they are amalgamated with the ideals of modern society. Only a few romanticists amongst the philosophers of life attacked the technical development as such (just as did a few ecstatics amongst the socialists, and a few pietists amongst the followers of Kierkegaard). Generally speaking the technical world was accepted as a meaningful creation of life. But the way in which this creation turns against its creator produces the wrath of all philosophers of life. They want to restitute the integrity of creative life by looking for something below the split into the subject and object. On their way they meet the depth psychology, the emphasis on the unconscious, or the instincts, or the demonic, or the unreflected and unbroken self-realization. From the beginning in the early nineteenth century to their full development at the end of the nineteenth and the first half of the twentieth century depth psychology, philosophy of life, and Existentialism were intimate allies. Their common enemy was and is the objectifying, depersonalizing power of technical society. They do not look for the religious liberation through the leap of faith as did Kierkegaard, nor to the political liberation through the social dialectics as did Marx, but they look at the liberation that comes out of the depth of the personal life itself, his unconscious ground, his drives and instincts, his unity with nature, his self-affirming will. Sometimes they look back into the past, not in order to return to it, but in order to discover in it examples of undistorted life, e.g., in the Middle Ages, or in the archaic periods of the ancient cultures, or in the so-called primitives. Some go even beyond this and use the unreflected animal life to symbolize the ideal they put against the realities of technical society (note the use of animal symbols in Nietzsche's *Zarathustra*).

Contemporary Protests

Again the protest is profound and forceful. But is it able to pierce the walls of the society and its depersonalizing magic? Obviously not. It is driven to fateful self-contradiction. It has to fight the state of reflection with the tools of reflection. Politically the fight against the intelligentsia, and for the primitive and the genuine—in its most extreme form for "blood and soil"—has produced the most sophisticated and technically elaborate tools for suppressing every genuine expression of life that did not fit the demands of the political system. Man in this society was pressed into a scheme of thought, action, and daily behavior that reminds more of machine parts than of human beings. Even the faces of the storm troopers, for example, were as stereotyped as normal industrial tools. Any indication of personality and individuality was removed. The attempt made in the name of life to overcome the rule of depersonalized things has produced the complete removal of humanity in the supporters of this attempt. And its victims (including many followers) were transformed by terror into slaves, no less obedient than the slave that is called machine. The only way in which the original emphasis on life was maintained was the unrestricted realization of formerly repressed drives toward power, pleasure, and destruction. This was done in the name of vitality, against rationality. But the result was a mutilated, self-destroying vitality united with bestiality and absurdity. The power of the technical world proved again to be overwhelming.

Recent Existentialism (Sartre) tried to break its power by isolating the individual from the embracing structure of technical civilization. It tries to save the person by asking him to create himself without norms, laws, and principles, without anybody else or anything else. True humanism is declared to be the message of the individual making himself. Since "man's essence is his existence," no criteria are given to him for his self-creating activity. The will willing itself, the decision deciding for the sake of deciding and not for the sake of a content, the freedom maintaining itself by the rejection of any obligation and devotion—all the descriptions of the existential situation express the protest of Existentialism against our technical world. They are an analogy to Kierkegaard's "leap"; and their freedom is as much a leap into the dark as Kierkegaard's leap would have been without his participation in the Christian Lutheran tradition. By surrendering all norms they deliver the person to the contingencies of the situation; they depersonalize him.

Much more successful in saving the person from the dehumanizing power of technical society seems to be the third ally in the fight for genuine life, the depth psychology, especially in its latest development in which all emphasis is put on the analysis and synthesis of the personal life. "Personality" has become the central concept of the post-Freudian psychotherapeutic development. The analytic attempt to liberate the unconscious from the repressions forced upon it by the society, to liberate the ego from the authoritarian representatives of the superego, to liberate the person from the compulsive drives that subdue the personal center and eliminate its power of making personal decisions—all this seems to be the way to the salvation of the person in the technical society. Many people believe that it is and feel that their own experiences support this belief. So we must ask: Is psychotherapy the way to break through the otherwise unconquerable fortress of technical society? Is it the way to save the person from becoming a thing amongst things? Or is there a similar problem as that in the other attempts to save personal existence, namely the problem of transition, "the leap," the breaking away from the tyranny of the technical civilization. For two reasons it seems to me that the situation is not essentially different: first, because the individual person is not isolated; second, because the method of liberating him may strengthen that from which it tries to liberate. The first reason points back to Marx, the second to Nietzsche. A philosophical analyst once said to me, "What is the use of my work with my patients even if most successful, when I have to send them back into *this* society?" More and more psychotherapists have discovered that the conflicts of their patients are partly and often largely conditioned by the social situation in which they live, the competitive, technical, postpuritan society with the repressions, the anxiety, and the compulsions it produces. This, however, means a limit to the healing power of analysis and the demand for a social transformation for the sake of the person and his salvation from the depersonalizing forces.

But psychoanalysis has not only its "Marxism" problem, it has also its "Nietzschean" problem. It is this question: can a method, a technically elaborate procedure, save the person from technical society? Two answers can be given to this question. The one would say that psychotherapy is indeed a technique and works like every technique through adequate means toward a definite end. The end is the healing of pathological states of mind; the means are determined by their methodological adequacy to their end. If this answer is accepted, the psychoanalyst no more saves the person than does the internist in bodily medicine. The opposite answer would say that within the psychotherapeutic method elements are present that transcend the mere technical sphere, above all a person-to-person relationship that may be saving for the patient as person. If this answer is accepted it means that the analyst implicitly and indirectly exercises priestly functions. This is quite possible and certainly very often real. But then it is not psychotherapy as psychotherapy that saves the person, but the spiritual substances in which both the analyst and the patient participate. And the question remains: What is this saving power?

Two Shortcuts

The result of all this seems to be quite negative. It seems that the Existential revolts against technical society have been futile. From Kierkegaard to present-day psychotherapy, the problem of transition is decisive for the failure to save the person within the technical society. The "leap" in all its variations is more an expression of despair than an answer. Nevertheless, the Existentialist revolt is the decisive event, theoretical and practical, of the last one hundred years. It has shown the problem and it has given different solutions, each of which proved the superiority of the technical society over all those who attacked it. But the attack itself was and is most significant. Whether victorious or not, it kept alive the consciousness that technical society is the great threat against the person. This is the reason why almost all important creations of the last decades were creations by those who belong to the movement of rebellion against the technical society.

These attacks have led to attitudes and systems of life and thought that challenge the contemporary bourgeois society. What, then, about this society and the attitude toward it by groups who largely agree with the criticism made by the one hundred years of Existentialist protest and who, at the same time, are aware of the tragic self-contradictions into which the protesting ideas were driven when they succeeded politically or spiritually? It seems to me that such groups, e.g., the contributions of this volume and the movement they represent, must avoid two shortcuts, the one to return in a state of disappointment to a full affirmation of present-day technical society; the other, to use the Christian message as a *deus ex machina* that solves all problems, unsolved by the other movements!

The first shortcut is an understandable reaction to the chaos of disintegration and the horrors of attempted reintegration that we have experienced in our period. A conservative mood today pervades: not only the disappointed members of the older generation, but also the younger people who, without a revolutionary impetus and without visions concerning the future, adapt themselves in a matter-of-fact way to the concrete demands of the given reality. It is a practical positivism, but without the forward-looking enthusiasm of the earlier positivism. It is a realism of resignation. One hardly can resist this mood in a world in which small groups under the protection of political and military secrecy rule mankind; and in which the dependence on production of a highly technical character subjects everybody more and more to a new kind of fate—as incalculable and threatening as that towards the end of the ancient world. Nevertheless, one can resist this mood, not by closing one's eyes to this actual situation, not by glorifying our own reality because it is not as bad as the reality elsewhere—certainly it is better, yet the threat is the same—not by pointing to the improvements of the social situation in the Western world—certainly there are improvements, yet the conflict between person and industrial society is not removed—but by transcending the whole situation and seeing it from a point beyond it.

This point, however, is not the Christian church and her traditional message. To say this would be another shortcut. One must ask, especially on Christian ground, why the church and her message are so powerless in their fight against the depersonalizing forces of the present world. The reason cannot be that they are in themselves without power. The opposite is true, not only for the vision of faith, but also for the sociological and psychological observation. The reason that the church and her message are unable to resist the progressive annihilation of the person within industrial society is something else. It is the unintended participation of the church in the essential structure of industrial society. Step by step, the church, including the way she has shaped and communicated her message, has been determined by the categories of life and thought that characterize the industrial society. The church became a section of that against which she was supposed to defend the person. The process of depersonalization has caught up even with the churches and their members. One should not close his eyes in face of this situation, and one should not glorify the churches as more protected against depersonalization. Certainly, they are more protected in principle, namely, by their foundation, their message, their community—but this is not a necessary protection in the actual churches. They have means of resisting depersonalization in their traditions, their symbols, their rites—but their means can be transformed into powerful tools of dehumanization. They emphasize the infinite value of the individual person—but they are in danger of depersonalizing the person in order to preserve his infinite value. One must transcend not only society but also that section in the society that is taken by the churches, in order to see the situation in its threatening power. Only from "beyond" can industrial society and its dehumanizing forces be resisted and finally overcome.

Humanity and the New Reality

Two shortcuts have been rejected: the conservative acceptance of the state of things within the so-called free world and the ecclesiastical acceptance of the churches as the means of saving the person in the industrial society. It is obvious that the widespread combination of the two shortcuts does not provide for the right way. What, then, is the direction in which we must look for the right way? It is the Christian message of the New Reality, seen in the light of the Existentialist criticism of the old reality, and of its special expression in the industrial society. This, it seems to me, must be the program of a group such as that which is represented by this volume. It is now possible to point to some basic implications of this idea.

The first critical statement to be derived from it is directed against the reality of such a thing as "Industrial Society." Its meaning is a society whose character is determined by man's industrial activity. Man certainly is *homo faber,* industrial man. The being that invented the first tool *as a* tool for permanent use transcends by this act everything given and was potentially the creator of a world beyond the given world. The importance of this fact can hardly be exaggerated in a theological or philosophical doctrine of man. But this power of transcending the given is not an isolated element in man's nature. It is interdependent with many other elements within a total structure. The industrial man is at the same time the man who is able to speak because he has universals, and he is social man because he is able to have I-Thou relations, and he is theoretical man because he is able to ask and to receive answers, and he is moral man because he is able to make responsible decisions, and he is religious man because he is able to be aware of his finitude and of the infinite to which he belongs at the same time. Man is all this because of the basic structure of being that is complete in him; he has a centered self in correlation with a structured world. He looks at both of them, he is free from and for both of them, and he can transcend them both.

If one element in this structure is developed in isolation and put into control over the others, not only the whole structure is distorted, but the special element loses its power and its meaning. If, for instance, industrial society transforms the universities into places of research for industrial purposes, not only the universities lose their function of asking radically for the truth, but the technical development itself will be stopped in the long run—the danger of present-day America. On the other hand, if the universities isolate their function of asking for man's existential concern, e.g., the social, they lose their significance and fall victims to unanalyzed ideologies—the danger of past Germany. Many similar examples about the self-destructive consequences of the isolation and imperialism of a special function of the human mind can easily be given. In all of them the result is depersonalization, for the person is a centered whole to which all his functions are subjected. As soon as one function is separated from the others and put into control over the whole, the person is subjected to this function and through it to something that is not itself. It *becomes* this function. This is even true of religion. The abominable word *religionist* implies that a man has dissolved his personality into the religious function, that he is, for example, not free to ask radically even for the truth of religion, that he cannot transcend his functional limits—an implication that is not in vocational names such as artist, economist, statesman, bishop. If religion makes "religionists," it destroys the person as much as industry by producing an industrial age. Not industry but the isolation and imperialism of industry is the threat for the person in our age.

Homo faber, the industrial man, makes tools; this is the only thing he can "make." The "world above" the "world" he produces is the world of means, leaving open the question of the ends. One previous consideration has shown that the person is either the end for which everything else is means, or the person becomes a means, and then not only the person but also the end is lost. There is no end in the chain of means and ends except the person. And if the person himself becomes a means, an endless chain of means-and-ends-and-means is established that crushes purpose, meaning, and person. But one may ask the question: Is it not the person for whose comfort and well-being the whole technical world is produced; and even more, is not the creation and the use of tools, from the hammer to the artificial brain, in itself an expression of man's superiority? To this one must answer that, certainly, only man as a person is able to produce this "second world," but that in doing so he can become himself a tool for the production of tools, spiritually as well as economically centered in "gadgets" and considered as a part of the production and consumption power. And although the tool serves the comfort of the person, it cannot serve the person as person, that which makes him a person. It can make communication easier. But that which makes the person is the content of what is communicated, and it may well be that the ease and the content of the communication are inversely proportional. Another question could be raised, namely, whether the person is the end that cannot become means without being destroyed. Is not the glory of God or the kingdom of God or, in more secular terms, the realization of values, the ultimate end for which everything must become means, even the person? But such a question is self-contradictory. The meaning of, for instance, kingdom of God is not the unity of things or their functions, but it is the unity of persons, including their relationship to the whole nonpersonal realm. Through persons, i.e., through beings who can decide for or against them, values and the glory of God are actualized. To say that God is the ultimate end is saying that the person is the ultimate end.

Conformity versus the Person

Western technical society has produced methods of adjusting persons to its demands in production and consumption that are less brutal, but in the long run, more effective than totalitarian suppression. They depersonalize not by commanding but by providing; providing, namely, what makes individual creativity superfluous. If one looks around at the methods that produce conformity one is astonished that still enough individual creativity is left even to produce these refined methods. One discovers that man's spiritual life has a tremendous power of resistance against a reduction to prescribed patterns of behavior. But one also sees that this resistance is in great danger of being worn down by the ways in which adjustment is forced upon them in the industrial society. It starts with the education of "adjustment,'' which produces conformity just by allowing for more spontaneity of the child than any preindustrial civilization. But the definite frame within which this spontaneity is quietly kept leads to a spontaneous adjustment that is more dangerous for creative freedom than an openly deterministic influence. At the same time, and throughout his whole life, other powerful means of adjustment are working upon the person in the technical society: the newspapers that choose the facts worth reporting and suggest their interpretation, the radio programs that eliminate nonconformist contents and interpreters, television that replaces the visual imagination by selected pictorial presentations, the movie that for commercial and censorship reasons has to maintain in most of its productions a conscious mediocrity, adjusting itself to the adjusted taste of the masses, the patterns of advertisement that permeate all other means of public communication and have an inescapable omnipresence. All this means that more people have more occasions to encounter the cultural contents of past and present than in any preindustrial civilization. But it also means that these contents become cultural ''goods,'' sold and bought after they have been deprived of the ultimate concern they represented when originally created. They cease to be a matter of *to be or not to be* for the person. They become matters of entertainment, sensation, sentimentality, learning, weapons of competition or social prestige, and lose in this way the power of mediating a spiritual center to the person. They lose their potential dangers for the conformity that is needed for the functioning of the technical society. And by losing their dangers they also lose their creative power, and the person without a spiritual center disintegrates.

The Struggle for Persons by the Church

To struggle for the right of the person under the conditions of technical society should not become a fight against the technical side of mass communications; it should not even become a fight against their adjusting power. The technical development is irreversible and adjustment is necessary in every society, especially in a mass society. The person as person can preserve himself only by a *partial nonparticipation in* the objectifying structures of technical society. But he can withdraw even partially only if he has a place to which to withdraw. And this place is the New Reality to which the Christian message points, which transcends Christianity as well as non-Christianity, which is anticipated everywhere in history, and which has found its criterion in the picture of Jesus as the Christ. But the place of the withdrawal is, at the same time, the starting point for the attack on the technical society and its power of depersonalization.

It is the task of the church, especially of its theology, to describe the place of withdrawal, mainly the "religious reservation." It is the task of active groups within and on the boundary line of the church to show the possibilities of attack, to participate in it wherever it is made, and to be ready to lead it if necessary.

Looking back at the three great movements of protest against the dehumanization in the technical society, we can say that he who fights today for the person has to become an heir of all three of them. He must join in the rebellion of creative life against the degradation of person into an object. This is the first frontier of a Christian action today. Together with the philosophers of life, the Existentialists, the depth psychologists, and whatever new allies appear, it must show how the "structure of objectivation" (transforming life and person partly into a thing, partly into a calculating machine) penetrates all realms of life and all spiritual functions. It must show especially how even the religious symbols have been misinterpreted as statements about facts and events within the whole of objectivity, thus losing their inborn power to transcend this realm of the subjective-objective and to mediate visions of that level of reality in which life and personality are rooted. Christian action must be as daring as that of the Existentialists in their analysis of the human situation generally and the present cultural and religious situation especially. It must be as conscious of the infinite complexity of the human soul as that of the depth psychologists, fully aware of the fact that religion is responsible as much for the complexities and conflicts of the mind as it can contribute to the solution of the conflicts. Christian action today must, like the philosophers of life, have the courage to join the rebellion of life against internal repression and external suppression—in spite of the risk of chaos. But in joining these allies, Christian action must show that it comes from a place of withdrawal where it has received a criterion and a power able to overcome the danger of losing the person while attempting to save him.

And Christian action today must be aware of the second front: together with all movements for social justice whether they are called socialist or not, it must show how the competitive society produces patterns of existence that destroy personality because they destroy community, and that increase that all-pervading anxiety that characterizes our century. Christian action today must preserve, in spite of political and social odds against it, the tradition of social criticism that runs from the enthusiasts of the Reformation period through the bourgeois revolutionaries of the eighteenth century to the social critics of the nineteenth century, of whom Marx was the most passionate, the most profound, and the most dangerous. In alliance with all these movements, Christian action must attack wherever social patterns become visible by which persons are treated as means or transferred into things or deprived of their freedoms to decide and to create, or thrown into anxiety or bitterness or hate or tragic guilt. But in joining these allies, Christian action must show that it comes from a place of withdrawal where it has received a criterion and a power able to overcome the danger of sacrificing the person in order to save him.

And Christian action today must be aware of the third front: Together with all the movements within and outside Christianity that have rediscovered, partly in dependence on Kierkegaard, man's existential situation and the ultimate conflict that underlies all other conflicts, his estrangement from the ground of this being and meaning, Christian action must point to the ultimate roots of personal being. It must show that man can maintain his nature and dignity as a person only by a personal encounter with the ground of everything personal. In this encounter, which is the living center of religion and which, against rational as well as mystical criticism has been defended by Christianity, the person is established. In showing this, Christian action shows also the place to which it withdraws from the technical society in order to attack this society. This place is that which transcends every place, even the Christian churches. It is the New Reality that is manifest in Christ and against which even technical society and its power of destroying the person as person cannot prevail. Only out of the ground of the personal can the personal be saved. Only those who withdraw from action can receive the power to act. Christian action today rests on two poles, the one that transcends the structure of technical society—the New Reality of which Christianity is the witness; the other that is present within the structure of technical society—the movements that struggle, from different sides, against its depersonalizing power. In the correlation of these two poles, Christian action must find a way to save the person in industrial society.

CHAPTER 11

Environment and the Individual

Environment, Surroundings, and World

The term *environment* seems simple and without problems. Actually it is complex and a difficult though open doorway for man's self-understanding. Man and his relation to his world are misunderstood if man's environment is defined as the totality of objects that are so close to the place where he lives that he experiences them in a continuous encounter. If taken in this sense, environment is identical with surroundings. In order to know the environment of a man, one has to register, within an arbitrarily chosen orbit, every single object that he may regularly encounter. For instance, every single tree along the road he uses daily, every single figure in the pattern of his drapery, every single car he sees passing his street, every color, every sound by which he is consciously or unconsciously affected. All this and an infinite amount of other objects surround him. But they are not his environment. Environment is made up of those elements of his surroundings that are relevant for him as man. A man and his dog have the same surroundings, but a different environment. The Bosch painting in my living room is environment for me; it is not environment for my dog for whom only the peculiar smell of oil and varnish may have environmental character. For my maid, the environmental character of the picture may consist of the awareness of the subject matter of the painting and of her duty to dust it from time to time. All this means that environment is not identical with surroundings and that it is correlative to him who has surroundings. The question is not environment and the individual, but the individual and *his* environment.

This means that the same surroundings are something quite different for different kinds of individuals. If one takes a New York Puerto Rican out of his slum surroundings and out of the environment that was his environment, and puts him into an apartment within a new housing project, he will bring his old environment into the new surroundings and deal with them in terms of his old. They soon will become a slum. Conversely, for somebody who grew up in a cultivated house and for whom the Bosch picture was a picture, he could make of a cave in a wartime trench a small underground living room. This is the first limit for the influence of surroundings on the individual. He selects from the surrounding what shall become his environment.

This man is not different from any other living being—the dog, the fly, the migrating bird. But there is a difference between man and all other beings: Man's environment has the character of world. The environment of animals remains environment. It can never become world. What is world?

The Greeks called it *cosmos,* which means beauty, order, structure. The Romans called it universe, which means the unity of an infinite manifoldness. A definition of man in which all other definitions are implied is that he has not only environment, but also world. World is the structured unity of an inexhaustible number of actual and possible things. It is *the structure* that makes the world world. If we encounter world, we encounter it as a whole that is structured in time and space, in geometrical and biological forms, in things and consciousness of things, in laws and spontaneity, in the positive and the negative. All this makes the world *world* and determines the relation of world and environment. One could say that in man's environment, world is present and that every piece of his environment points beyond itself to his world. This is decisive for any attempt to change man's environment. The criterion of every change in the environment is the character of the world that is manifest in the changed surroundings and that determines the character of the environment that people can make of it.

Expressions of World

The presence of world in an environment expresses itself in many ways. And each of these expressions has symbolic character. It points to a particular self-understanding of man within his world. As such it reveals something about man and world in themselves and their encounter. The environment as the result of an encounter wins spiritual significance. Let me give a few examples.

Environment is by its very nature limited in space. But world, present in environment, drives beyond any limited space. The world-space is open in all directions without a noticeable or even imaginable end (whatever physical theory may say about the limited space of the universe). This infinite space is potentially present in the limited space of the environment, producing two reactions, each mixed with anxiety and courage. The infinite space is both threatening and liberating. It threatens to take away any space upon which one can stand by its endlessness and emptiness. It liberates from the bondage to a particular space its narrowness and its tendency to isolate from the world. Narrowness, on the other hand, has given the name to anxiety, *augustiae* in Latin. It is the cutting off of life potentialities that produces such an outbreak of basic anxiety. At the same time the narrow place is the protected place—the mother's womb, the cave, the narrow streets of the wall-protected medieval town. The modern functional house with its large, open glass walls seems to express the same courage that has conquered the space above the surface of the earth and is conquering the cosmic space itself. But man remains man, and often just in contrast to his wide openness, needs the place that is a separated part of endless space to give him a feeling of psychological as well as physical protection.

Connected with the question of the endless and limited space is that of environment that gives privacy and that prevents privacy. The spiritual problem in this respect is even more urgent than that in the former example. External privacy makes inner solitude possible or at least easier. And nothing is more needed in a period of loneliness within the crowd than solitude with oneself and the divine ground of one's being. The interdependence of the individual and his environment has produced an environment in which solitude is less and less possible. Both time that leaves no time for solitude and space that is organized without a space for privacy work against it. There is no privacy in houses for the individual member of the family. This is being caused by owners and builders under the false assumption that family is a unity that must always appear together. But the family consists of individual selves who need self-encounter. Otherwise, they become lonely within the family group and hostile to it, or they resign to their fate of losing their individuality. It is here that a large responsibility lies with the architectural profession.

Connected again with this problem is that of environment and conformity. Its spiritual significance is still greater. Driving through the housing projects that are found throughout Long Island in commuting distance from New York, I ask myself, what does this mean in terms of human existence? Settlement after settlement with little distance between them, each with exactly the same model of house, small differences in color and design, each for itself in immediate vicinity of the others, each surrounded by a small garden. The whole thing seems to me a disturbing symbol of loneliness in a crowd, breeding as well as confirming the patternization of present-day industrial society. The impression given by the metropolitan apartment house developments is different. They lie more in the direction of mass concentration, but they seem to leave more freedom for individual nonconformism—as big cities always do. What will these developments do to the individual is the question that now arises. In the daily movement of people between model homes, office, factory, school, train, social-togetherness with people who live under the same laws of existence, are there symbols left that break the conformist compulsion?

The answer may be: It canot be done from outside. Neither the city planners nor the architects nor those who direct the movement of the population can produce such symbols. They must come from inside. They are the concern of education and religion. But if we look in the light of this answer at the educational institutions, from family and school to public communications and at the way in which the churches consecrate conformism every Sunday morning, we shall become skeptical about this answer. Adjustment to the demands of our competitive mass society is the aim of most directly or indirectly educational activities. Such developments are useful for the ruling groups in a society and they have given security to the others, not only in dictatorial but also in democratic systems. But there is a limit to their usefulness. When man becomes dehumanized in patternized security, the whole system loses those who can support it in the future, those who can say no to a given pattern, those who are able to experience the new in a creative spirit, those who take the risk to fail. Are there elements in the environment of our society that have symbolic power for this no out of which a new yes can spring? Let us remember that environment is a correlative concept and that surroundings are not yet environment. It may be that the surroundings develop in a way that makes nonconformism almost impossible. But they cannot suppress it completely. Every man has a source of uniqueness in his self. Participation is only one pole of being, individualization is the other. And every man has a direct approach to the ultimate ground and meaning of life—the divine. Certainly, solitude seeks for privacy. But it can even be experienced within the crowd.

And since this is so, symbols of nonconformism will always appear in the midst of surroundings that try to compel adjustment to models and patterns. We are made by our environment, and we make it at the same time. Out of this follows our task, the task also of a group like this today. We should not imagine that we can change our cultural trend, either as architects or as theologians or as educators. But where there are trends there are also opportunities. Symbols cannot be produced intentionally. They are born and grow and die. But one can tell how they are conceived and born: Out of the personal passion of individuals who in total honesty and total seriousness penetrate into the demands of the material with which they work, who have a vision of the form that is adequate to their aim, and who know that in the depth of every material, every form and every aim, something ultimate is hidden that becomes manifest in the style of a building, of a poem, of a philosophy. Out of this depth, symbols can and will be born that, by their very character, say no to present conformity and that point to an environment in which the individual can find symbols of his encounter with ultimate reality.

CHAPTER 12

Conformity[1]

Conformity is a word that does not necessarily have negative connotations. We all must conform to some given forms of life and thought. Education—even if it has a better ideal than adjustment—aims at giving us a form. And in doing so, it makes us conform to the sources and bearers of such form. There are cultures, highly advanced as well as primitive ones, that in this way produce conformity for long periods of history. It was in Great Britain that my unqualified rejection of conformity was shaken, for there I found a powerful conformity that does not destroy the creative potentialities in the individual. This is so, I realized, because Great Britain lives consciously out of the past. Her conformism has an historical dimension.

Conformity is a negative force if the individual form that gives uniqueness and dignity to a person is subdued by the collective form. If this happens—often in connection with the loss of the historical dimension—a structure appears for which it probably would be more adequate to use the word *patternization*—the process in which persons are modeled according to a definite pattern. Patternization is what determines our period, both in learning and in life. And the questions I want to ask now are: What are the patternizing powers in our present culture, and are we able to resist them? Are we still able to say no in matters of serious concern, in spite of the tremendous strength of the patternizing forces?

In recent years several scientific books have appeared that describe the contemporary process of patternization and add criticism and warning. Such warning was anticipated in fiction, in Huxley's *Brave New World* and, in a more sinister way, in Orwell's *1984*. In both novels a kind of negative utopia is presented—a total reversal of the positive utopias that opened the

[1]This paper was delivered by Professor Tillich at the annual commencement exercises of the New School for Social Research, 1 June 1957.

modern period of Western history. The conquest of nature by reason, which in the utopias of the Renaissance was considered the main liberating power, is now seen as a means for the enslavement of man by patterns of life and thought that deprive him of the possibility of freedom and individual self-affirmation. According to the negative utopias of the last decades, an age of total patternization is about to come upon us.

The series of scientific books to which I referred confirms this diagnosis. Sociological analyses as given in *The Lonely Crowd, The Organization Man, The Hidden Persuaders, Mass Culture,* and others—besides several significant magazine articles—show what one of these books, written in German, expresses in its title: *The Future Has Already Begun.* The material presented in all these writings is rather impressive. One can distinguish three main causes of the present process of patternization: our technical civilization as such; the intentional imposition of patterns on the masses by interested groups; and the striving for security in many people, especially in the youngest generation.

That technical civilization as such, in its objective structures, is conducive to patternization is in complete contrast to its origins. It was born out of the courage of people who asked the questions that soon undercut the security of medieval conformity. How then could it happen that the answers to these questions became the principles under which present-day patternizing conformism developed? It happened because in the new structure of society the subject who asked the critical questions, that is, man as man, was more and more pushed aside and almost removed. The human self that once had the courage to say no to a thousand years of sacred conformity could not find a place in the world created by it. Man was interpreted theoretically as a bundle of conditioned reflexes without a determining center; and in practice he was treated as a commodity, a cog in the big machine of production and consumption, an object among objects, to be tested, calculated, and managed. This refers to everyone within industrial mass society, even to the central wheels of the machine. Even those who determine are determined by the structure of the society they control. Therefore, as the communist revolutions have shown, the replacement of one ruling group by another does not change the patternizing structures of mass industrial society.

This is the objective situation. Like every human situation, it becomes reality through human action and reaction, and most conspicuous among those whose actions make for patternized conformity are the political manipulators of mass reactions. The manipulation of men is not, of course, a one-way road. It is successful only if the reaction of the manipulated is not negative. Even the totalitarian systems are established by revolutionary armies, not seriously resisted by the masses, and after their establishment their controlling groups cannot afford to neglect the reaction of the people in the long run; from time to time they observe signs of a silent resistance and change their methods of control. But political patternization, whether it has a more one-way or a more two-way character, works to eliminate the possibility of a nonconformist no. Concentration camps and labor camps are not so much tools for the exter-mination of actual enemies as threatening symbols of the transformation of human beings into manageable objects.

In the democratic section of the world, political manipulation is much more a two-way road, but there too it drives millions toward a model con-formity. The schizophrenic split of mankind into East and West, and the secrecy connected with it, makes an independent political judgment al-most impossible for most people. It prevents the rise of fresh political phi-losophies, since every nonconformist political thought is denounced as neutralist or worse. Courage is demanded for the expression of serious po-litical disagreement even by a student, because it may later wreck his ca-reer. But if students and the generation they represent are silenced, where can we turn to hear the voice of nonconformity? Certainly not to the con-trolling powers in economy, in advertising, or to mass culture—those three powerful tools of patternization?

As to the first of these, I do not need to dwell on the screening and test-ing that precede an appointment to even the lowest executive position in big business and civil administration. It is well known that they delve into hidden trends of the unconscious, into all phases of private life, into mar-riage and the relation of the wife to the enterprise and her willingness to subject herself to its social requests. Sociologists believe that the image of the executive will become the pattern, vigorously imposed on all groups of society. And they even derive from this pattern the peculiar character of the present movement toward religion. They may be right!

The political as well as the economic manipulation of our society is supported and often controlled by the managers of advertising. This also is a two-way road. The advertiser can create needs only if he knows the hidden desires of the people. Out of this necessity the "depth approach" in advertising has developed. When I first read about this method I re-membered that once I had given a sermon about the meaning of depth—

and I shuddered. And I believe that Freud too would shudder at the use of his discoveries in advertising depth research. Certainly, there are hidden motives that determine the buying of a special brand of shaving cream or car, the attention to a special advertisement. But when the managers of advertising and their allies and customers in business and politics use this knowledge to direct our lives and thoughts, they actualize just those elements in us that do *not* constitute our real self but come from our childhood memories, our resentments, our daydreams, our contingent desires. All this does belong to us, but it is not we ourselves in our deciding, responsible center—the point of our freedom and personal dignity. This center must be avoided by the manipulators, because out of it may arise the no that could destroy their attempts to condition our reactions. We could cease to be a calculable object, and this would be disastrous for all methods of manipulation. We would again become individual persons and cease to be examples of one of the several types of reaction defined by the depth approach of motivation research.

The problem of mass culture and its patternizing effect is an inexhaustible subject in itself. It too is ambiguous, not simply good and not simply bad. But in any case, it is one of the driving forces toward model conformity. It is a matter of mass distribution, and for this very reason it cannot avoid the stereotype, standardization, and the lowest common denominator. Cultural creations of past and present become manipulated consumer goods. One can hardly avoid the impression that the means of mass communication through which these cultural commodities are distributed to everybody have the effect that children receive much too early the status of adults, while adults remain children, never allowed to grow into maturity. Maturity, personal as well as cultural, presupposes a suffering under problems, a necessity to decide, a possibility of saying no. Unfortunately, one gets the further impression that the methods used in some places for producing a religious revival are essentially of the same type as those we find in the marketing of mass culture. This is tragic, because religion is supposed to be the place where the ultimate source and power of nonconformism becomes manifest, the place where the prophetic no to all patterns, religious as well as nonreligious, is heard and pronounced.

These are the conditioning forces in the process of patternization. But they would not be so powerful as they are if it were not for the third factor I mentioned: a state of mind, especially in the youngest generation, that is

ready to subject itself to these forces. One can observe in many young people an intense desire for security, internal and external, a will to be accepted by the group at any price, an unwillingness to show individual traits,
a conscious rejection of nonconformist attitudes in the older generation, an
acceptance of a well-circumscribed happiness without serious risks. It is
difficult for my generation to understand this attitude. Therefore we should
restrain ourselves from harsh judgment. But nobody can doubt that it confirms the assertion that "the future has already begun."

This is the picture. How do we react it? A few weeks ago I gave a speech
to a large group of architects and referred to the patternizing effect of many
suburban housing projects, not only through the monotony of the buildings
but also through the abolition of privacy and with it of the possibility of
the self to encounter itself in solitude. I was then asked whether this does
not agree with human nature, which makes collectivism unavoidable. My
answer is no, and must be, as is shown even by the possibility of asking
such a question. The totally patternized man would have lost the capability
of asking questions and deliberating about answers. He would cease to be
a man.

Today as always there are symptoms of resistance to patternization,
symptoms that reveal something about human nature. The first is what the
French call *ennui*, being bored with existence itself. This is an important
potentiality of man. It saves our children from being drowned by comics
and television. It forces the managers of mass culture to change the fashion
of music and dance and all their other products from time to time. And to
do this, they have to follow the guidance of a less conformist minority.

Another symptom of resistance to the patternizing processes is the awareness of these processes in science and art. We have become conscious of he
threat of dehumanization. The literature to which I referred has abundantly
exposed the dangerous forces. And as an old religious symbol teaches us, an
exposed demon has lost much of its power. This is why the manipulators of
conformity try, often unconsciously, to make the books of exposé just another
in the line of goods for mass consumption.

A third symptom of the presence of nonconformist forces in human nature is the spirit of rebellion, which still exists in many places in the Western world, even in the lonely-crowd attitude of the younger generation. It
is a spirit that in its best manifestation is the courage to say yes to one's
birthright as a unique, free, and responsible individual, and consequently
to say no to whatever would destroy the freedom and dignity of man—even

at the price of taking socially unpleasant and dangerous consequences upon oneself. Such courage is able to do what is even more difficult than resisting external pressures: it is able to resist internal compulsions, such as a socially conditioned, uneasy, and anxious conscience. It is not in willfulness but in the courage to take a moral risk that one has the right to say no even to the commands of an anxious conscience.

The courage that resists patternized conformity is ultimately rooted in a dimension of human experience that transcends fashions and patterns, anxieties and compulsions, generations and nations. It is the dimension that appears if somebody asks with radical seriousness the question of the ultimate meaning of his life. Whether or not one calls this the religious question, it is one that is rooted in the true, unfathomable depth of every human being. Out of this depth arises the courage to resist patternization. In religious language one would call it the prophetic spirit. But this spirit is not restricted to historical religion, which often has betrayed it. It can and must appear in our daily life, in our professional work, in our social behavior, in our political conviction, in our cultural preferences, in our human relations, in our creative eros.

The future of our country would look brighter if at each commencement in every college and in every university at least a few students entered their vocational life with the decision to resist the seemingly irresistible powers of patternizing conformity. It is my wish and my hope that many in this outgoing class will remain determined to preserve their human integrity and their power to say no, even under severe pressures by the patterns of life and thought prescribed by society. We hope for nonconformists among you, for your sake, for the sake of our nation, for the sake of humanity.

CHAPTER 13

The Relationship Today
between Science and Religion

Principles

If the theologian deals with the sciences, he is caught in a contradictory situation. Either he is tempted to give a summary judgment about scientism and to dismiss the whole problem of religion and science, or he is tempted to keep away from the problem because of unlimited awe towards the sciences. Both his arrogance and his humility are expressions of the fact that his subconscious has been shaped by the consequences of the historical battles between religion and science and their disastrous effects on theology. Almost every theologian who has to deal with the relation of religion and science is anxiety-ridden; and I certainly do not to conceal my own anxiety.

The Definition of Science

The word *science* is a stumbling block, especially if one comes from continental Europe. One does not know whether science is supposed to mean the mathematical sciences alone, or natural science generally, or the scholarly approach in all spheres, like the German word *Wissenschaft*. I feel that the idea underlying this lectureship demands restriction to the natural sciences. Such restriction, even if systematically not justifiable, allows the concentration on some problems that are most representative for the relation of religion and science today.

The Definition of Religion

The statement that religion and science do not interfere with each other (in their essential nature) presupposes above all a sharply defined concept of religion. Such a concept is a summary of a whole philosophy of religion and must be presupposed here. But this does not introduce a completely strange element into our problem. For the philosophy of religion presupposed is largely conceived of under the impact of the problem, religion and science. It is partly created under the necessity of drawing the dividing line between religion and science so sharply that both must trespass this line in order to interfere with each other.

Religion can be defined as the encounter with the holy, and the holy can be defined as the manifestation of what concerns us ultimately and with unconditional seriousness. The holy is a dimension of reality that shines through the bearers of the holy, be it stars and trees, ocean and earth, paintings and buildings, music and words, or persons and historical events. Through all of them one can encounter the holy. Through all of them human beings have encountered the holy, although none of them is holy in itself. They are holy as bearers of the holy. They are holy because in them something is encountered that is a matter of ultimate concern, something in which the question of the meaning of our life is asked and answered in symbols and myths.

The unconditional seriousness of the encounter with the holy shows itself in the double effect of the holy upon us. It has an irresistible fascination as that which gives to our life ultimate depth. And it has an awe-awakening strangeness. We cannot touch it as we can touch with hands and minds everything in time and space. We can touch the bearers of the holy, but not the holy itself. It remains the unapproachable mystery of being.

The Conflict
between Science and Religion

If religion is understood in this way, no conflict between religion and science is possible. Someone could say, "I have never had the experience of the holy as you describe it." Perhaps this is correct. But from this it does not follow that he never had the experience of an ultimate concern, of something that is sacred to him. I have never found a human being who has nothing that is sacred to him—at the very least, there is his cynicism of trying to have no ultimate concern. But then he will answer, "That is not what usually has been connected with the word *religion*." And in this he is right.

For there is another concept of religion out of which inescapably the conflicts with science follow. It is the concept of religion as the belief in the existence of a being, called God, who surpasses everything in power and value and with whom men communicate in terms of knowledge, adoration, obedience. The activities of this being in our world produce extraordinary effects, like miracles or revelations, that can be experienced like any other event. These last words already show where the conflict with science occurs. The realm of God's activities in our world is the realm where science becomes a competitor to religion.

But in order to become a competitor, science itself has to develop out of the stages in which, as in a mother's womb, it was still united with myth. In this stage there could be no conflict because the world was "full of gods," as Thales, the first Greek philosopher, still says. The divine was not supernatural and the things were not natural. In Homer the divine is ever-present, working out the destiny of man. The course of events and the actions of the gods are one and the same thing.

The great change began when the Greek philosophers approached what they called *physis* (that which grows out of itself, *natura,* nature) in terms of exact observation and calculation. In this moment a long process of the demythologization of the world followed, and so did the first conflicts with religion. Anaxagoras, in the fifth century, made the tremendous step of depriving the heavenly bodies of their divine character and describing them as mere bodies. He was exiled for this early act of demythologization. Other acts of demythologization followed, not so much by Socrates—who was condemned to death as the incarnation of pure critical rationality, undercutting the unquestioned authority of the traditional ways of life—as by his schools. In them, for instance, Euhemerus explained the gods as deified heroes and rulers of the past, while the later schools tried to remove them from the universe of scientific discourse—the Epicureans by pushing them into the sleeping happiness of the empty spaces between the worlds, the Stoics by interpreting them as metaphors for natural powers.

These conflicts are examples. Slowly, partly with the help of the all-embracing and all-restoring Neoplatonic system, the gods returned as inferior powers; finally Christianity removed them radically, but replaced them with angels and saints. Science, except mathematics and Ptolemaic astronomy, was subdued; and Augustine thought that the dealing with natural objects is a matter of the demons, because it involves the mind into what is farthest removed from the divine. Serious conflicts were never possible under these conditions; natural and miraculous processes were accepted as equally valid. The myth ruled again in the tripartite world: heaven, earth, hell.

But in the underground the scientific approach gained momentum. At the end of the Middle Ages it could not be stopped any longer. The doctrine of the double truth saved the philosophers from persecution, until in the Renaissance they came into the open and new conflicts arose.

As in the Greek philosophy, it was the shock produced by demythologization that produced the conflict. When Galileo defended the Copernican system it was not a new astronomical theory that aroused the protest of the church but the decentralization of the earth, and with it the decentralization of mankind, and with it the decentralization of the Christ. Mankind has become a particle in an infinite universe in which the spatial distinctions of up and down, of heaven and hell, have lost any literal meaning. When Kepler fought against even the astronomers of his time for the noncircular, parabolic movement of the planets, he undercut the mythological assumption that the heavenly bodies, according to their divine nature, have a perfect circular movement. When Newton developed the cosmic mechanism of classical physics, it was the anxiety of man who felt dehumanized into a part of this machine that produced resistance and rebellion. Pascal represented both the scientific attitude that had brought about this model and the resistance against it in the name of the God of the patriarchs. When Darwin announced his theory of evolution in which he derived in mechanical terms all species of life including man, it was the reduction of man to subhuman forms of life that produced the resistance of the churches. Again, it was not the scientific analysis as such that created the conflict, but its demythologizing influence on the self-interpretation of man.

These examples—which are somehow a summary of the main historical conflicts between religion and science—show one thing clearly. In every scientific approach there are two elements: the first is genuinely scientific—the approach to reality is in terms of observation, hypothesis, experiment, theory, and all this is related to the processes in time and space with their mathematical and logical structure. In this element, science is autonomous, determined by its object alone, and obliged to resist any interference from any side, be it a religious or a quasi-religious political organization, or democratic conformity and conventional fashion. Science in all realms, not only in the natural sciences, but also in psychology, sociology, and history, is continuously threatened by these powers, especially if they are internalized and have become unconscious in the scientist himself.

For there is another element in science: its participation in the whole of man's spiritual life and, therefore, in the self-interpretation of man in the universe. Out of such self-interpretation in mythological and metaphysical terms has science once grown; and in no stage of its development has it left the ground completely. This is the point where science itself reaches into the religious dimension, for both myth and metaphysics express in symbols or concepts the encounter with ultimate reality. Here is the realm of conflicts, humanly unavoidable, but not necessary according to the nature both of religion and of science. This latter point has been acknowledged by both sides since the second third of our century when the spirit of the nineteenth century was finally conquered. The decisive point that underlies my own analysis is the distinction of the dimensions in which lie the religious and the scientific encounters with reality. Science is the cognitive approach to the whole of finite objects, their interrelations and their processes. Religion is the total approach to that which gives meaning to our life and, therefore, concerns us unconditionally and ultimately. Dimensions cross each other, but they do not conflict with each other. All conflicts occur if the difference between the dimensions is denied and the two functions of man's spiritual life are seen on one and the same level. And this happens under two conditions, the one, if science confuses its religious and metaphysical matrix with its methodologically gained results. Whenever this happens the scientist becomes a theologian, and in some respect, every scientist is a theologian, however hidden and absurd his theology may be. But if he expresses his theology as an implication of his scientific method and as a result of his research, he confuses the dimensions; and then people with another theology necessarily conflict with him.

The same problem is actual in religion and theology. They are continuously in the state of confusion of dimensions. All statements about facts, structures, processes and events in nature, man and history, are objects of scientific research and cannot be made in the name of religion. Nothing factual can in principle produce conflicts between religion and science. But religion is always in danger of overstepping this boundary line, and some theologians always have tried to defend these trespasses. And they have done even more. They have tried to use scientific results that seemed advantageous to theology as proof for theological statements. But whether they used science or fought against science, they fell into the error of confusing the dimensions. In both cases it was religion that was most damaged.

Discursive and Symbolic Language

One cay say in the semantic terminology of our time that they confused two kinds of language, the discursive and the symbolic language. Religious language is symbolic, for the holy cannot be grasped like any object among objects. It cannot be grasped directly or literally. Any attempt to do so is an unconscious desecration of the holy. In the struggle between the atheist and the theist, the theist seems more in danger of becoming blasphemous than the atheist. I intend to give some examples for this basic thesis by discussing some religious symbols that have produced conflicts between religion and science by the interference of religion in science, in consequence of the belief in divine interference in the scientifically describable world.

Religious Symbols
and Scientific Observations

The Symbol of Creation
and the Ontological Relation of God and the World

Creation is a basic religious symbol that expresses two things. It expresses man's own experience of his creatureliness, philosophically speaking, of his being finite, and it points to something from which his creaturely existence is derived—the Creator, or more generally expressed, the creative ground of his being. If the symbol of creation is interpreted literally, God is made into a being who out of heavenly *space,* once upon a *time, caused* a new *substance* to come into existence. Such interpretation uses all the categories (space, time, causality, substance) that ordinarily are used for the interrelationship of existing things. In this way God becomes a thing and the world another thing. But the description of the relationship of things is the task of science, and so it can happen that a scientific statement, for instance, about the beginning of the world, is used as an argument for the religious symbol or is rejected in the name of the religious symbol. Extreme fundamentalists maintain that the world had been created a few thousand years ago in six days, while the late Pope declared that all scientific arguments point to the creation of the world by God five billion years ago. Both positions are untenable. They are based on a confusion of dimensions.

The Symbol of Consummation
and the Relation of Time and Eternity

Consummation is, like creation, a basic religious symbol that can be found in most developed religions. It also expresses the experience of man's finitude of his world, but it does so, not from the side of the beginning, but from the side of the end. Usually the end is symbolized as a cosmic catastrophe pointing to the transitions of the temporal into the eternal. If this is taken literally, one thinks of eternity as a continuation of time without end, and one attributes such endless being to an immortal soul. But time is not like a river bed in which things move along like a stream, but is like a form that is dependent on the character of the thing to which it belongs. Atoms, trees, animals, man have a different time, and the human time is the time that comes from the eternal and returns to the eternal. Here and now, in a present moment, eternity can be experienced. It is neither timelessness nor endless time. The end, therefore, is here and now for everybody and everything, no matter how science may describe the probable end of living organisms on earth, or of the solar system, or of the universe as a whole. No conflict is possible if the dimensions of the eternal and the temporal is are not confused.

The Symbol of Providence and the Interaction
between God and the World

The basic symbol expressing the interaction between God and the world is providence. Providence is the continuous directing activity of the creative ground of being here and now in past and future. The symbol of providence should not be confused with a deterministic description of the process of being. And certainly, the divine activity within and through this process should not be described as a preestablished divine mechanism with which God sometimes interferes. Such interference is the definition of miracles in the distorted meaning of this word. Originally, the word meant that which produces astonishment by a special constellation of factors and that points into the dimension of the eternal. If *miracle* is understood as a destruction of the structures and laws of natural processes, science rightly protests against such a confusion of dimensions. But on the other hand, science cannot give a foundation for a nondeterministic interpretation of reality. It is a temptation for some theologians to use the principle of indeterminacy. It transcends both of them and is a creative act of a total and centered being. Providence creates and directs through human freedom as it creates through the spontaneity of all living beings and the centered structures of everything that is.

The Symbol of Revelation
and the Cognitive Approach of Religion

The last great symbol I want to give as an example is revelation. It expresses the ecstatic experience of the presence of the divine out of which new religious symbols arise. Again a literal interpretation of this symbol distorts it into the idea of divine information, or even dictation. Such information then gives divine authority to the message of those who have received it, or to every word of the divine dictation. Here again, scientific research into the historical development of sacred literature would come into conflict with such an idea of revelation. Literalism, in this sense, is one of the worst confusions of dimensions, and it has most devastating consequences both for the social and the personal life. It causes destructive conflicts between religious faith and scientific honesty. Such conflicts can be avoided if the dimension of ultimate concern is distinguished from the dimension of processes in time and space. The former are a matter of religious experience, the latter are a matter of scientific research. They are within each other, but since they are not on the same level, they cannot stand against each other.

CHAPTER 14

Religion, Science, and Philosophy[1]

Mr. Chancellor, Ladies and Gentlemen, this is a second lecture. Therefore, I must start by repeating some of the fundamental ideas that are presupposed in the other lecture this time.

The Two Concepts of Religion

In my first lecture I distinguished between two concepts of religion. And this is the foundation for everything I have to say in these lectures, because on them depends what one can say about the relationship of religion and culture in all different realms.

The first concept, the fundamental or universal one, has been called by me and by others by different terms. And I leave you the choice; whichever of these terms fits what you feel expresses something in you, you may choose. For instance, "being unconditionally concerned about the meaning of one's existence." That's one definition of the fundamental concept of religion. Or, "taking something absolutely seriously." That's another possibility of expressing it. Or, "being grasped by an infinite interest and an infinite passion." That is a line of the Danish theologian and philosopher of the nineteenth century, Kierkegaard. Or, "the self-transcendence of life experience," a self-transcendence toward the ultimately sublime or instead of ultimately sublime, one can also say *holy,* because that is what holy means. Then, I use an abbreviation of all this, a simple two-word phrase, *ultimate concern.* Being ultimately concerned is religion in this sense. Now this is the fundamental concept and this is the judge of all concrete religion and it is the foundation for the second-level concept of religion.

---

[1]This was the second of four Regent Lectures delivered by Professor Tillich in 1963 at the University of California, Santa Barbara.

The second concept is "a social group with symbols of thought and of action." Symbols of thought are, for instance, myths, liturgical words, theological formulations, and even metaphysical conceptualizations. And symbols of action are ritual activities and ethical consequences of them. All these things express a particular direction of our ultimate concern, something that concerns us ultimately but which is expressed in particular form. And such a thing constitutes a church, or a sect, or a monastic group (in early Buddhism and of course very much in Catholic Christianity), or a fanatic movement, often of a very valuable kind, often on the boundary line of irrationality.

The Conflict between Religion and Culture

My main thesis is that all conflicts between religion and culture generally, or religion and its special cultural function, are dependent on the reduction of religion to the narrower concept of religion. If you understand religion only in the narrower concept, then of course conflicts are practically unavoidable (although in principle they could be avoided as I will try to show). But if you understand that in all these concrete religions there is something present that is more than this concrete religion, the fundamental concept or meaning of religion, then you have a tool to overcome such conflicts. The reason why there are conflicts between the narrower concept of religion, or the concrete historical religions, and cultural activities is obvious. Every concrete religion is in itself a cultural phenomenon. It appears in the whole of the cultural life of the society. It plays a great role in it even today, and it is a part of this culture, an element in this culture, while the fundamental concept transcends both religion in the narrower sense and culture. For instance, the church is a social group, and every social group has a larger or smaller amount of power. And in this power it is possible that conflicts arise between the power of the group we call church and the power of the group that we call a state. And out of this, then, conflict and separation, and gaps between them, and wars between them arise. The danger in this situation is that the church represents what I call ultimate concern, and in the power of representing the ultimate in meaning of human existence, it tries to elevate itself above everything, above family and state. And out of this, then, of course, conflicts with both arise. That is the reason for these conflicts or these separations in this country. The same conflicts can arise in all other realms: in the realms of law, in the realms of political aims, in the realms of artistic style and in the realm where it is especially found, in the educational realm.

Therefore, we have now one point that is fundamental: all conflicts between religion and culture are based on the identifying of religion as religion in the narrower sense, religion as a piece of culture that claims to be more than culture and therefore comes into conflict with other cultural realities. And the same is true when both religion and culture affirm the possession of, or the methods to, truth—culture in terms of science and philosophy, concrete religion in terms of myth, symbol, and dogma. And then conflicts arise between this part of culture and the other part of culture. This is perhaps—in this country at least and in the modern world today—the most serious of these conflicts. The solution of this conflict is something we all attempt, (we are responsible for thinking about these problems all the time), but that I also want to try in this hour.

This brings us directly to our subject, and I believe that beyond this it gives us the weapon to overcome the conflict, and that I will try to do. Beyond this reason, it gives us a way of reunion of the functions of the human spirit and, in our case, of religion with science and philosophy. They belong together, but they are separated because of the situation of man's estrangement from his true being.

Science and Religion

In the first consideration I want to speak about science and religion. The term *science* shall not be restricted to natural sciences, but shall include every methodologically disciplined scholarly research, for instance, psychology, sociology, and history. Philosophy shall not be treated as a particular science beside others. It is a pity—but we cannot help it that we have philosophical departments—that we have a particular religious section of our culture. But philosophy should be embodied in every department, and religion should be embodied in every section of culture and in every moment of life. But this is not the way reality is. We have disciplines that go their way without caring for their mother's womb, namely philosophy. And we have daily life that goes its way without caring for the ultimate meaning of life. That this is so is an expression of what I call man's estrangement from his true being. Philosophy, therefore, shall be treated as the cognitive eros toward the whole. *Eros,* the Greek word for the love towards the good and the true and the beautiful, was developed fundamentally and grandiosely I would say in Plato. And this meaning of philosophy underlies everything I want to say here both about science and about philosophy in their relation to religion. And I repeat, philosophy is the cognitive eros towards the whole. There is also the aesthetic eros, which is satisfied in the arts. There is the personal eros, which is fulfilled in the development of personality. And there is the community eros, which is fulfilled in community life. In all of them we have the human mind or the human spirit (as I prefer to say) driving towards the whole, towards fulfillment not in isolation, but in unity with the whole. And in reality, if you look carefully, the whole is effective in all its parts. And the philosophical eros reaches into all particulars of life and of culture.

Theology and Science

This leads to questions about the relation of philosophy to science and to the place of the scientist in the whole of human existence, especially in our present situation. The great problem of the past is almost obsolete today, namely, that about the relation of theological and scientific statements. I believe that this problem has been solved. And if we know what is going on today in the most advanced philosophy and theology, then it is easy to see that the conflicts—of which all of us still have scars in the depths of our souls—namely, the conflicts between Galileo and the church, the struggle against the Newtonian universe by the church, the struggle against the Darwinistic interpretation of the development of life on earth are very deep in the intellectual life of Western man. And there is always a hesitation even at a distance when one makes a statement as I just did, that this conflict—the causes of this conflict—are overcome and that this conflict therefore has become obsolete. It is not actual any longer.

Here, for instance in philosophy, the language analysis that is done from philosophy and the interpretation of religious symbols, or of the religious language that is thoroughly symbolic from the theological side, has shown that the conflicts can be overcome. One notes that scientific language is predominantly calculating and detached and that religious language is predominantly existential or involved. (These words mean the same here.) And it is very satisfying for me to state how in the recent schools of analytic philosophy an awareness of this situation has appeared. From this follows that all religious statements are analogous or symbolic. Catholic *analogia* theology always has called it ''analogous'' and has spoken of *anaogia entis,* the analogy of being, with which we alone can speak of God. I prefer, for certain reasons, the term *symbolic.* And all religious statements are distorted and become idolactric—they serve idols of our imagination—if they are taken literally. One can more directly say that these two types of statements belong to different dimensions. The dimension of finite interrelations, that is science; and the dimension of the meaning of being or of infinite concern, that is religion. And speaking in the one dimension is different from speaking in the other dimension. Of course, this can be forgotten from both sides, and there are many discussions going on, on campuses especially, in which it is forgotten.

Symbolic and Literal Statements

Theology, for instance, can take on ecclesiastical or biblical authority statements about things and events that are, according to the theologian, religiously authorized. They have the authority of ultimate concern behind them. And then physical, biological, psychological, or historical statements are taken as authoritatively verified statements about things in physics, in the sciences of life, in history, or in psychology. For instance, when you take symbols as "creation" or as "consummation," the great symbols of the Christian drama of salvation, concerning the beginning and the end of the world, and then calculate that the creation has happened six thousand years ago as fundamentalists say, or five billion years ago as the preceding Pope has said, then you confuse the dimensions. The symbol of creation has nothing to do with the calculation of the period of construction or extension of the physical bodies. Or if you take other myths literally, then they become superstition. They lose their power, their meaning, their power greater than any scientific statement. They open up dimensions of life that no scientific statement can, but they are something else. And if you bring them down to the level of scientific statements they become superstitious and have to be rejected by science, or, taken as suppositives that might be rejected very soon.

The same is true of the astronomic views of the biblical writer that are in the line of the whole ancient world and the Middle Ages. Even by the greatest fundamentalists, these are not maintained you ask them whether they reject the astronomy of Copernicus and Galileo. They then become silent. Or, if some miracle stories that are expressions of the healing power of Jesus, the power of God over everything in reality, are taken literally—with a very poor and distorted concept of miracle (miracle is that which produces astonishment because in it the dimension of ultimate meaning is revealed)—and become photographically open events (which a *Times* photographer could have taken), then we are in the realm of absurdity and superstition.

The same is true of biological statements about man, and psychological statements about human nature. In all these cases science has to reject any such claim if it lies in the realm of vertifiable statements about facts and the relations of facts. And this is also true of historical statements. Historical research has the same strict and disciplined rules of dealing with sources as natural sciences have with experiments, and they must be taken as seriously as the other. Every historical statement has lower or higher probability, but it never has certainty. On the other hand, science should not interfere in the world of religious symbols and deny religion because many religious people take symbols literally, and make them superstitious, and put them into conflict with scientific results or processes. What is symbolic and therefore on a quite different dimension of language should not try to become literal and then interfere with the scientific world. There is an interesting phenomenon with some of my antitheological colleagues. I criticize them because they do that trick: they attack some of these things that I just have rejected, some of these superstitious elements in primitive theology or primitive religious symbolism. And then I say, yes, but I do not attack your natural science on the basis of pre-Copernican ideas about the stars, or even earlier ideas by primitives about the tides. But I would attack you (if I were a scientist) on the latest results that happened yesterday at the University of California in the scientific laboratories. I do not go back five hundred years in order to attack you. But with theology this is always being done. One attacks the theological primitivism, or better, mostly the religious pretheological primitivism. I have nothing against this. The human beings who live in symbols shall live in symbols. Only if they claim that these symbols have to be taken literally do I have much against them. And if then my critical colleagues attack me on the basis that this is Christianity, then I get angry (which not often happens). This you should not do in your own discussions. You should not say, here are the doctrines of Bible and church; now science has this and that. Of course science does not have a tripartite world: hell down, earth in the middle, and then heaven up where the stars are in the nearness of God. This is not our worldview. And the fact that it is biblical does not make it truer. It belongs to a world view of a much earlier period of our inquiry into the structure of reality. It is beautiful to be used in symbols, as we use continuously "sunset" and "sunrise," but this does not bring us back to the pre-Copernican idea that the sun really runs around the earth.

Now, this is the situation. There is no religious statement that can contradict a scientific statement if religion is understood in its fundamental sense as ultimate concern and science is understood as the inquiry into the finite facts and their relations. But of course, there are always scientists and theologians—and I must add often more theological laymen who are not theologians but who have taken over the theology of fifty to one hundred years ago—who are often even more guilty of what I call the confusion of dimensions. That is the real basis for the conflict: the confusion of dimensions, the dimension of the ultimate with its language and the dimension of the finite interrelations with scientific language.

But there remains still the question of the basic attitudes and their contrast. And this is deeper today and more important and not really obsolete: the question of the attitude of the scientist in relation to the attitude of the theologian. The scientist is detached, calculating, trying to formulate it in mathematical terms, counting on many possible errors in observation, cautious in making statements, only admitting preliminary assertions, separating his scientific work from the other concerns of life, from those concerns in which emotion and will, moral tradition, and religious or political loyalty are included. And then, the other type, the religious man, is living in the tradition of a particular set of symbols in which he moves as the expressions of the meaning of life for him, resisting doubt, accepting biblical or ecclesiastical authority, giving unconditional loyalty to the manifestation of the holy in his particular religious tradition. This seems to be the situation from the point of view of the inner attitude of these types of human beings. But is this the real situation? Is this the true reflection of what is and therefore is unavoidable? The scientist claims not. I have heard him speak in many conferences. When the theologians speak, the scientist says, "I don't understand." And that is not an understanding in the sense that the theologian—for instance *this* theologian, certainly—would say that he does not understand the mathematical formulas for atoms. It is another kind of understanding. It is a strangeness to the attitude and the language of religion. Hence the religious man speaks of the atheistic scientists—for which he has no justification at all, even if these scientists behave as if they were atheists; they have their ultimate concern just as much as a religious man, and if atheism means this, then they are often much less atheistic than the religious man. Their ultimate concern has many traditional formulas, but very little life. And I know so-called atheistic scientists who have an ultimate concern that is very much alive. Now is this the situation?

An exact analysis shows that this is not the case. First, the thinking religious man and the theologian know that faith is not a restful certainty on the ground of which one can sleep, but faith is only certain in the experience that we belong to something that has unconditional meaning. Faith is not certain in the particular expressions that are objects of courage and risk. It is a matter of courage and risk that we are Christians in a world in which there is non-Christian reality. And this means the possibility of failure and the necessity of getting the courage to say yes again and again, and, therefore, it is subject to doubt. I have formulated it the following way: faith embraces itself and the doubt about itself. And that is the inner tension of faith that makes it alive. Any other kind of faith is belief that is accepted on the basis of tradition, authority, convention, or for other reasons that have nothing to do with faith. The scientist has his own ultimate concern, not only as a human being, but also as a scientist. First, there is his belief in scientific honesty, for which a large number of scientists would be willing to become martyrs, just as the Christians and other religions and quasi-religions have become. He also has often to believe in the ultimate significance of science over and against all other life. But if he has this, he has faith; but it is distorted faith. I would call it with the stronger word, a *demonized* faith, making something relative and finite absolute, just as Communism is demonized socialism, making the faith in social transformation into an ultimate concern and therfore demonic, destructive. And the same is true of nationalism, making the justified affirmation of one's nation into the ultimate, which then becomes Fascism and the Fascist movement, which we have also in this country today. The idolatry of scientism is something that is very important, but we must go beyond this and ask now the second problem in the philosophy and the sciences, where we may solve this problem of scientism to a certain extent.

The first step in relating religion and the sciences has been done. The boundary line has been drawn, and that is what I wanted to do first. This is extremely important in view of the history of the conflicts from Galileo to Darwin and Freud. It is still important in theology. The church authorities as well as Christian laity resist, for instance, historical research into the biblical books, resist what happens in this research, namely, the discovery of the mixture of historical, legendary, and mythical elements in these books. It is very dangerous if ministers hide the scientific results of the two-hundred-year-old research into the biblical books, and then people by chance encounter books concerning these researches and are shocked because they feel it undermines their faith. I had this experience when Edmund Reardon in the *New Yorker* wrote the story about the Dead Sea Scrolls, and wrote this story in such a way that it seemed as if these scrolls undercut the originality of Christianity. We have known for two hundred years the relationship of John the Baptist to these sects of the Dead Sea. We know that they had many ideas that appear in our biblical records. But these people, in some way kept unaware of this—I wouldn't use the sharp word *betrayed,* but kept unaware like children from what has happened in scientific research into the biblical books—discovered these things and then they had the feeling, "Now this undermines everything I had believed." For two hundred years theologians knew this, and it has not undercut because it cannot undercut, as no scientific statement can undercut the faith and the religious meaning of the biblical message.

But there is also the other side. These historical scholars should not derive from their work negative or even positive judgments about the validity of the Christian message. History never can do this. History can only show how this has happened. But the attitude towards it is a matter of our being grasped by an ultimate concern about these things. It is a matter of personal decision. But this is not all that can be said. The scientists with whom I was friends at Harvard University indicated that our relationship had to be much more intimate. When I asked them about this, they said to me again and again that they see in their own work a religious dimension. And they thought this true not only of actual scientists, but also of the psychologists and the physicians with whom I had a continuous collaboration. In these places—as well as before in New York—and in many places where I was asked to speak and to discuss the problems of the medical understanding of reality in relation to religious problems, these scientists did their work with what I called before philosophical eros, and with a full consciousness of their own philosophical presuppositions. They knew that they never could escape, however they tried, the philosophical mother's womb. They are always tied to it, and there are always philosophical elements in what they do and how they do it. The sciences are born out of philosophy, which asks the question of the universe, the whole of being, of simple being itself. And philosophy found the same universal characteristics of being almost everywhere, however they were differently expressed. For instance, the categories of time, space, causality, the polarities of form and matter, freedom and necessity, the relation of potentiality and actuality, of subject and object of knowledge, of logical and linguistic structure, of being and ought to be, different dimensions of reality and their relations, concepts like nature, life, history, person, mind—all this is philosophy. It can also be considered scientifically, but the background is philosophy. And this is what makes the philosophical substance in every scientific research. You can have two attitudes to it. You can repress it and go on your way as a scientific technician. Or you can be aware of it and ask about the meaning of your interpretation about the element of universal truth in it, and the significance of it for human existence, besides the technical applicability.

No scientific inquiry is possible without the use of all these concepts I have just mentioned, openly or hiddenly. I just yesterday had a conference in which a friend of mine with great refinement showed how in the figures of logical calculus and symbolic logic, the old metaphysical problem of potentiality and actuality, of subject and object and so on return, but hidden, covered. People do not dare to express them. This element is effective in the scientific procedures that, of course, conversely contribute to the vision of the whole, tentative solution that they give to the vision of whole. Most of the creative scientists in the past and many in the present were driven in their work by the eros towards the universal in their particular fields. They were more than scientific technicians. They were more also than solvers of logical riddles.

Now what of the whole? I must say a few words about this. The eros, the love for the whole, for the cosmos, for the universe, is not directed toward the sum total of all particulars. Such a sum total does not exist because in the moment in which it is even imagined, it is already changed. But what is meant with the term of the *whole* is the underlying unity within the infinite diversity and change. Philosophy, in asking this question, was driven by the experience that what seems to be real proved to be not real. And so the question arose for a more real formulation, more adequate, more in accordance with what happens and can be foreseen than the ordinary look at reality. And they were driven step by step to deeper and deeper levels of reality. Finally—or even in the every beginning of philosophy—they asked the question of the really real or ultimately real, of ultimate reality, that which underlies and transcends everything that seems to be real. But everything here (as with you, as what happens in your minds and souls and your bodies in this very moment) is oscillating between being and no more being or not yet being. And so philosophy asks the question of that which has ultimate reality.

Thus question of ultimate reality arose with the beginning of philosophy. And in it the ground of both the unity and the manifoldness of the whole was seen. So the eros of the whole became the passionate desire to find cognitively the ultimately real, as the artist tried to find aesthetically or artistically the ultimately real, the true real itself. And even in logical analysis, seemingly so far removed from this, a hidden image of the real itself is present. I spoke with many philosophers about this, and last time with professor Heidegger in Freiburg, in Germany. And he was completely in agreement with the impossibility I suggested: to escape into logical analysis without having some image of the relationship of the logical structure of the human mind to reality as a whole. This eros and passion for ultimate reality has led to contradictory answers. But in the eros for it, all philosophers, and not only those of the West—perhaps even more, those of the East—are united. The answers divide them into different philosophical schools. Their eros, and that towards which this eros is directed, the inner power of reality itself, unites all true philosophers. And insofar as the philosophical element is effective in all sciences, this eros is also effective in the philosophers.

Philosophy and Religion

And now let me come to a third and last consideration: philosophy and religion. The search for the unity of the existing and for ultimate reality is an element in the religious concern as it is in the philosophical. The cognitive eros, as I called the philosophical eros, is never missing in religion. The only difference is that the religious concern is more embracing. It will not only recognize ultimate reality, it will reunite with ultimate reality. And it will shape him who is driven by this eros and the world in which he lives according to the reality that is discovered. This leads to the assertion of a point of identity between philosophy and—by implication of all sciences—and religion: the desire to unite cognitively with ultimate reality in traditional symbols. This would be expressed, "the longing of the human soul to know God." This is not a god in the sense of the second concept of religion, but of the first concept, ultimate concern about the ultimately real. This is understandable out of the birth story of philosophy. The background of philosophy is mythology. In mythology the experience of ultimate reality is expressed in the powerful symbols that underlie all great cultures of mankind. They all are built on the basis of fundamental mythological symbols. But these symbols of the myth combine an aesthetic and a cognitive element. They are beyond poetry and science. They unite both of them. We can see this in the Old Greek mythology, and we can see how slowly these two elements separate. The early transition mythology from Greek mythology to Greek philosophy are the *theogonies* and the *cosmogonies,* the birth stories of the gods and of the world as we find it in the old Greek tradition. The conceptual element becomes independent of its unity with the poetic. And the mythological symbols are transformed on the one side in myth and poetry, as in Homer where they already start to become myths, and they are transformed into concepts in the early Greek philosophers. We call today this process "demythologization," the dissolution of the myth into its two elements, the poetic and scientific elements. But behind these two elements there is the intuition of ultimate reality that is now taken over by the philosophers, and the poets, and artists. These philosophical concepts, which are in this way based on a religious background, now are conversely used by theology in order to interpret religious symbols in a culture that has both experiences, the mythological and the demythologizing. This is the way in which the Christian dogma was created, with symbols coming from the Old Testament partly and partly from the other surrounding religions that were already largely demythologized—the prophets did the work of demythologizing in the Old Testament—and then these Greek concepts were used in order to create the Christian dogma, *dogma* meaning those doctrines that distinguish Christianity from the other schools of religion. Conflicts between theology and philosophy are based on a lack of distinguishing the elements in both the mythological background and the religious substance in the philosophical concepts, and on the other hand the philosophical concepts in expressing the religious substance through the *logos*. Theology is logos, that means the "word" and the "concept." In Greek it means both reason and language. Genuine conflicts are possible only if the religious substance in a particular philosophy contradicts the religious substance in a particular theology. Certainly the Dionysian philosophy of Nietzsche in our time, and the moralistic Calvinism coming from the Old Testament contradict, but this is not a contradiction between the philosopher Nietzsche and the theologian Calvin. This is a contradiction between two different different religious substances, the old Testament in Calvin's case, the Dionysian Greek in the case of Friedrich Nietzsche. All the conceptualizations of a particular philosophical school contradict the conceptualization used in a particular theology. In the whole Middle Ages we have the struggle of the great scholastic schools, the one based on Plato, the other based on Aristotle. This is not the conflict between philosophy and theology. And therefore such conflicts again are based on a failure to understand of the true nature of theological concepts and philosophical concepts.

Now, let me slowly come to a conclusion. I believe that one interest you have has not been satisfied, namely, the interest in the role of the scientist and of science at all in our present culture. And I will tell you a few things about this, because some of you will become scientists, many of you will be educated in the natural sciences and biological sciences, sciences of life. And what I want to do is to show you one profound problem that is symbolized in Christian myth, in the myth of the paradise, namely the temptation of Adam and Eve to eat from the tree of knowledge. Knowledge of what? In the traditional translation it is knowledge of good and evil. In the original Hebrew it means the good and evil powers in nature in order to be able to control them. Man wants to have knowledge. But you cannot have it without awakening from what I like to call "the dreaming innocence" in which we are created. And so man had to decide not to remain in the paradise of dreaming innocence—this of course is a psychological term, taken from early childhood—and the reality of a full life in which knowing starts. And it starts very early. A child very, very early awakens out of dreaming innocence, both out of dream and out of innocence as every parent knows.

Now, this is the general destiny of mankind. And the myth of the paradise is so great because it shows the alternative of human existence: the alternative either to stay in dreaming innocence or to know the power and pay the price, namely, to leave paradise. This is a problem that is more actual today than ever before. Every knowledge includes spiritual dangers. Every transition from potentiality of knowledge, which man has by nature, and actualizing it in time and space, is a dangerous thing. It is always dangerous spiritually.

This leads to a problem that we have today, the problem of the responsibility of the scientist for these dangerous consequences. The problem is as old as scholarly thought and was for a millennium a source of the conflict between the priestly guardians of the holy and the prophetic or philosophical critics of the traditional beliefs. Even if the sociological, political, and economic causes of such conflicts are taken into account, there is a genuine tragic element in it. This is a tragedy of all mankind in which we all live, namely, we are driven to go to knowledge and we are barred.

The prohibition of God is a warning that is in us, namely, the danger of the consequences. The priest is aware of the catastrophic consequences that criticism of holy traditions can have on the spirit of many people, but neither the prophet nor the philosopher can resign his vocation to fight for justice and truth even if sacred beliefs must be destroyed, as the prophets did and the philosophers did. This is the earliest example of the conflict, which I can call the conflict between the safety of the given and the risk of the new. The dangers connected with present scientific discoveries do not refer to the salvation of souls but the very existence of mankind. But the problem and the tragic implications are exactly the same. The tragic consequences of the discovery and expression of truth are no reason for giving up the attempt to discover and to express truth. The danger for the soul of the believer should not stop the prophet or the reformer or the philosopher from pronouncing truth. And considering the danger of destructive consequences of scientific discoveries—and here I want to point to the social scientists and psychologists where the danger is perhaps deeper and even more tragic in many cases than the natural sciences—they should not stop the expression of truth. It is bad to avoid tragedy if the price is to avoid truth. Man cannot be kept in the state of dreaming innocence. Of course, what we can do is to try healing power in the application of what we can do: healing power for disturbed minds, for anxiety, for the use of scientific power for self-destruction. The problem of truth remains as a problem where the results cannot protect against going ahead, even if the results are tragic. Again, I should state a restriction, of course, so that you do not misunderstand me. You can not use tools for finding truths that are poisonous for souls or bodies. You can perhaps learn something from experiments as the Nazis did them on living human beings, but this learning is the creation of the satanic distortion of the problem of truth. But truth itself must be pursued even if tragedy follows.

Now this brings me to an end. And I sum up saying, the period of conflict between religion, science, and philosophy is in principle over, although there are still individuals who are back in older periods of thought. We are living in the period of tolerance. It is never satisfactory because it admits, but it does not unite. Tolerance can have in itself, as a result, a strict consciousness if it is not more than tolerance. And so we always strive for a period of reunion, and in this case, of cooperation, and this is a possible thing today. It has started in many places, and I want to express my hope that it may become a reality in ever-increasing power.

PART V

The Symbols and Ambiguities of Technical Society

CHAPTER 15

Science and the Contemporary World in the View of a Theologian

The word *a* before theologian in the title of my paper implies that there is a typical theologian who, by the very fact that he is a theologian, gives a more or less predetermined answer to the question of the relation of religion and science. In this sense I am neither typical nor even unambiguously a theologian. I am a Protestant theologian who stands on the boundary line between religion and culture, both theology and philosophy, between religious symbol and scientific method. And I don't feel that this boundary line situation is an uncomfortable one. On the contrary, I believe that it is the position from which the truth about the interrelation of both sides of the boundary line is best discovered.

To be a theologian means to see the world from the point of view of what concerns man ultimately, namely the meaning of *his* existence and of that of his world. From this point of view the theologian asks: What is the most adequate answer to this question, what are the most expressive symbols for this answer, and how are they related to the symbols that are alive in the tradition from which he comes? On this basis then, the theologian tries to relate his answers and his symbols to the answers and their conceptual expressions that philosophy and science have given to the question of the structures and laws of the universe.

Religion and Science in the Present World

Religion, Science, and the Confusion of Dimensions

On the basis of this understanding of the task of a theologian, I venture to give my first answer to the problem: "Religion and Science in the Present World." I believe that the inherited mutual suspicion between religion and science has been overcome in the most advanced representatives of both functions of man's spirit. This does not exclude that much suspicion has remained, and that some of it is justified in view of the attitudes of orthodox theologians and philosophically dogmatic scientists. The reason why the mutual suspicion has been removed to a large degree is the fact that both sides have learned to distinguish the dimension of the religious from that of the scientific. While religion is the reaction of man to experiences of the holy, experiences in which he is grasped by an ultimate concern, science is the cognitive act in which man tries to analyze and describe the structures and interrelations of finite objects. If these dimensions are confused, religion, in the name of an ultimate, makes statements about facts, the knowledge of which is the proper function of scientific (and historical) investigation, and conflicts are unavoidable. From the side of science, the confusion of dimensions leads to statements that, in the name of the scientific method, give expression to the metaphysics and with it to the hidden theology of the scientist. Creative relationship and cooperation between religion and science is only possible if, first of all, such confusion is overcome and the difference of the dimensions is acknowledged.

The Ambiguity
of Life Manifest in Science

If this is done, a theological evaluation of science within the whole of man's existence is possible. Science is a part of the processes of life and of human life particularly. As such it shares the ambiguities of all life, a fact that came out clearly in the preceding discussions, and frequently through the mouths of the scientists themselves.[1]

Life, under all its dimensions, is both self-productive and self-destructive in every particular process. In man's cultural functions—in those that receive reality in cognitive perception and artistic intuition and those that transform reality through technical, personal, and communal activities—life produces itself, creating something new above the naturally encountered world. Science, in alliance with technical production, has created a realm of tools and products that has gained a kind of independence and has partly transformed its own creator, man. The glory of this process is before

---

[1]This lecture was delivered in the context of a "Conference on Science in International Education and Cultural Affairs," sponsored by the Department of State and the National Science Foundation, at the Massachusetts Institute of Technology in Cambridge, Massachusetts, on 16-17 December 1960.

everybody's eyes. It has given to man an incredible amount of power over nature and society. It is not wrong to consider it as a continuation of the originating creation through man. It has liberated him from the slavery to mechanical functions and has broken through the limits of the biological time and the biological space to a surprising degree. At the same time, science, supported by technology, has opened up the macro and micro realms of being with the knowing subject fulfilling man's eros towards the knowable and his search for truth in an astonishing way.

But the other side has become equally manifest. For the first time in history, the alliance of science and technology has produced tools of complete biological destruction, not only of historical mankind, but of all living beings on earth. This has become a possibility, and since possibility is temptation, it may become reality. Beyond this immediate external threat, a more longtime spiritual danger has resulted from the alliance of science and technology: It has caused a perversion of means and ends. It enabled man to produce tools without limits and to make this production into an end itself. In this way it suppressed the question of an end, of the meaning not only of the process of production and consumption (under the control of advertisement), but of life as such. The feeling of emptiness and meaninglessness in innumerable people is a result of this perversion.

And science itself, even without its alliance with technology, had the effect of directing the cognitive eros exclusively towards the finite objects and their interrelations. The question of the "qualitatively infinite," the ultimate in being and meaning that had aroused people in millennia of Western history was pushed into the corner of subjective feelings. The eros towards the true and the good itself was swallowed by the eros towards its finite manifestations. And this increased the experience of meaninglessness that simultaneously was produced by the state of Western industrial and business society.

Risk and Freedom in Science

This statement of a boundary-line theologian about the ambiguity of science can be supplemented by an even more critical statement about the ambiguities of religion—and beyond this of every function of the human spirit. But this would trespass the scope of my paper. Only one thing I want to add at this point. Since the ambiguities of science are expressions of the ambiguity of life as a whole, science should not be restricted even if it can become dangerous. This it shares with all functions of life, and perhaps above all with religion. *Any* restriction of science, even the smallest one, would destroy it altogether, for the forbidden point might, if inquired into, have changed the whole scientific interpretation of a subject matter. As a theologian I may add that we have exactly the same situation in historical research. One religious prohibition against the methodological inquiry in the biblical literature would destroy not only the scientific honesty of this particular inquiry; it would also undercut the foundation of our understanding of human history universally. Since "the truth is one," every interference in the search for it is an attempt to prohibit truth altogether.

This, however, means that mankind must take upon itself the risk of being destroyed by the consequences of its search for truth. It can try to overcome the temptation of infinite possibilities of action. Everybody is called to fight against this temptation. But there is no guarantee that mankind will succeed. It might be destroyed, physically or spiritually. Religion does not give a guarantee against it. For man is free to act against himself. And even if he ever reached a centralized humanity, the dangers of his eating from the tree of knowledge of the good and evil powers of nature would not have been removed. Man is a risk; and in spite of all the greatness this risk has brought about, it might finally fail: Historical man may come to an end by historical man!

Religion does not guarantee the conquest of this danger—the physical as well as the spiritual. But religion may receive better weapons than it has now to resist this danger. It may collaborate with science to create symbols of ultimate reality that are able to speak to the scientifically transformed mind of our contemporaries. This at least is the task of a theology that dares to listen to the concrete reality of our time.

The problem we have discussed is not only important for America and the Western world, but for the whole world, including the primitive cultures of Africa as well as the high cultures of Asia. It is a telluric problem concerning all mankind. In the light of this analysis I venture to say to this group of scientists and officials: Whatever we do in the context of our worldwide involvements, we should not do with the idea that it is good for America, but with the idea that it is good for man and the meaning of his existence. Only then will it be good for this country too!

CHAPTER 16

The Technical City as Symbol[1]

Thing and Symbol

Every human artifact is simultaneously *thing* and *symbol*. As thing it serves a purpose and is determined by it. As symbol it expresses a being and is determined by this. Of every human artifact it can be asked what purpose it serves, what means it uses. But it can also be asked: What being is being expressed in it; what symbol does it represent? The answer to the question regarding the "technical city" as a thing is the development of all that which the word signifies, for example, the obvious display that is presented at an exhibition. Here the thing content [*Sachgehalt*] of the "technical city" is exhaustively represented. Not so the symbol content [*Symbolgehalt*] that simultaneously lies within. It cannot be outwardly presented; it cannot be empirically perceived. And yet it can be seen in the introspection in which we grasp our *human* being—our spiritual and our social being. In this way it can become clear how our being, our common human being and our particular, historical being, expresses itself in the "technical city" as a thing. It can become clear the extent to which the technical city is a symbol for the condition of our souls, for our feeling for life, for our will to be creative. We want to pose this question of the symbolic element in the technical city here in the conviction that, if answers to it should be forthcoming, they also would not be entirely insignificant for the empirical consideration. Above all, however, the question will be discussed with the conviction that through it the decisive human question can be pressed: the question of meaning.

---

[1]Translated by John C. Modschiedler, College of DuPage.

The Uncanniness of Existence and of Things

Every human being can discern within his soul a feeling in relation to the world that one might call a "feeling of uncanniness" [*Unheimlichen*]. It is not as though we were continually encountering uncanny things. The so-called uncanny things are merely the changing symbols of a basic sense of uncanniness that humankind feels in relation to existence itself. Our existence, this existence that we in fact *are,* is what is characteristically uncanny for us. Uncanny, i.e., not homelike, not familiar, foreign and threatening is our situation in the world as such, even if there are no particular threats and feelings of uncanniness present. Indeed, exactly then, for if we are threatened by something specific, we defend ourselves, and the act of self-defense already takes a part of its uncanniness away from the thing. When, however, we cannot defend ourselves because nothing is there that tangibly opposes us, that is where uncanniness is in power.

In order to escape this uncanniness, the human being seeks to make himself at home in existence. He tries to take what is strange, what is threatening, away from existence. An excellent symbol of this intention is the house (including its forerunners, the cave and the tent). The house has its materially intrinsic value, its purpose that it must serve and according to which it is shaped and modified. But at the same time it has a symbolic value. In a house a part of existence is made homelike, is brought into the realm of familiarity. The uncanniness of infinite space, which wants to swallow us up, is held at a distance by the bounded space that we can fill with our existence. And at the same time, the uncanniness of the totally bounded—of the cave, the labyrinth—the experience of constrictedness (with which anxiety is connected), is partially overcome in the union with infinite space by means of the window, the balcony, the tower, the courtyard, and the garden. Between the uncanniness of the unbounded and the totally bounded lies "the coziness of the house," a coziness that, depending upon the awareness of life of a particular time and culture, takes its comfort from a nearness to the one pole or the other. The modern house, e.g., with its transformation of the wall into a window, with its reciprocal permeation of infinite space and bounded space, with its base raised above the level of the earth, is a symbol of the modern awareness of life that thrusts into the infinite, and its fear of the confinement of the cave.

The house is the cell of the city, and the city, like the house, is the symbol of primal humanity's flight from uncanniness. The Lower Saxonian farmer who lives in isolation defies the uncanniness of the wide open spaces that surround him and confine him to loneliness by the familiarity of his house: a symbol and at the same time a primal factor in his own quiet individuality. The city dweller of the Middle Ages crowded himself into the constrictedness of the city in order to escape the uncanniness of wide open spaces. Only in the towers that stretched upward did the city dweller break through the constriction, but the direction was up, toward the other-worldly, not into the breadth of existence. We experience the close familiarity of the cities, but at the same time the uncanniness of their confinement, the cavernous, subterranean quality of their streets. (One thinks of Meyrink's portrayals of the Jewish ghetto in Prague.) The modern city is broad and bright. The brightly lighted boulevards and squares of our great cities are symbols of an overcoming of confinement without allowing the unrestrictedness of wide open spaces to enter in. The typical suburb has neither the narrowness nor the breadth of the inner city, and because of the uncanniness of its "monotony," which also estranges, it drives people back into the center of the city.

Just as house and city are the means of adapting ourselves to human existence, so also is all technology an overcoming of the uncanniness of things. Even perception, the ordering of things according to laws and relationships, is a restraint upon their demonic depth, their incomprehensibility, their strangeness, their threatening character. Perception of the world is always also becoming at home in the world, and the history of science is also a history of the victory over uncanniness. This victory only comes to its fulfillment, however, in technology. It is the great experiment that verifies science and that at the same time places it in the service of some goal or purpose. A thing that is fully determined by its utility has also become fully transparent; it conceals no threatening depths, no more shocking, unexpected reality. It is subject to the laws upon whose perception it is dependent; it is calculable in every one of its parts and aspects.

In the union of technology and science, humankind has subjugated the earth, has made the whole earth into a house for itself, as it were, just as the utopians at the time of the Renaissance predicted. The earth as the home of humankind, as the place that humankind has appropriated, which has become thoroughly familiar, deprived of its uncanniness—this was the consequence that the human being of the Renaissance derived from the revolution in astronomy. The earth had become a star just like all the others. The divine is no closer to the stars than it is to the earthly sphere, as the Greeks and the Middle Ages had still believed. Human beings need not yearn for the stars. They themselves live on such a star and must shape it into a home for themselves within the infinite universe. The means for accomplishing this is the technical "magic" of which human beings are capable because they stand at the point of intersection of all the spheres of existence. This is what the philosophy of the Renaissance demands, and this is what the technological age seeks to fulfill. However, among all its creations, the "technical city" is its most powerful symbol. It unites the thought of the domination of being with that of making a home within being. In the technical city certain effects come into immediate concentrated view that encompass the entire earth: the earth as the "home of humankind," the mastery of all the powers of being, the victory over the uncanny, the strange, the threatening character of human existence.

It is not necessary to point this out in the individual structures that are the products of the technical city. Each one represents humankind's appropriation of being to its use in enormous profusion. Each represents a freeing of humankind from the enormous burdens of mechanical labor. Each is a symbol of the de-demonizing of the world. Each is a creation of a new, often wonderful, form of being. The technical house, the technical city, the earth dominated by the technical city and made into a home for humankind: this is the symbol of our age, the age of the fulfillment of the technical utopia, the age of humankind's making a home of the earth and of the appropriation and transformation of the earth by human beings.

Precisely thereby, however, has the technical city become the symbol for the uncertainty that hangs over our age, over the fulfillment of the technical utopia. For with the technical city there arises a new threat, a new uncanniness that can no longer be banished by knowledge and technology; on the contrary, it is called forth itself by these. The stronger and more complicated the technical structures are, the more they take on a life of their own, independent of human beings, the more difficult it becomes to control them, the more threatening they become, especially for those who know and understand them best. As the technical structures develop an independent existence, a new element of uncanniness emerges in the midst of what is most well known. And this uncanny shadow of technology will grow to the same extent that the whole earth becomes the "technical city" and the technical house. Who can still control it?

And at the same time a characteristic contradiction arises: the technical thing has indeed lost its original uncanniness as a thing, but despite this it has not really become familiar. The technical house, the technical city remain strange. The thing has had its own life taken from it, and therefore no eros can unite it with our own life. It has become lifeless, and it induces lifelessness in us. The soil, the bond with the living earth, is taken away. Hewn or artificial stone separates us from it. Reinforced concrete buildings separate us more than loam, wood, and bricks from the cosmic flow. Water is in pipes; fire is confined to wires. Animals are excluded or else they are deprived of their vital powers. In the technical context, trees and plants are arranged to serve the rational objective of "relaxation." Strangeness remains despite all efforts to appropriate things for our own use, and it reaches a degree of insurmountableness in the metropolis, where it rules everything. Along with the strangeness of the technologized world of things, however, a new uncanniness arises, a kind of dread of the lifeless world, which serves us but which cannot speak as life speaks to life. And there comes a moment when (mostly in false Romanticism, at times in genuine despair) we would like to plunge into all the uncanniness of bygone eras, in order to escape the horror of the strangeness that arises out of the subjugated world of things.

The New Uncanniness of the Technical City

Or, we ourselves are being deprived of our vitality, deadened by our being in the service of that which we ourselves have brought to lifelessness. This applies to us all, but most of all to those who are most deeply involved in the service of the technical city, the technical house "earth," who have nothing to make up for the powers of life of which they have been deprived, who do indeed have dominion over things, but nevertheless as ones who are themselves ruled over, stunted in their vital and spiritual life: the proletariat. And this gives rise to a new threat, the threat of an emptied humanity condemned to be servants of the servant of humankind. And this threat will become even more menacing because it takes its power from the insecurity, the impoverishment, the disintegration of the proletarians and their fear of life, which constantly nourishes itself on all this. (The basis for this fear is the demonic power of an economic process that has long since gotten out of hand.) Here also there arises from the very foundation of the "technical city" a new shadow of uncanniness that raises doubts about its luster and its durability.

Behind these threats, however, there remains at the deepest level the question of the essential meaning of technical dominion itself, of the meaning of the "well-furnished house of the earth." We do not dwell in order to dwell, rather we dwell in order to live. When, however, life, our whole life, is spent in the service of dwelling, in service to the technical city, then what is the purpose of this life? The technical city gives no answer to this question, but it *poses* this question. And if "The Technical City" exhibition,[2] and with it the centennial celebration of the Technical Institute, would pose this question to many people, then it would truly have become a symbol in which we would have seen ourselves in the power and in the uncertainty of our being.

---

[2]Translator's note: This was an exhibition in connection with the Dresden Technical Institute centennial of 1928.

CHAPTER 17

Has Man's Conquest of Space Increased or Diminished His Stature?[1]

The subject under discussion has two sides: the one is the effect of space exploration on man as such, and the other is its effect on man's view of himself; the first requires more a report about man's condition, the second more a valuation of man's stature in consequence of the space exploration. But this distinction cannot be maintained when one goes into the concrete problems that have arisen as an effect of space research and space travel. A decisive part of man's condition, as it is caused by his penetration into space beyond the gravitation of the earth, is his self-evaluation on the basis of this achievement. On the other hand, its conflicting evaluations are brought out by the contrast of the negative and positive effects of space exploration on the human condition. Therefore I intend to deal with the problems of our subject without any sharp demarcation between the effects of space exploration on the situation of man, and on his view of himself.

The Historical Situation

The present situation is the result of many steps made by Western man since the Renaissance. It would be unrealistic and would prevent an adequate answer if the last step, however important and unique it is, were considered in isolation from the previous steps. Many effects, both on man himself and his view of himself, appeared long ago; and it leads to a distortion of facts and valuations, if contemporaneous writers overemphasize the uniqueness of the present achievement in comparison with what has

[1]Originally published in *The Great Ideas Today 1963*, Robert M. Hutchins and Mortimer J. Adler, eds. (Chicago: Encyclopaedia Britannica, 1963) 49-59, this article also appeared as "The Effects of Space Exploration On Man's Condition and Stature," in *The Future of Religions*, Jerald C. Brauer, ed. (New York: Harper & Row, 1966) 39-51.

been done and thought before in the series of steps that have made the present one possible.

The Renaissance is not the rebirth of the ancient traditions as the term is often misunderstood, but it is the rebirth of Western society in all respects, religious, cultural, and political with the help of the ancient sources of the Mediterranean civilization. In this process the traditions were transformed in many respects, due to the Christian background of the Renaissance. One of the most important transformations is the turn from the Greek contemplative and the medieval self-transcending ideals of life to the active, world-controlling, and world-shaping ideal. This implied a high valuation of technical sciences and the beginning of that fertile interaction between pure and applied sciences that immensely contributed—and is still doing so—to the fast development of both of them. There was little of this interaction in Greece, the late ancient world, and the Middle Ages; it was something new, not a repetition, but a rebirth. One way to express the situation is in three geometrical symbols: the circle for the fulfillment of life within the cosmos and its potentialities—as found in classical Greece; the vertical or the striving of life toward what transcends the cosmos, namely the transcendent One, the ultimate in being and meaning—as found in late antiquity and in the Middle Ages; the horizontal or the trend toward the control and transformation of the cosmos in the service of God or man—as found in the period since the Renaissance, Reformation, and Enlightenment. The "discovery of the horizontal" is the first step in a development in which exploration is the preliminary last step. Both are victories of the horizontal over the circular and the vertical line.

The transition from the vertical to the horizontal line in the determination of the telos, the inner aim of human existence, was greatly helped by the astronomy of the Renaissance and the related "utopian" literature. The Copernican astronomy had thrown the earth out of the center of the universe—the least divine of all places—and elevated it to the dignity of a star amongst other stars. About the same time a highly influential philosopher, Nicholas of Cosa, taught the immanence of the divine within the finite, e.g., in earth and man. This raised the significance of everything in the world by making it an expression of the divine life, and it gave impetus to the expectations of a fulfillment of history on this planet. The "utopian" literature shows visions of a future that unites religious, political, economic, and technical elements. This again raised the importance of technology in relation to the pure sciences far above what it was in Greece and the intermediary periods. Typical for this situation is Leonardo da Vinci, who combined the anticipation of the ideal in his paintings with empirical studies of natural phenomena and with technical experiments—in which, just as today, techniques of war played a great role.

In the seventeenth century the realization of the problems implied in these beginnings of the modern period of Western history increased and found a characteristic expression in Pascal's confrontation of man's smallness and his greatness. He experienced with many of his contemporaries the shock of man's smallness in view of the universe of recent astronomy. At the same time, he experienced in his own work as mathematician and physicist the power of the human mind to penetrate into the calculable structures of nature, his greatness even in the face of the quantitative vastness of the universe. In Pascal many problems of man's present self-interpretation are anticipated. The human predicament in its contradictory character is shown just as we see it today. And he also asked the question that is highly relevant for our problem: What has become, under the control of the horizontal line, of the vertical one, the line toward what transcends the cosmos? He answered with his famous words that contrast the "God of Abraham, Isaac and Jacob" with the "god of the philosophers." He himself was struggling to save the dimension of the ultimate, which transcends the greatness as well as the smallness of man. He found it for himself, but the development followed the horizontal line in the eighteenth-century belief in human progress; in the nineteenth-century belief in universal evolution; in the ideologies supporting the industrial, social, and political revolutions of the three last centuries. There were always theological, mystical, romanticist, and classicist attempts to recover the vertical line or to return to the circular world view of classical Greece. But the drive towards that which lies ahead proved to be stronger than the longing back to a world in which it is more important to look at the eternal essences of the cosmos than to anticipate a future to be created by man.

One of the shocks connected with the removal of man and his earth from the cosmic center was basically theological. Since the biblical literature as well as its interpretation in fifteen hundred years of church history was based on a world view in which the earth was in the center of the universe and human history the ultimate aim of the creation of the earth, and the Christ the center of human history, an urgent question arose: What about the position of man in the providential acting of God; what about the cosmic significance of the Christ in the universe as a whole? Does not the moving of the earth out of the center undercut both the central significance of man and the cosmic significance of the Christ? Is not the whole "drama of salvation" reduced to a series of events, happening on a small planet at a particular time without universal significance?

With these problems, already alive in the Western world, the age of space exploration started.

The Emotional Reactions to Space Exploration

The first reaction to the break through the gravitational field of the earth was naturally astonishment, admiration, pride, increased by the national pride of those who achieved the breakthrough, diminished but not annihilated by the feeling of national humiliation of those who could have achieved it but did not. Yet there was almost no exception to a feeling to astonishment about man's potentialities, hidden up to then, but now revealed: Man is not only able to explore transterrestrial space, he is also able to change the astronomical picture by adding something to what was given to him by nature. Admiration was particularly directed to the theoretical and technical intelligence of those who were responsible for the successful penetration of the earthly sphere, and to the moral courage of those who risked their life in actualizing what was a human potentiality and had now become real. A consequence of this admiration was the status of heroic pioneers given to the astronauts, even to those in the enemy camp, and of bearers of esoteric wisdom unattainable for most human bengs, given to the atomic scientists. The emotional power of these reactions is very strong and not without important sociological effects. They became symbols, and thus decisive for the formation of a new ideal of human existence. The image of the man who looks down at the earth, not from heaven, but from a cosmic sphere above the earth became an object of identification and psychological elevation to innumerable people.

The Imaginative Transcendence of Earth

The same image unlocked streams of imagination about encounters inside and outside the gravitational field of the earth with nonearthly, though not heavenly (or hellish), beings. The largeness of the literature of scientific fiction, often done as a sideline by scientists themselves, preceded as well as followed the actual progress of space exploration. But it reached its full extension only after actual achievements in this direction had been attained. Its real importance is not the occasional anticipation of scientific or technical discoveries, but it is the fulfillment of the desire of man to transcend the realm of earthbound experiences, at least in imagination. The so-called Gothic novel did this with the help of supranatural divine and demonic interferences in the natural processes of life; the spiritualistic novel did it through the ambiguity of psychic phenomena that appeared as neither unambiguously natural nor unambiguously supranatural. Science ficton, especially if connected with space exploration, transcends the bondage to the earth by imagining encounters with natural but transterrestrial beings. Mythological as well as psychic supranaturalism are replaced by a transterrestrial naturalism: the earth is transcended, not through something qualitatively other, but through a strange section of something qualitatively the same—the natural universe.

At this point an observation can be made that should have some restraining effect on the drive toward earth-transcending imaginations (whether they are called experiences or mere phantasy): the content of these imaginations is always a combination of elements taken from earthly experience. The "beings" whose pictures are given are either glorified (angels and heavenly saints), or vilified duplications of the human figure (demons and inmates of hell), or they are combinations of elements by which the human figure is disfigured, as in science fiction. This shows a definitive limit on man's possibility of escaping the bondage to his earth even in imagination. The imagined worlds are construed with parts or elements of earthly experiences, even if these experiences are religious or artistic.

The last remark leads to another basically negative group of emotional reactions to space exploration. It has somehow concretely raised man's awareness of the immensity of the universe and the spatial distances in it. Just the experience of bridging some of these distances, and consequently imagining the bridging of more of them, have increased the sensitivity to the actual remoteness of even the nearest solar system beyond our own. The dizziness felt by people at Pascal's time facing the empty spaces between the stars has been increased in a period in which man has pushed not only cognitively but also bodily into these spaces. His anxiety of lostness in a small corner of the universe, which has balanced pride in his controlling power since the time of the eighth Psalm, has grown with the growth of the controlling transcendent above the greatness and smallness of man— the answer to the question of man's predicament by the Psalm as well as by Pascal. The other, more particular reason, unknown to both of them, is the fact that man can use his controlling power for self-destruction, not only of parts of mankind, but of all of it. The intimate relation of space exploration to preparation for war has thrown a deep shadow over the emotionally positive reaction to space exploration. And this shadow will not recede as long as production of weapons and space exploration are tied up with each other.

Ethical and Spiritual Problems of Space Exploration

In describing the emotional effects of space exploration and its scientific precedents we have avoided value judgments except in an implicit way. It is, however, necessary to make them explicit and to discuss some ethical problems connected with our subject.

The Objectification of Earth and the Emptiness of "Forwardism"

One of the results of the flight into space and the possibility of looking down at the earth is a kind of estrangement between man and earth, an "objectification" of the earth for man, the depriving "her" of her "motherly" character, her power of giving birth, of nourishing, of embracing, of keeping for herself, of calling back to herself. She becomes a large, material body to be looked at and considered as totally calculable. The process of demythologizing the earth that started with the early philosophers and was continued ever since in the Western world has been radicalized as never before. It is too early to realize fully the spiritual consequences of this step.

The same is true of another radicalization: the flight into transterrestrial space is the greatest triumph of the horizontal over the vertical. We have gone forward in directions that are practically limitless while the farthest distances on earth are restricted to a half-circle that, if continued, leads in a full circle back to the beginning. However, this triumph of the horizontal raises serious spiritual problems, which all come down to the basic question: "For what?" Long before the break through the gravitational field of the earth, the question "for what?" had been asked with increasing seriousness and concern. It had been asked in connection with the endless production of means: machines, tools, gadgets! It has been asked in connection with the question of life; and it has been asked, whenever the ways of modern civilization in technology and business were subjected to prophetic criticism, be it in religious or in secular terms. If the question is now asked in connection with space exploration, it becomes more abstract and more urgent than before. For here the horizontal line is almost completely formalized. The aim is to go forward for the sake of going forward, endlessly without a concrete focus. Of course, one could call the desire to learn more about cosmic space and about astronomical bodies in it a concrete aim. But this is only an accidental aspect. The desire to go ahead whatever may be encountered gives the real impetus. But just as the *exclusive* surrender to the vertical line (in skepticism) leads to the impossibility of expressing anything and acting in any direction, so also the *exclusive* surrender to the horizontal line (in what one could call "forwardism") leads to the loss of any meaningful content and to complete emptiness. The symptoms of this emptiness are already conspicuously among us in the form of indifference, cynicism, and despair. And space exploration is not the means of healing it, but it may become a factor in deepening it after the first enthusiasm has evaporated and the pride in man's almost divine power (Psalms 8) has receded.

These spiritual dangers, however, should never lead to a decision to give up either the production of technical tools or the attempts to penetrate into the outerterrestrial spaces (as the danger of radical mysticism should not lead to a rejection of the mystical element in every religious experience). For danger is not a reason to prevent life from actualizing its potentialities.

The Ethical Responsibilities
of Science and the Scientist

This leads to another problem, connected indirectly with out subject, the problem of the responsibility of the scientist for dangers implied in his discoveries. The problem is as old as scholarly thought and was for millennia a source of conflict between the priestly guardians of the holy and the prophetic or philosophical critics of traditional beliefs. Even if the sociological, political, and economic causes of such conflicts are taken into account, a genuine, tragic element remains: The priest is aware of the catastrophic consequences that criticism of the holy traditions can have on the spirit of many people. But neither the prophet nor the philosopher can resign from his vocation to fight for justice and truth, even if sacred beliefs must be destroyed. This is probably the earliest example of the conflict between the safety of the given and the risk of the new.

The dangers connected with present scientific discoveries do not refer to the "salvation of souls" but to the very existence of mankind. But the problem itself and the tragic implications of any possible solutions are the same. And the answer should be the same: Tragic consequences of the discovery and expression of truth are no reason for giving up the attempts to discover and the obligation to express truth. The danger for the soul of the believer should not keep the prophet or the reformer from pronouncing truth in the vertical dimension; and the danger of destructive consequences of scientific discoveries (including those in the social sciences and psychology) should not keep the scientist from searching for and expressing truth in the horizontal dimension. It is bad to try to avoid tragedy if the price is to avoid truth. Therefore, even if space exploration, through its military implications, increases the chances of tragedy, this would not be a reason for stopping it. But such danger would be a powerful motive to balance the horizontal by the vertical line, in order to receive from there weapons against ultimate tragedy, this would not be a reason for stopping it against ultimate tragedy. In other words: The answer to the tragic implication of the pursuit of the horizontal line is not to break off this pursuit but to continue it under the criteria coming from the vertical line. But, one asks, is this still a possibility? Has not the power of the horizontal drive, especially in its scientific expressions, almost cut off the relation to what transcends the universe and its scientific exploration? Has not man's image of himself in all Western religions been made obsolete by the horizontal dynamics of the last five hundred years? And does not space exploration pronounce the last word in this respect?

The Contemporary Possibility of the Vertical within the Horizontal Dimension of Existence

There is no doubt that science has undercut the cosmic frame within which man has seen himself in biblical literature and ecclesiastical teaching, namely, as the bearer of the history of salvation for the universe, as the *only* creature in whose nature God could become fully manifest, as he who will experience his own historical end as the end of the universe. Today's astronomy considers the possibility of other religiously meaningful histories in other parts of the universe, with other beings in whom God could have become fully manifest, through with another beginning and another end. If space exploration is seen in this context, as the preliminary last step in a long development, one can say that it has changed tremendously the cosmic frame of man's religious self-evaluation. But one must add that it has not changed the divine-human relationship that had been experienced and symbolically expressed within this frame. Therefore one can answer the question, whether the dynamics of the horizontal have cut off the vertical, with a definite no! It is still possible for man to transcend tragedy and break through the horizontal movement with its tragic implications for the vertical and with its power to restrict. This "stature and condition" of man has not changed, although the way of its actualization must be different from that of periods in which the horizontal line had not yet shown its driving power.

Sociological Consequences of Space Exploration

Space Exploration within Economic Justice

While the question of the right of scientific inquiry to go ahead without considering possibly dangerous consequences was answered affirmatively, another question arises to which an answer must be given. It is the economic question: How much of the income of a nation (or of all nations) should be given to space exploration? A main argument against space exploration is the immense amount of money needed for it which, according to the critics, should be used for more important projects, e.g., cancer research or study of the best ways of restricting the increase of the world population. In both cases it is the conquest of bodily evils—disease and hunger—to which priority is given. This seems to be natural from the point of view of justice and agape. But actually it is neither natural nor was it ever real. Agape requires that the individual be always ready to help the sick and poor in personal encounters as well as in social projects. And justice demands of society and its political representatives the continuous fight against the structures of evil in all its forms. Neither justice nor agape prohibits the use of economic power for cultural production. Otherwise no human potentiality, neither scientific nor technical, neither artistic nor ritual, neither educational nor social could ever have been actualized. But they *have* been actualized at a tremendous cost, and in their development they have produced powerful weapons against the structures of evil (mostly without intending to do so).

"Priority of needs" cannot mean that the whole cultural process should not have been started before the most immediate needs, e.g., conquering hunger and disease, had been satisfied. The term *priority* in the context of our problem is meaningful only in a particular situation. The question is: Which demand on the economic reserves of any social group has priority in this moment? And if a definite preference is established, the next question is: In which proportion shall economic aid be given to the preferred project in relation to other important projects? Finally it must be considered whether the rejection of one project, e.g., the next phase of space exploration, implies the certainty, or even a real chance, that one of the alternative projects will be accepted by the responsible authorities. It is, for example, highly improbable that the money saved by the stopping of space exploration would become available for cancer research or a restriction of the population explosion. Beyond this, all these considerations would become academic in the moment in which it is manifest that space exploration has military consequences and belongs to the realm of competition with a potential enemy. Then it has priority over against all projects without direct military importance. The decision lies in the hands of those who have knowledge of the relevant factors and the power to balance the different points of view in terms of priorities and on the basis of the actual situation. They cannot be bound by a static hierarchy of priorities. Their only criterion should be the human aim of all political decisions (which certainly transcends national power as well as scientific progress). In this they are subject to the judgment of their conscience, the criticism of their contemporaries, and the later judgment of history.

The Growth of a Scientific Elite

But here a conflict arises that is intensified by the sociological implications of space exploration: It contributes greatly to a general trend in our period, the growth of esoteric groups who through their knowledge and their inventiveness by far surpass what can be reached even by highly learned and productive people, not to speak of the vast majority of human beings. Such elites are esoteric and exclusive, partly through natural selection, partly through public prestige, partly through skillful exercise of their power. An aristocracy of intelligence and will to power has developed in the West as well as in the East and equalized to a considerable degree the two originally opposite social and political systems. Space exploration in the democratic world strengthens the antidemocratic elements, which are present in every democratic structure. There is a tendency in the average citizen, even if he has a high standing in his profession, to consider the decisions relating to the life of the society to which he belongs as a matter of fate on which he has no influence—like the Roman subjects all over the world in the period of the Roman empire, a mood favorable for the resurgence of religion but unfavorable for the preservation of a living democracy.

Space Exploration
and the Ideal of Education

It seems strange to raise the question of the consequences of space exploration for the ideal of education. But it is pertinent to the actual situation. If only the most extraordinary mathematical and technical intelligence can reach the top of the hierarchy of space theoreticians, and if only the most extraordinary bodily and psychological fitness can reach the top of the hierarchy of practical space explorers, it is understandable that these two types of man are raised to the place of ideal types according to which every individual should be formed, though in many degrees of approximation. This demand was made in this country most urgently after the success of the first Russian Sputnik. There was a strong reaction on the part of the humanistically minded educators and also of many students who did not want or were not able to undergo the rigors of the education that would bring them to the top of the new hierarchy.

But the question is not solved by a transitory balance between the two ways of education or by the serious attempts to combine them. The preponderance of the nonhumanistic way can hardly be overcome because of the actual structure of a social pyramid. Education cannot resist the solid structure of a social system and its demands on every individual in it. But again, this is no reason for cutting off space exploration or the developments on which it is based. For human nature is not expressed in its full potentialities by the horizontal line. Sooner or later it will revolt against the latter's predominance. And then space exploration will be judged in the light of the meaning of life in all its dimensions.

CHAPTER 18

Seven Theses
concerning the Nuclear Dilemma[1]

1. Ethical problems underlie all political considerations. They become predominant when the political situation puts alternatives before the statesmen that cannot be escaped by compromise. They must anticipate them, even while negotiations aiming at compromises still are going on.

2. The ethical problem is not, as in discussions with older forms of pacifism, the rightness or wrongness of power-groups using force. The negation of this right, I am glad to say, did not come up in the present conversations. The primitive identification between personal and social ethics was hardly noticeable. But there are social ethics; and the question of their principle must certainly be asked. It is, as I call it, creative justice—a justice whose final aim is the preservation or restitution of a community of social groups, subnational, or supranational.

3. The means for reaching this aim must be adequate to the aim: negotiation, diplomacy, war (if necessary), a peace that not only does not destroy but also makes a new community possible. War occurs when a social group feels attacked and decides to defend its power to exist and the ultimate principles for which it stands (e.g., democratic freedom in this country).

---

[1]This article was originally published as a "Contribution to the 'The Nuclear Dilemma—A Discussion,' " in *Christianity and Crisis* 11:19 (1961): 203-204. Professor Tillich remarks, "The best comment I can make on John Bennett's paper is contained in the following theses. I prepared them originally for a recent discussion with Dean Rusk, Max Freedman, Henry Kissinger and James Reston on Eleanor Roosevelt's television program, 'Prospects for Mankind.' I am glad to publish them in connection with John Bennett's congenial article."

4. The decision to enter a war is justified only if it is done in the service of creative justice. Each such decision, however, is not only political and military but also a moral risk.

5. In the light of the aim of intergroup justice, a war fought with atomic weapons cannot be justified ethically. For it produces destruction without the possibility of a creative new beginning. It annihilates what it is supposed to defend.

6. In the present situation this ethical principle leads to the following political-military preferences:

   (a) Defense—political and military—not only of its power to exist but also of its ultimate principles for itself and those who adhere to the same principles and who are likewise threatened, is a clear, ethical demand.

   (b) If such defense is in particular situations impossible with conventional weapons (as it would be in the case of Berlin and perhaps parts of Western Europe), even then this does not justify the use of atomic weapons; for they would not be the means of defense but of mere destruction of both sides.

   (c) Nevertheless, atomic armament is justified because it shows the potential enemy that radical destruction would take place on his side as much as on the other side if he attacks first with atomic weapons.

   (d) For the American strategy this means that no atomic weapon can be used before the enemy uses one, and even then not for "retaliation" but in order to induce him not to continue their use. (Practically, the very existence of atomic weapons on both sides is probably a sufficient deterrent.)

   (e) If this includes—as it very probably does—a temporary military retreat in Europe on our side (by no means a total surrender), this is a most ordinary phenomenon in most wars and can be redressed by the arrival of the total Allied military power.

7. This suggestion makes, on the basis of ethical principles, a sharp distinction between the atomic weapons of total destruction (including the tactical atomic weapons) and the so-called conventional weapons, that can be directed against the enemy army and its bases. Of course, the atomic weapons remain in the background, but our awareness of the social-ethical imperative must prevent us from ever using them first again.

CHAPTER 19

The Hydrogen Cobalt Bomb

The increasing and apparently unlimited power of the means of self-destruction in the hands of men puts before us the question of the ultimate meaning of this development.

The first point that comes to my mind is the possibility that it is the destiny of historical men to be annihilated not by a cosmic event but by the tensions in his own being and in his own history.

The reaction to this possibility—this is the second point—should be the certainty that the meaning of human history, as well as of everyone's life within it, is not dependent on the time or the way in which history comes to an end. For the meaning of history lies above history.

The third point is that everyone who is aware of the possibility of mankind's self-destruction must resist this possibility to the utmost. For life and history have an eternal dimension and are worthy to be defended against man's suicidal instincts, which are socially as real as they are individually.

The fourth point is that the resistance against the suicidal instincts of the human race must be done on all levels, on the political level through negotiation between those who in a tragic involvement force each other into the production of even stronger means of self-destruction; on the moral level through a reduction of propaganda and an increase in obedience to the truth about oneself and the potential enemy; on the religious level through a sacred serenity and superiority over the preliminary concerns of life, and a new experience and a new expression of the ultimate concern that transcends as well as determines man's historical existence.

The fifth point is that the resistance against the self-destructive consequences of man's technical control of nature must be done in acts that unite the religious, moral, and political concern, and that are performed in imaginative wisdom and courage.

Bibliography

These works are organized as far as possible according to the earliest date of their public appearance, either in spoken or written form.

Abbreviations

PTA   The Paul Tillich Archives. Andover-Harvard Theological Library, Harvard Divinity School, 45 Francis Avenue, Cambridge, Massachusetts, 02138.

PTATC   The Paul Tillich Audio Tape Collection. The Library of Union Theological Seminary, 3407 Brook Road, Richmond, Virginia, 23227.

GW   *Gesammelte Werke,* Stuttgart: Evangelisches Verlagswerk, 1962.

PJ   From the collection of the Rev. Peter H. John, East Windsor, Connecticut

AT   Audio Tape

LN   Tillich's handwritten lecture notes

TS   Typescript

NM   No manuscript is available

V   Included in this volume

1923

Das System der Wissenschaften nach Gegenstädnen und Methoden. Ein Entwurf. Göttingen. Vandenhoeck & Ruprecht, 1923. This early work was published in translation as *The System of the Sciences According to Objects and Methods.* Translated with an Introduction by Paul Wiebe. Lewisburg PA: Bucknell University Press, 1981.

1926

Die religiööse Lage der Gegenwart. Berlin: Ullstein, 1926. Interpreting science, technology, and capitalism as the determining spiritual powers of the contemporary situation, this work made what Tillich called "the original impact" upon his German audience.[1] It appeared in translation as *The Religious Situation.* Translated by H. Richard Niebuhr. New York: Meridian Books, 1956. *The Religious Situation* and "The World Situation" (below) were identified by Tillich as primary contributions to his "theonomous" interpretation of culture.[2] The present volume lies directly within this lineage.

1927

"The Logos and Mythos of Technology." This address was delivered at the 99th anniversary of the Founders Day of the Dresden Institute of Technology, where Tillich was Professor of Philosophy and Religious Studies from 1925 to 1929. It was originally published as "Logos und Mythos der Technik." *Logos* 16 (November 1927): 356-65, and appears here for the first time in English translation. (GW 9:297-306, V)

1928

"The Technical City as Symbol." This lecture was delivered in conjunction with an exhibition celebrating the centennial of the founding of the Dresden Institute of Technology. It was published subsequently as "Die technische Stadt als Symbol." *Dresdner Neueste Nachrichten* 115 (17 May 1928): 5. It appears in English translation for the first time in this volume. (GW 9:307-11, V)

1931

"Wissenschaft." *Die Religion in Geschichte und Gegenwart.* Edited by Hermann Gunkel and Leopold Zscharnack. 2d ed. Tubingen: Mohr, 1931. (GW 4:36-39)

1932

"The Freedom of Science." The date ascribed to this lecture ("Freiheit der Wissenschaft") was estimated by Jack Mouw and Robert P. Scharlemann in the bibliography they provide to *The Theology of Paul Tillich.* Edited by Charles W. Kegley. New York: The Pilgrim Press, 1982. If this date is correct, this document would have been written during Tillich's tenure as Professor of Phi-

---

[1]Pauck, Wilhelm and Marion, *Paul Tillich: His Life and Thought: Volume 1* (New York: Harper & Row, 1976) 98.

[2]Paul Tillich, *The Protestant Era,* trans. James Luther Adams (Chicago: University of Chicago Press, 1957) xiii.

losophy at the University of Frankfurt, the same year that *The Socialist Decision* was published. It has not appeared previously in English translation. (PTA:TS, GW 13:150-53, V)

1935

"The Doctrine of Man and the Scientific Knowledge of Today." This series of four addresses was delivered as the Taylor Lectures of 1935 at Yale University. (PTA:LN)

1940

"Science and Theology: A Discussion with Einstein." In *Theology of Culture,* edited by Robert C. Kimball, 127-32. London: Oxford University Press, 1959.

1942

"Nature and Sacrament." In *The Protestant Era.* Translated with a concluding essay by James Luther Adams, 94-114. Chicago: University of Chicago Press, 1948.

1945

"The World Situation." In *The Christian Answer.* Edited with an Introduction by Henry P. Van Dusen. New York: Charles Scribner's Sons, 1945. Like Tillich's *The Socialist Decision,* which was written in the context of the "Kairos Circle," "The World Situation" was written in conversation with a group of some twenty-five people called first "The Younger Theologians," and later "The Theological Discussion Group." Tillich was asked to give a "diagnosis of the present situation," and this essay was the result. It was circulated and critiqued by the group—along with the four others of this volume—prior to publication. It has been reprinted by Fortress Press of Philadelphia, 1965.(V)

"The Redemption of Nature." *Christendom* 9 (Summer 1945): 299-305. This sermon, delivered at Union Theological Seminary on 25 March 1945, was also published as "Nature, Also, Mourns for a Lost Good." *Shaking of the Foundations,* 76-86. New York: Scribner, 1948.

1946

"The Tragedy of Autonomous Reason in the Growth of Industrial Society." Delivered to the Annual Minister's Convocation, Wilbraham Academy, 9 September 1946, this lecture was the first of a series with the general theme "The Contemporary Spiritual and Moral Situation." (PTA:LN)

1949

"Religion and the Social Sciences." This lecture was delivered at Upsala College in East Orange, New Jersey, on 23 April 1949. (PTA:LN)

1950

Tillich, Paul, et. al. *The Christian Conscience and Weapons of Mass Destruction.*
New York: The Department of International Justice and Goodwill of the Federal Council of the Churches of Christ in America, December 1950. This document was produced by a committee of nineteen appointed by the executive
committee of the Federal Council of Churches.

1952

"Man in Late Industrial Society." This lecture was delivered in conjunction with
the Christian Frontier Council in Windsor, England, 26 June 1952. (NM)

1953

"The Person in a Technical Society." In *Christian Faith and Social Action: A
Symposium,* edited by John A. Hutchinson, 151-53. New York: Charles
Scribner's Sons, 1953. It appears also in *Social Ethics,* edited by Gibson Win-
ter, 120-38. New York: Harper & Row, 1968. A manuscript, "Mench in der
Technisierten Gesellschaft," may have been a German language version of
this essay, but no record of this lecture having been delivered has been found.
(PTA:LN, V)

1954

"The Spiritual Situation in Our Technical Society." This title essay was one of
the lectures given at the Wesley Foundation at the University of Mississippi
during Tillich's visit, 3-4 April 1954. (PTA:LN)

"The Hydrogen Cobalt Bomb." *Pulpit Digest* 34 (June 1954): 32, 34. (V)

1955

"Participation and Knowledge: Problems of an Ontology of Cognition." In *Sociologica,* edited by Theodor W. Adorno and Walter Dirks, 201-209. Frankfurt am Main: Europasche Verlagsanstalt, 1955. (V)

"Theology and Architecture." *Architectural Forum* 103 (December 1955): 131-
34.

1957

"Religion, Science, and the Current Crisis." This work was a lecture delivered
in conjunction with the "Institute on Religion in an Age of Science" on 27
April 1957, on the campus of the Massachusetts Institute of Technology.
(PTA:LN)

"Environment and the Individual." This address was given to the American Institute of Architects in Washington, D.C., during its meeting, 13-15 May 1957.
It was published in the *Journal of the American Institute of Architects* 28 (June
1957): 90-92. (V)

"Conformity." Delivered as the Commencement address at the New School for Social Research on 11 June 1957, this lecture was published in *Social Research* 24 (Autumn 1957): 354-60. It has appeared subsequently in *Readings in Human Relations,* edited by Keith Davis and William G. Scott, 456-61. New York: McGraw-Hill, 1959; and in *Humanitas* 1 (Fall 1965): 117-22. (V)

1958

"Expressions of Man's Self-Understanding in Philosophy and the Sciences." This was the second of six Lowell Lectures delivered in King's Chapel, Boston, Massachusetts, beginning on 4 February 1958. (PTATC:AT #T78, PTA:LN, V)

"Thing and Self." This was the fifth of six Lowell Lectures delivered in King's Chapel, Boston, Massachusetts in 1958. (PTATC:AT #T81, PTA:LN, V)

"The Lost Dimension in Religion." *Saturday Evening Post* 230 (14 June 1958): 28-29, 76, 78-79. This essay has also appeared in *Adventures of the Mind.* Edited by Richard Thruelsen and John Kobler. New York: Knopf, 1959, and in *Issues in Christian Thought.* Edited by John B. Harrison. New York: McGraw-Hill, 1968. (V)

"The Relationship Today between Science and Religion." This address was delivered as one of the Ingraham Lectures in Philosophy and Religion during his stay at Colby College, 24-25 April 1958. It appeared in print in *The Student Seeks an Answer,* edited by John A. Clark, 296-306. Waterville ME: Colby College, Press, 1960. (V)

"Theologians and the Moon." *Christianity Today* 3 (13 October 1958): 31.

1959

"Religion, Science, and Philosophy." This essay was delivered as one of the Cole Lectures on Religion and Culture at Vanderbilt University held from 6-9 April 1959. (Vanderbilt University Archives: AT)

1960

"Religion and Culture: Application to Science and Arts." Under the general rubric of the primary title, this was a second lecture delivered at Antioch College in Yellow Springs, Ohio, during Tillich's stay there on 5-6 April 1960. (PTA:LN)

"Science and Religion." This essay was read at the Massachusetts General Hospital in Boston on 19 October 1960. (PJ:AT)

"The House We Live In." Broadcast Lecture, WCAU Television, Philadelphia Educational Series, 5 November 1960. (PΓA:LN, PJ:AT)

"Religion, Science, and History." The second of the Danforth Foundation Lectures for graduate students delivered at Columbia University on 13 November 1960. (PTA:LN)

"Science and the Contemporary World in the View of a Theologian." An address delivered at the Massachusetts Institute of Technology on 16 December 1960, in one of four conferences sponsored by the U. S. Department of State, this work was published in *Public and Private Association in the International Educational and Cultural Relations,* 67-70. Washington: United States Department of State, 15 February 1961. (PTA:TS, V)

1961

"Zur Theologie der bilden Kunst und der Architecktur." *Kunst und Kirche* 24 (1961): 99-103.

"Seven Theses concerning the Nuclear Dilemma." This short essay was published as a contribution to "The Nuclear Dilemma—A Discussion." *Christianity and Crisis* 21 (1961): 203-204. It was offered in response to an essay by John Bennett in the same issue, but it had been prepared for an earlier discussion with Dean Rusk, Max Freedman, Henry Kissinger, and James Reston on Eleanor Roosevelt's television program "Prospects for Mankind." (V)

"How Has Science in the Last Century Changed Man's View of Himself?" Delivered as a lecture during the centennial celebration the Massachusetts Institute of Technology on 8 April 1961 (PJ:AT), it appeared in *The Current* 6:1-2 (1965): 85-89, a periodical published by the Catholic community of Harvard University. A German manuscript titled "Die Wandlung im Selbstverständnis des Menschen durch Wissenschaft und Technik" (PTA:LN) was revised in Tillich's hand and was apparently the text for a lecture in Hamburg in July 1961. (V)

1962

"Contemporary Protestant Architecture." In *Modern Church Architecture.* New York: McGraw Hill, 1962.

"Nuclear Morality." *Partisan Review* 29 (1962): 311-12.

"Man, the Earth, and the Universe." *Christianity and Crisis* 22 (1962): 108-12.

"Man and Earth." This sermon, first delivered at the Harvard University Memorial Church, 11 February 1962, was also given at the Unitarian Church of Germantown, Philadelphia (18 March 1962), Union Theological Seminary (1 April 1962), Sage's Chapel of Cornell University, Ithaca, New York (15 April 1962), and Battell Chapel of Yale University (13 May 1962). It was published in *The Eternal Now,* 66-78. New York: Charles Scribner's Sons, 1963.

1963

"Has Man's Conquest of Space Increased or Diminished His Stature?" In *The Great Ideas Today*. Chicago: Encyclopaedia Britannica, 1963. This essay appears also under the title "The Effects of Space Exploration on Man's Condition and Stature" in *The Future of Religions,* Edited by Jerald C. Brauer. New York: Harper & Row, 1966. Jerald Brauer refers to this essay as a "lecture," but no date or place is fixed to it.

"Religion, Science, and Philosophy." This lecture was one of four Regent Lectures delivered in a series called "Religion and Culture," beginning in February to 25 March 1963, at the University of California, Santa Barbara. (PTATC:AT #T107, V). Essentially the same lecture was delivered at the University Meeting in Harmon Gymnasium at the Pacific School of Religion on 20 February 1963. (PTA: TS, PTATC:AT #T130) A lecture by the same title was given at Louisiana State University in New Orleans, Louisiana, 8 April 1963. It is not certain whether this lecture was delivered from the same notes as those above. (NM)

1964

"Religion, Science, and Philosophy" The note written at the top of these handwritten lecture notes says "Durham, New Hampshire, March 1964." It may have been delivered at the University of New Hampshire. This is the fifth lecture by the same title, but with different content. (PTA:LN)

"The Decline and the Validity of the Idea of Progress." Delivered on 19 May 1964, as one in the series of The Edwin and Ruth Kennedy Lectures at Ohio University, Athens, Ohio, this lecture appeared in *The Future of Religions.* Edited by Jerald C. Brauer. New York: Harper & Row, 1966. (V)

1965

"Christian View of Man in the Light of Contemporary Science and Philosophy." No exact date or place of delivery can be given to this 1965 lecture. (PTA:LN)

No Date

"Protestantismus u. Wissenschaft." (PTA:LN)

"Religion und Technik" (PTA:LN)

"Religionese Dimension der Wissenschaften." (PTA:LN)

"The Line of Thought in Religion and Physics." (PTA:LN)

"Man and Nature in Existence: The Mark of Man's Estrangement." (PTA:LN)

"Man and the Universe." (PTA:LN)

"Modern Science and the Eclipse of Religion." A note at the top of this manuscript, which does not appear to be in Tillich's handwriting, reads "Occidental College, Jan. 1960." However, the convocation address Tillich delivered
at Occidental College on 6 January 1960 was titled "The Meaning of Health."[3]
When or where Tillich actually delivered this lecture on science and religion
remains unknown. (PTA:LN)

"The Person in an Impersonal Society." (PTA:LN)

"Religion and Culture in the Arts and the Sciences." While these brief notes are
neither dated nor given a place, they may have been for Tillich's course in
"Religion and Culture." (PTA:LN)

"Religion and the Sciences." (PTA:LN)

"Religion, the Arts, and the Sciences." (PTA:LN, PJ:AT)

"Religion and the Technical Realm." (PTA:LN)

"Truth in Architecture." (PJ:AT)

In his lecture on "Religion, Science, and Philosophy," of 20 February 1963, Tillich wrote that the title of his lecture represented "the subject matter of a two
year course, four hours every week." He may have had reference to a course
called "Religion and Culture," offered at Harvard. Some handwritten notes
from the Tillich Archives are for a "First Lecture: Problems and Concepts
(Religion, Scientific, and Technical Culture)." These undated notes probably
come from this course. (PTA:LN)

---

[3]This information was obtained through Michael C. Sutherland, Special Collections
Department, Occidental College, Los Angeles, California.

Index